The world's leading expert on the life of America's greatest military hero, LADISLAS FARAGO served with the Chief of Naval Operations during World War II and later as confidential consultant to Radio Free Europe. An acclaimed writer, military historian and biographer, his international bestseller, PATTON: ORDEAL AND TRIUMPH, became the basis for the award-winning film, *Patton* with George C. Scott.

THE LAST DAYS OF PATTON, written in the last days of Ladislas Farago's life, stands as one of his greatest works and an enduring monument to his outstanding career.

"Compelling. For military history buffs it is a must, for anyone else it is a gripping book no matter what one thinks of Patton."

—Pittsburgh Press

"A clear-eyed portrait of one of the ablest, and surely most colorful, American commanders of the Second World War."

—New Yorker

"As Farago describes it, Patton's death is movingly human."

—Publisher's Weekly

"Provides marvelous insights into the last thoughts and actions of the General."

—King Features Syndicate

"This book sheds new light on Patton's eclipse."
—*Kirkus Reviews*

"A movingly written historical profile of a great general."
—*Milwaukee Journal*

"Written with the control and flourish of an outstanding work of fiction."
—*Booklist*

"A superb job...eminently readable."
—*Houston Post*

THE LAST DAYS OF
PATTON

LADISLAS FARAGO

BERKLEY BOOKS, NEW YORK

*To Frank McCarthy
with affectionate regards*

This Berkley book contains the complete
text of the original hardcover edition.
It has been completely reset in a typeface
designed for easy reading and was printed
from new film.

THE LAST DAYS OF PATTON

A Berkley Book / published by arrangement with
McGraw-Hill Book Company

PRINTING HISTORY
McGraw-Hill edition published 1981
Berkley edition / April 1982
Seventh printing / November 1986

ISBN: 0-425-09881-8

A BERKLEY BOOK ® TM 757,375
Berkley Books are published by The Berkley Publishing Group,
200 Madison Avenue, New York, New York 10016.
The name "BERKLEY" and the stylized "B" with design
are trademarks belonging to Berkley Publishing Corporation.

PRINTED IN THE UNITED STATES OF AMERICA

ACKNOWLEDGMENTS

THE NEW MATERIAL gathered for this book amazed me for its richness and for the difficulty of access to it. This was why the writing of *The Last Days of Patton* took much longer—five years, in fact, instead of the two originally scheduled. During those years, I spent many months in Germany—in Bad Toelz and in Bad Nauheim, following Patton's footsteps; in Heidelberg, at his bedside, so to speak; and in the Kaeferthal near Mannheim, conjuring up his ghost.

In the end, I managed to piece together the story of his last days in a mosaic that, I hope, is complete, fair, and balanced. This book, therefore, is based almost entirely on primary sources: on documentary evidence supplemented by, rather than substituted for, interviews. Foremost among my sources are General Patton's 201 File in the Office of the Adjutant General of the United States Army and the private papers of Professor Walter L. Dorn, in the possession of his daughter, Mrs. Ellen Dorn Warburton.

I must therefore acknowledge my debt to Mr. Waldemar A. Anderson, who was instrumental in arranging access for me to General Patton's official file. And I am also deeply indebted to Mrs. Warburton, who agreed to bring a battered old suitcase from her attic in Washington, D.C. She had preserved her father's papers, including an unpublished manuscript he had completed shortly before his death in 1961. It was to be called, characteristically, "The Unfinished Purge." Also in the suitcase were Professor Dorn's notes on his historic clash with General Patton. I am also grateful to Professor Lutz Niethammer of Essen University,

West Germany, who guided me to Mrs. Warburton, and who showed me his own pioneering research on Professor Dorn's activities in Germany in 1945.

Other individuals whose help proved invaluable in the preparation of this book (in alphabetical order):
Dr. Abram J. Abeloff, Colonel, Medical Corps, U.S. Army (1942–46); Herrery Akkermans, Assistant Curator, American Battle Monument Commission, Luxembourg; Hollis Alpert, historian, Third U.S. Army (1943–45); Samuel Atkin, M.D.; Senator Peter K. Babalas, Lieutenant, 818th Military Police Company (1945); Colonel Lawrence C. Ball, Commanding Officer, 130th Station Hospital, Seventh U.S. Army, Heidelberg, Germany (1945); Major Abraham L. Baum, U.S. Army (Ret.); Victor M. Bernstein; Major Martin Blumenson, U.S. Army, historian, Third U.S. Army, editor of *The Patton Papers;* Philip M. Cavanaugh, Director, Patton Museum, Fort Knox, Ky.; Colonel Horace B. Clarkson, Commanding Officer, 130th Station Hospital (1978–79); William F. Cunliff, Deputy Chief, Military Records Branch, National Archives and Records Service, Washington, D.C.; Major E.C. (Ernie) Deane, chief press officer, Third U.S. Army (1945); Lieutenant Marjorie Ettinger, executive officer, 130th Station Hospital (1978–79); Charles Fisher, M.D.; Lieutenant Paul Gauthier, U.S. Army, assistant press officer, Third U.S. Army (1945); Lieutenant Hobart R. Gay, U.S. Army (Ret.); the late Lewis Frederick Gitler, intelligence officer, U.S. Army in Germany (1945); Judge Horst von Glasenapp, Bad Homburg, West Germany; General Paul D. Harkins, U.S. Army (Ret.); Colonel Paul S. Hill, chief of surgery, 130th Station Hospital (1945); Carl Levin; the late Frank Earl Mason; Brigadier General Frank McCarthy, Secretary to the General Staff and Military Assistant to General George C. Marshall (1943–45); Professor Rolf Nutzmar, University of Essen, West Germany; Dean Saul K. Padover, Intelligence Officer, U.S. Army in Germany (1944–46), Dean, School of Politics, New School for Social Research (1950–55); David J. Pucket, Senior Curator, American Battlefield Monument Commission; John M. Purdy, Curator, Patton Museum;

Colonel of the Waffen-SS Richard Schulze, last commandant of the *Junkerschule* under the Nazis; Mortimer F. Shapiro, M.D.; Andreas Szegö; Lieutenant Colonel Harry P. Tech; Dr. Thomas Thalken, Director, Herbert Hoover Library; Hans M. Weindl, public relations director, Flint Kaserne; Robert Wood, Associate Director, Herbert Hoover Library; Horace L. Woodring; and the brilliant and helpful staff of the Army's Center of Military History, in whose ranks Hannah Zeidel was particularly cooperative.

Throughout the preparation of this book I was immensely gratified by the impressive and incomparably astute editorial work of McGraw-Hill Senior Editor Gladys Justin Carr.

I found nothing but understanding and generosity from Leslie Meredith, Assistant Editor, and I appreciate the care and industry of Rita Stein, a superb copyeditor.

To Arthur Neuhauser, my old friend and veteran editorial consultant, who was my editor on *Patton: Ordeal and Triumph,* go my thanks for another mission so well accomplished; thanks also go to Isabelle Bates for a typing job that was nothing less than inspired and constructive throughout.

I would like to celebrate here the twentieth anniversary of my friendship and association with Maximilian Becker, literary agent extraordinary, who puts up with my moods and whims valiantly and with elegance.

To my wife Liesel, my son John, and my daughter-in-law Sharon—words cannot express my gratitude. They know how I feel, and how much strength and solace I am gaining from their love and support, and from their understanding.

LADISLAS FARAGO
Lenox Hill Hospital

IN A SERIES of tragic ironies, *The Last Days of Patton* is inextricably intertwined with my father's own last days. As he had just completed the final version of this manuscript for his publisher, he checked into Lenox Hill Hospital in New York City for what he thought would be a rather routine battery of tests. He never left the hospital, and died there six weeks later on October 15, 1980. I write this two days before his funeral.

When he first entered Lenox Hill I worked with him on the copyediting and final detail work that he had brought with him. But one test stretched into another, his stomach condition was revealed as cancer, and a relentless siege of complications and unrelated ailments set in. He suffered a small stroke while in the hospital; his lungs became congested and he ran a continual fever; he contracted endocarditis, which had an unnerving and unpredictable impact on his ability to think, see, or move. Like Patton, he ultimately was for all intents and purposes paralyzed. His kidneys weakened, and finally the cancer extended to his liver and he experienced total organ failure.

Throughout most of this he remained himself, curious, inquiring, at times angry because none of his doctors could help him piece together the entire picture of his illness. Irascible, like Patton, but also charismatic and possessed of a childlike vulnerability, he drew the hospital staff to him during those last days. It was therefore not easy for me to work on the last portion of this manuscript, as its words echoed my father's life.

Indeed, there was much of the General in my father—his bluster, his strength, his willingness to tread firmly where others feared to tiptoe. Perhaps it is this subliminal kinship that breathes life into the Patton described in the pages that follow. Certainly it explains why my father was drawn to the General's career, even though Patton was a fighter and my father's field was espionage and psychological warfare.

I add this brief final note because there are several people whose help must be acknowledged. In completing the copyediting and in working with the page proofs (the final stages before a manuscript becomes a book), we have had to do without my father's encyclopedic knowledge of the events and of his material. I have drawn upon the kindness of Major Ernie Deane, General Paul Harkins, and General Frank McCarthy, each of whom read the manuscript under very pressing time constraints, and each of whom helped correct minor details in the book. I have tried to retrace some of my father's research in verifying names and dates, but time, the fact of my father's illness, and my responsibilities for my own job, have necessarily combined to make these final stages of preparation less precise than they would have been had my father been able to participate. Nonetheless, John Wilson, Third Army Historian of the Pentagon, kindly helped with many such details.

There are others who must be thanked: Dr. Abe Abeloff, who read the final page proofs for medical accuracy, and who, together with other close physician friends of my father and my family, was at my father's side almost daily. These included Sam Atkin, Carl Paley, and Mort Shapiro. They were led by Dr. Harry Fein, a dear friend for many years, a consummate physician, and a source of much solace for my father and my mother during these last weeks.

I must thank Charles J. Rubin for his help with the manuscript and the logistics. And Ian Cookridge, an associate of mine for many years. If it had not been for the flexibility evidenced by Dean Charles A. Ehren, Jr., of the Valparaiso University School of Law (where I am assistant dean and assistant professor), I would not have been able to spend the time necessary to coordinate this final push to bring the book to print.

And, of course, I thank my father . . . for this book, for my life, but most especially for his.

JOHN M. FARAGO
Valparaiso, Indiana

CONTENTS

PUBLISHER'S NOTE

★ ★ ★ ★

LADISLAS FARAGO died several weeks before this book went to press. His indefatigable commitment to the completion of this work during the months just prior to his death inspired all who worked with him.

The final vetting of *The Last Days of Patton* was completed by the author's son, John M. Farago.

GLADYS JUSTIN CARR

There is one great thing you men will be able to say after this war is all over and you are at home once again. And you may thank God for it. You may be thankful that twenty years from now when you are sitting by the fireplace with your grandson on your knee and he asks you what you did in the great World War II, you won't have to cough, shift him to the other knee and say, "Well, your Granddaddy shoveled shit in Louisiana." No sir! You can look him straight in the eye and say, "Son, your Granddaddy rode with the great Third Army and a son-of-a-bitch named Georgie Patton."

*Third Army speech
May 31, 1944,
to the men of General Gerow's
Sixth Armored Division
in England*

INTRODUCTION

☆ ☆ ☆ ☆

Years of the Jackals: The Mysteries of General Patton's Death

. . . All, which makes death a hideous show.

—MATTHEW ARNOLD, *"A Wish"* (1867)

THE DEATH of George S. Patton, Jr., at Yuletide in 1945 has become second only to the assassinations of John F. Kennedy and Martin Luther King, Jr., in controversy and obfuscation.

One of the reasons for the prosperity of the "assassinologists" is that the official investigations of these cases have left much to be desired. Pearl Harbor, for example, underwent seven separate investigations, including the spectacular hearings in the Senate's ornate Caucus Room, and still left enough open wounds for the revisionists to pour salt on. By contrast, there were only two serious major probes of the Kennedy assassination, and only one on a large scale of the murder of the Reverend Dr. King—and all of them left gaps and raised more questions than they answered.

The strange death of General Patton was never properly probed. The failure of the authorities to close the case with a definitive solution produced myths and legends—theories that Patton had been assassinated in an elaborate plot in which, some implied, General Dwight D. Eisenhower may have been an accomplice.

1

Patton died in the early darkness of a winter afternoon, eleven days and six hours after an auto accident on Highway 38 near Mannheim, on his way to his last pheasant hunt in Germany before returning home. He died prostrate on his hospital bed—an incongruous death for the U.S. Army's fightingest general—not as Patton had willed or hoped when he had said that if the Lord wanted to be really kind to him, he would see to it that he would be killed with the last bullet of the war. That last bullet missed him. He went on to postwar adventures and mishaps that ultimately deprived him of all the *gloire et victoire* he had earned in three and a half years of combat.

Nobody raised the issue of foul play while Patton was in the hospital. But within hours of his death, it was rumored throughout Germany that Patton was the victim of premeditated murder in a sinister plot to get him out of the way. Apparently, the story went, his superiors had several reasons to get rid of him. For one thing, he had become pro-German since the end of the war—*"unser Patton, unser Freund"* was the way Carl Vogel, who had been Nazi foreman of a prisoner-of-war camp, was referring to the American general. For another thing, he was hellbent on provoking a *casus belli* for a head-on clash with the Soviet Union—in alliance, *horribile dictu*, with intact divisions of the Waffen-SS. As long as Patton was around, it seemed, the specter of World War III would haunt the world.

The rumor was not folklore. It was not the product of popular fantasies. And it did not, in fact, originate with the bewildered German populace. Actually, the people in the vanquished land hardly knew who Patton was and what he had done—not even what he was doing then and there, right or wrong, as the American proconsul in Bavaria.

German interest in Patton was still so spotty many years later that the famous motion picture with George C. Scott, a smash hit everywhere else, flopped dismally in Germany. After a week or two playing to empty houses, its showing had to be cancelled. Rommel, yes. Zhukov, surely. Montgomery, maybe. But the vast majority of the Germans simply did not know why General Patton rated a film.

Patton never really entered the German consciousness

either as foe or friend. Even in 1978, when I was in Bad Toelz, at the very spot where Patton had his penultimate command post and endured his greatest humiliation, I placed ads in the local newspapers soliciting the help of natives for my research. Not a single person came forward, not one man or woman who had memories or recollections of the general. "I was a boy then," said Hans M. Weindl, son of the town's police chief under the Nazis, then public-relations man in the Flint Barracks under the Americans. "All I remember of General Patton is the earsplitting noise he made when driving between his villa in St. Querin and his office in the *Kaserne* with that damned foghorn going full blast on his huge limousine."

THE TALE of Patton's violent end was *invented* by a group of former Nazi officers who had visions of a triumphal return to power. It was their second-best prospect of one day snatching victory from the embarrassment of defeat. At first, the Nazi plotters thought of creating a vast redoubt in the Austrian Alps to accommodate cadres of the Party and government, defended by the cream of the crop of the SS, and supported by the fabulous gold hoard of the Gestapo. In that impregnable fortress, these diehards had dreamed, the miracle would happen—the Führer would be resurrected somehow and Nazism would continue its thousand-year course after a brief interruption.

But the miracle did not happen—thanks largely to General Patton and his Third Army. As soon as the plan became known to Allied intelligence, General Eisenhower moved to smash it. He ordered Patton to regroup the Third Army and capture those Alpine peaks. Today the site is cold and deserted, populated only by bearded vultures and Alpine goats, visited from time to time by wayward treasure hunters looking for the Nazi gold.

After the stillbirth of their vaunted *Alpenfestung*, the Nazi jingos hit upon a cunning device that had been tested before, and worked. It was the *Dolchstosslegende*—the "Legend of the Stab in the Back," anchored to the myth of the invincibility of German arms after World War I. It was not that the Allies, so the fable went, had succeeded in defeating the indomitable German armies of the Kaiser. Rather, Germany had succumbed to the domestic forces of the radical left.

Memories of the *Dolchstosslegende* cropped up during the closing days of World War II. But the design to blame the leftists for Germany's disgrace had to be abandoned when it was realized that the German radical left had spent the war either in exile or in concentration camps. And then it became evident to the average German that it was Hitler, indeed, who was the architect of the catastrophe.

Something else was needed on which to jerry-build the future, and Patton came in handy, with his apparent new awe of all that was German—impressed as he was with their discipline and industry. He also appeared to be their potential ally because of his alleged distrust of the Red Army and hatred of the Communists. Although headlined in the United States, his attitudes and opinions were not widely known in Germany. They were known only to the small circle of his own intimates—in Bad Toelz, where he had his see, and in Frankfurt, where General Eisenhower ruled supreme.

But they were also becoming known to a tiny group of Germans who had managed to establish themselves within Patton's entourage. There was, for instance, Baron von Wangenheim, former colonel of cavalry, captain of the German equestrian team during the Olympic Games in 1936. He had wormed himself into Patton's confidence and had become not only the groom of his small stable of horses but his daily companion on outings on horseback. Another German in this inner circle was a kind of major domo in the general's palatial villa on the Tegern Lake—a mystery man remembered but vaguely as a stranger in Bad Toelz. It took more than ordinary diligence to find out that he was a Herr Brehm, an executive agent of the *Sicherheitsdienst*, the Nazi secret service operating underground. He had been hand-picked by the plotters and the dreamers to spy on Patton for them.

Last but not least, confirmation came when a group of these stubborn Nazis, kept in a special camp set aside for them, heard it from Patton himself—that the United States had fought "the wrong enemy."

IT WAS THUS of Nazi design, devised as a major implement of their comeback stratagem, that the drama of Patton's untimely death was turned into a melodrama. But it was two British writers who gave it respectability and circulation. The mainsprings of their motives were spelled out by Lieutenant General Sir Frederick Morgan, Ike's brilliant British chief of staff at SHAEF in a letter to me. He identified Field Marshal Montgomery as the spiritual source of the anti-Patton campaign. He blamed its widespread acceptance on the new inferiority complex that seized the British people after the war—unreasonably at that, for "we had no reason in the world," General Morgan wrote in his melancholy note, "to feel inferior about our share in the victory."

Strange as it may seem, the Nazi idea blossomed into a British plot and eventually spread to millions throughout the world. It produced first a strange little book by one Christopher Leopold, called with deliberate affront, *Old Blood and Guts Is Going Nuts*. An Irishman with an Oxford education, Leopold's qualifications for making such a diagnosis were neither academic nor psychiatric. He "has traveled the world as a free-lance journalist," the jacket copy described him, "and as an international consultant to a large American corporation."

Leopold used real names—those of Generals Patton, Gay, Eisenhower, and Bedell Smith—even, gratuitously, of Captain Kay Summersby, described in the book as "one of Ike's most sensitive memories." He then spun his yarn around them, giving a semblance of authenticity to the figments of his imagination. No Britons appeared among the principal characters. And the Germans were cushioned from the author's sardonic bent. They were given pseudonyms.

When the book crossed the Atlantic, its American publisher described it as a black comedy of politics and paranoia. "A bawdy, rollicking tale about the first few months of so-called peace in Europe" was the way Doubleday advertised the book with its provocative title, "full of unforgettable characters, zany, knockabout action, and harrowing suspense."

LEOPOLD'S BOOK vanished shortly after publication. But it was soon followed by a major motion picture produced by Metro-Goldwyn-Mayer, based loosely on a book called *The Algonquin Project,* written by an Irish-Anglo author, Frederick Nolan. Unlike Leopold, Nolan changed the names of his characters. He called the general "George Robinson Campion, Jr." The time of the accident in which "Campion" was killed was advanced to October 4, 1945. And Nolan included the familiar disclaimer, insisting that "the characters and the circumstances of the book [were] purely fictional." But the situation was still there, and the resemblances could not be ignored. By the time Nolan's opus was recycled as a motion picture called *Brass Target,* the names were all real.

MGM compiled a confidential dossier of its "research" for the decision to use Patton's name and weave the circumstances of his accident into a motion picture: "Thirty-three years after Patton's death," reads the dossier (called "Conspiracy Research Manual"), "it seems impossible that a minor traffic accident could have had such devastating effect. MGM's *Brass Target*... proposes that Patton's death was not an accident, but part of a daring criminal conspiracy."

The authority for this statement, containing the buzzword "impossible," was John Hough, an Englishman, who directed the motion picture with a star-studded cast. Hough dismissed lightly any possible *reasonable* objection to his theories: "Without entering into any discussion of reasons, it's obvious to us that the damage to Patton's car could not have been caused in a minor accident. . . . In *Brass Target,*" he wrote, "Patton's death is part of a conspiracy and I intend to leave very serious doubts in the minds of the audience about the General's death being merely an accident."

The cynical exploitation of the "conspiracy theory" originated in Soho Square in London, in an office suite occupied by Bill Edwards, international publicity director of MGM. From Edwards the wires led to Richard Kahn in Culver City, California, MGM's vice president in charge of publicity and exploitation [sic]; and to Rick Ingersoll, executive officer of ICPR, an independent public relations firm, hired on the outside to put additional clout into this all-out effort.

Masterminded by Bill Edwards and Dick Kahn from their respective command posts, the "exploitation" of the conspiracy theme had a dozen high-powered, highly paid PR persons working around the clock on two continents toward a single goal. It was spelled out in one of Bill Edward's first memoranda to Dick Kahn. "[The] key to our production publicity approach on *Brass Target*," he wrote on February 13, 1978, "should be variations on the theme—the world believes that General George S. Patton died following an automobile accident. But *was* it an accident? Conspiracies and cover-ups continue to fascinate the media. *Brass Target* offers both and we should take full advantage of this two-pronged opportunity to call attention to the film."

If there were any qualms about setting up an authentic American hero for a con game in his death, they were dispelled in March, in another report from Edwards to Kahn. "I met Frederick Nolan, author of *The Algonquin Project*, last week," he wrote. "After five minutes he convinced us all there was no doubt Patton was put away, in fact so persuasive was he, I think he could convince us of anything. He has an extremely bright, quirky sort of personality . . . and in my opinion would make a big hit on TV talk shows."

WHILE THIS was going on the motion picture was in the making from a screenplay that had been prepared under the supervision of the American producer Arthur Lewis *before* Nolan had convinced the powers at MGM that "Patton's death was part of a daring criminal conspiracy." The schedule was approaching the moment of truth—the shooting of the picture's key segment—what Edwards, by April 27, called "the assassination scene."

The concept of Nolan's book is that a group of Eisenhower's friends are grooming him for the presidency, and they fear that Patton might do or say something that could jeopardize Ike's chances. A scheme to kill Patton evolves so that he will no longer be a threat to Ike. Patton's death results from their ingeniously engineered murder plot. At the moment the decoy truck crashes into the general's car, a sniper fires a rubber pellet into the car, hits Patton's head, and breaks his neck.

An elaborate subplot suggests another reason for getting rid of Patton—the theft of a huge hoard of German gold by members of the American high command. Patton signs his death sentence when he takes personal command of the investigation and is believed to be close to catching the thieves. To complicate matters still further, the screenplay injects the Russians into the plot. Since the stolen gold apparently belongs to them, for it had been found in their zone, they hold Patton responsible for its disappearance.

Most of this was already in the can. Now that the "assassination scene" was about to be filmed, Bill Edwards shifted the publicity into high gear. He engaged David Douglas Duncan, the renowned photographer, for a fee of one thousand dollars, to take a set of still pictures of the shooting of the scene for magazines like *Paris Match* in France and other illustrated weeklies throughout the world. Conscientiously prepping for the assignment, David Duncan read my biography of General Patton and changed his mind. The man Edwards had described as "one of the world's best-known photojournalists" saw his integrity at stake and resigned from the job. "He said," Edwards wrote to Kahn, "there was no doubt in his mind Patton did die *accidentally* and because of his own special reputation did not see how he could accept the assignment. In short, he did not buy our story."

Still unwilling to give up the idea of covering the "assassination," Edwards now hired a British photojournalist who was prepared unconditionally to shoot the scene for two hundred fifty pounds. George Kennedy played Patton and Max von Sydow, the assassin.

The publicity and exploitation department gave the signal to release the picture—"on or around the 22nd of December." It would be the thirty-third anniversary of Patton's death—a "date [that] could be used to advantage." *Brass Target,* however, was an unequivocal failure at the box office.

• • •

THE CONSPIRACY theory that trailed Patton's death ever since General Jodl had hit on the idea refused to be put to rest. It gained viability—even popularity—from the decision of the American authorities not to subject Patton's accident to a proper probe. In fact, the accident of a four-star general, one of the greatest masters of warfare and an American hero on the grandest scale, was "investigated" more casually, superficially, and perfunctorily than any ordinary traffic mishap would have been under similar circumstances.

Military policemen in their fleet jeeps had flocked to the scene—among them Lieutenant Joseph Shanahan of Lambertville, New Jersey, a former deputy Provost Marshal in Patton's Third Army, now charged with the reorganization of the Mannheim police. Interviewed in 1979, by his hometown newspaper, Shanahan was anxious to stress that contrary to the books and the movie, the accident did not kill Patton. He died, he pointed out, in his hospital bed, three weeks *after* the crash.

According to Shanahan, no official report was ever made of the accident, because, as he put it, the nature of the crash did not warrant one. "By the time the MPs got there," he said, "there was nothing to report. They considered it a trivial accident at the time. No one thought that Patton was hurt at all."

As for the movie's "conspiracy theory"—well, Shanahan said, "it was known that General Patton was hated by all his men, including me." Any one of them *could* have arranged the trap. But none actually did. "I do know," Shanahan said, "that the accident was an *accident*."

The MP officer whose seniority of jurisdiction at the scene burdened him with what turned out to be a debt to history was Lieutenant Peter K. Babalas, a bright young Greek-American lawyer attached to the 818 Military Police Company at Mannheim. Babalas was destined to go far in his profession and in politics, becoming a state senator in Virginia in a distinguished postwar career. He was as puzzled about the accident as was Lieutenant Shanahan, but on different grounds. Nearer to the scene and closer to the case, Babalas knew that the accident was "trivial," to be sure, but General Patton's injury was not. And he did make an investigation of the mishap, concluding in his preliminary findings that both drivers of the vehicles had been guilty of careless driving.

What really puzzled Peter Babalas was the question of what happened to his report. On January 11, 1971, he wrote to the Department of the Army. Describing himself as "the officer who [had] made the automobile accident investigation in which General George Patton was involved," he asked for a copy of the official report that he had "submitted at the time of the investigation."

When no reply was received, he repeated his request on March 25, 1971, and was given the usual runaround—until July 21, that is, when the case was closed with a letter from M. W. Lawrence, an official at the National Personnel Records Center of the General Services Administration in St. Louis, Missouri, a civilian agency. "A review of the military personnel record of George S. Patton, service number 02 605, has been bade [sic]; however, the report of investigation which you request has not been located."

All we have extant from the probe is a deposition by Horace L. Woodring, Patton's driver, an obviously doctored document, for it includes statements far beyond the competence of the young soldier Woodring was at the time he signed the deposition. There is nothing in General Patton's 201 File, which contains *all* his personal papers bearing on his career in the Army, including his medical records and efficiency ratings; nothing in the archives of the Office of the Adjutant General; nothing among the documents of the Medical Corps or in the vast collection of the Military Police. There is nothing, for that matter, in the admirable array of documents in the Army's Military History Center—nothing that bears on the accident except a brilliant post mortem by Colonel Spurling, the neurosurgeon on the case. And that is still classified.

Thus is the mystery compounded, either by the inscrutable ways the bureaucracy works—misfiling or misplacing documents as often as not—or by some higher intervention that removed these records from the files. Because of the latter possibility, General Patton's accident has acquired sinister connotations.

Interviews with Senator Babalas convinced me that his

report contained little if anything that could have shed il-
lumination on what was by no means a trivial accident. The
car was badly battered and General Patton was already paralyzed when the ambulance took him from the scene. But,
Babalas said, Patton himself trivialized the accident. Lying
motionless and bleeding in his badly smashed-up limousine,
he was pale and in shock, but lucid and articulate. "What
an ironical thing," he said to Lieutenant Babalas, "for this
to happen at this time."

Babalas asked him what he meant, and the general said
in a soothing voice, even forcing a wan smile: "Nothing,
Lieutenant—except that I want to say that this here was a
stupid accident—only an accident! Neither of the drivers
was responsible for what happened!"

Patton had no way of judging the exact course of events
that had resulted in the crash. He could not possibly have
determined whether it could have been avoided. Yet he felt
a sudden warm surge of compassion, perhaps even gratitude.
As he saw it, the two drivers were mere pawns in the hands
of a Greater Force that was, at last, granting him the end
he craved.

WHAT WAS left carelessly undone thirty-five years
ago, was brashly undertaken by me, with the not inconsid-
erable resources at my disposal as the biographer of General
Patton. With the help of a panel of distinguished medical
specialists, highway safety experts, military police officers,
and a key group of eyewitnesses (including General Hobart
R. Gay, Patton's fellow passenger in the car, and PFC
Horace L. Woodring, the driver of the limousine), I have
reconstructed the general's last days as they really were and
subjected the accident to thorough scrutiny. My investigation was conducted in Washington, D.C., Fort Riley, Kansas, and Fort Knox, Kentucky; and also in Germany—Regensburg, Bad Toelz and Munich, St. Querin and Holzheim,
Bad Nauheim and Frankfurt, and, of course, on the tortuous
road of his last journey into the Kaeferthal.

WORLD WAR II was over and Patton's big job was
finished. At the time of his death, he commanded the Fifteenth U.S. Army—so-called, the quipsters said, because

there were altogether fifteen persons in it. It was a paper force, in more ways than one. It existed mostly on paper. And it was engaged in some obscure paperwork. Its assignment was to prepare the history of the great American crusade that began in Normandy on June 6, 1944, and ended in some frustration and futility just inside the western border of Czechoslovakia on May 8, 1945.

Although this looked like a shabby payoff for a victorious general, it was not really so incongruous an assignment for Patton as it appeared to be. For he was not only a soldier. He was a military historian. Patton himself affirmed the importance of history when he considered his transfer to the Fifteenth Army as more than just a consolation prize. "From a personal standpoint," he wrote to General Thomas T. Handy, one of his mentors, on October 2, 1945, "the new assignment is more in keeping with my natural academic tendencies than is that of governing Bavaria."

As it turned out, his few weeks of "moonlighting" as a historian did no damage to his fame as a fighter. But his untimely death was a tragedy on another score. An eloquent and articulate man, Patton left behind highly literate compositions about such diverse topics as strategy and tactics, the marvels of antiquity, the Arabs' way of life, the comparative value of English and French tanks in World War I, and the art of playing polo. But he did not tell all. He still had a great story to tell. As General Geoffrey Keyes put it, "The accident that killed General Patton destroyed what could have been the greatest book to come out of World War II."

LADISLAS FARAGO

BOOK ONE

★ ★ ★ ★

A War Too Late,
A Peace Too Soon

*Our success has been chiefly due to luck, I told him. "No,"
he replied, "to audacity," and I believe he was right.*

—*Note of a conversation with*
GENERAL HENRI HONORÉ GIRAUD *on March 30, 1945*

PROLOGUE

$$\star\ \star\ \star\ \star$$

Encounter
in the Haymarket

NINETEEN HUNDRED FORTY-FOUR.

Foggy and wet, and cold even for this harsh winter, it was truly a night to remember. London was under siege again. The frightful days of the Battle of Britain returned with vengeance. Attacked by a hundred Heinkels of the new 177 variety each night—twice in January, seven times in February so far—the year began with what seemed to be the revival of the Luftwaffe, more powerful and savage than before. Their 1,000-kilo bombs were hitting precious targets. One of them fell on St. James Square, chipped off old stones from the low palace of Henry VIII, and shattered the windows of Norfolk House where Eisenhower's new staff of invasion planners was at work. Tremendous fires were left burning in the wake of every raid.

By mid-February it seemed the new Blitz was raging out of control. Yet somehow this reprise of the famous battle seemed to be different from the holocaust of 1941. Life was going on now, and business was apparently as usual amidst the recent rubble. In the West End, the theaters were playing to packed houses, the audiences groping their way to and fro through the blackouts, between alerts and all-clears— the show was going on.

The stars in the Haymarket Theatre, between Piccadilly and Trafalgar Square, were the Lunts—Alfred Lunt and his wife, Lynn Fontanne, he a farmboy from Wisconsin, she the London lass, the smartest, slickest, most sophisticated couple on the stage. They were repeating in London their great Broadway success in Robert Sherwood's play *There Shall Be No Night*, about the heroic Finns during the Soviet invasion in 1941.

In the audience on a couple of passes were two American generals freshly arrived in London on busmen's holidays. One was Alexander M. Patch, in transit from the Pacific to North Africa where he was to take command of the Seventh U.S. Army, General Patton's former outfit. The other was Patton himself—Lieutenant General George S. Patton, Jr., just out of the doghouse.

Patton had arrived in Scotland on the morning of January 26, then flew down to see Ike the same day, sharing a plane from Prestwick to Chaddington with Caacie, one of Ike's pet dogs. Later in the afternoon in Eisenhower's office he was told that he had been chosen—"tentatively, mind you,"—to command the Third U.S. Army in the upcoming invasion of Fortress Europe.

It was one of the great switches in the plot of this war. Patton had come in from the cold. And now he was given an army by Ike who himself had just been named the Supreme Commander of "Overlord," the code name, newly coined, for the historic return to the Continent. Patton had been in exile in Palermo, sweating and fretting between the prospects of reassignment and retirement. The uncertainty of his future had borne down on him as the cruelest part of his punishment for the slapping of two shell-shocked soldiers at an evacuation hospital in the heat of the campaign in Sicily.

During his first couple of weeks now in London, while waiting for his new army to materialize, he spent his time seeing historic sights, among them a Druid ruin so big that it dwarfed Stonehenge. Dropping in at Faulkner's, his boot-makers in Mayfair who had had his custommade wooden last since his honeymoon in 1909, he ordered two pairs of boots—one for riding, the other for the tanks he was to lead in "Overlord." At his tailors in Savile Row, Mr. Weatherill fitted him for a new overcoat. "Damn the expense." He was back in the civilization he liked, spending his own money and living in his accustomed style.

He was seeing old acquaintances and making new friends

among people not usually known by American generals—
the aristocracy of both birth and the arts, where high society
blended with cafe society. Lady Cavendish was an old
friend, the former Adele Astaire from Omaha, Nebraska,
Fred's sister and partner in the footsteps of the Castles.
Lady Astor, the former Virginia belle, was another. And
Lady Duff Cooper. And the Lunts.

Just being in London was an exhilarating experience, for
it was the true capital of the big war, the microcosm of the
global conflict. Victory was no longer but a prayerful hope,
a remote chance on which bookmakers offered dismal odds.
It promised to be the Sure Thing, in the mightiest military
operation the world would ever see. Elsewhere the Red
Army was pushing forward all along the immense eastern
front. In Italy, the American Fifth Army had just reached
the Rapido River. And "Overlord." It was scheduled for the
late spring. The late spring. That was barely four months
away! Was it really possible to make it happen in only four
months?

Patton had no doubts. He, on his part, would be ready.
"I think," he mused, "that more and more my luck is holding
up. It sounds complacent but the slapping incident was a
good thing. At least Destiny seems to think that someone
must do something, and it will probably be me."

It was natural for him to snap out of gloom and swing
into euphoria—elated by Ike's choice, the abrupt return to
harness. And yet, he was disappointed. Who would get
command of the army group? And who would be named
to the overall ground command? Bradley? Jake Devers?
Montgomery? Forgetting that even a few weeks before he
was facing the possibility of going home, for some goddamn
sinecure behind a desk in the Pentagon, he now belittled
the command Ike was giving him. For he saw himself—
most of the time—as greater than any of the others. But
they failed to appreciate his greatness.

Now, there was time for everything. He went to the
pound and bought himself a dog—the ugliest he could pick,
an orphaned bull terrier with the smooth skin and the face
of a pig—and named him Willie. And when he found out
that the Lunts were at the Haymarket Theatre, he phoned

Alfred and got two tickets. He went to see the play with Sandy Patch, but the presence of the two American generals went unnoticed. Patch had no claim to fame in England. Patton had done great things in this war, yet his fame did not catch up with his deeds. He was a feuder and fusser, old Blood-and-Guts, notorious if anything—Ike's bad boy.

A few people recognized him, it seemed, but those who did were staring at him—the face was familiar, but who was he? This halfway mark between limbo and fame was bad for his soul, as he put it. He liked the play and loved the Lunts. But they could not keep him in his seat. In the middle of the second act he slunk out of the house, into the thick fog in the street to breathe the wet air and smoke a cigarette in violation of the strict blackout rules.

The Haymarket was pitch dark, and it seemed to be deserted, except for a few wanderers of these nights. Patton was accosted by one of them, whom neither snow, nor rain, nor sleet, nor the gloom of these nights could stay from the completion of her appointed rounds. She approached him with the most ancient proposition in the world.

She seemed to be a chubby little chippie, a mere girl, a Cockney lass by the sound of her few words. Patton remembered having been in London in World War I, a young man, a mere captain then, commanding General Pershing's palace guard at Hampton Court. Now he smiled in the darkness.

"I'm sorry, young lady," he told her. "But you're one war too late."

1.

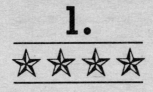

"What a War!"

"We are having one hell of a war."

—GENERAL PATTON in a letter to
    MAJOR GENERAL A. D. SURLES
in the War Department, on
                  December 15, 1944

*"Your Army has written a great page in history of
which the American people will always be very
proud."*

—GENERAL GEORGE C. MARSHALL *to* GENERAL PATTON,
                       on December 5, 1944

ON NOVEMBER 11, 1944, when George S. Patton, Jr., turned
fifty-nine, he was confronted by a vexing paradox. He hoped
this war would go on and on, in Europe, in Asia, somewhere—anywhere. But he was fearful that he was aging
out of it. "I celebrated my birthday," he wrote to his wife
in a somber mood, "by getting up where the dead were still
warm."

The man his friends called "Georgie," and regarded with
bemused tolerance as the eternal *enfant terrible,* was entering his last year—and though this is said in hindsight,
he himself was not entirely unmindful that these might be
his final days. He still had his voracious desire to fight but
no longer a matching will to live. When, during the year,
he saw his daughters in Boston, he startled them by saying,

19

"Well, girls, goodbye. I won't be seeing you again." And to his wife he wrote, "It is hell to be old and passé, and know it."

Some who had been close to him now thought he had matured of late, others believed he had grown a little quieter, but all agreed he had changed and grayed. He himself noticed strange signals, like a succession of semaphores. He had the funny feeling that the shells that struck near him now were landing closer, and the luck that had gotten him out of so many scrapes was running out. His vision was slightly blurred, a sure sign of age. And his values were getting mixed up—he spoke more and more of the beauties of war and the horrors of peace.

GEORGE SMITH PATTON, JR., was the descendant of warriors and scholars—of Hugh Mercer, Scottish physician and American patriot, former surgeon to Bonnie Prince Charlie, Charles Edward, the Young Stuart Pretender, and to John Forbes and Edward Braddock, British Generals in the Indian Wars. Mercer was killed in the battle of Princeton in 1777, at the head of his militiamen from Virginia. He was grandson of the first George Smith Patton, a brigadier general of the Confederacy at the age of twenty-six, who fell mortally wounded in the Battle of Cedar Creek near Winchester, Virginia, in 1862.

Patton himself learned the love and lore of war from their examples. Their memories were first kindled in his young heart by an old soldier he had befriended, John Singleton Mosby, the Virginia lawyer, who became the greatest partisan leader on either side of the Civil War. Mosby was a formidable teacher. He had served brilliantly in Jeb Stuart's cavalry, then turned guerrilla. Soon called the "Mosby Conspiracy," his private army, which never numbered more than two hundred men, routed the Union cavalry in northern Virginia, destroyed their supplies and smashed their communications, and became the scourge of the Army of the Potomac. Still fighting after Lee's surrender, but paroled eventually by Ulysses S. Grant himself, Mosby moved to California after the Civil War and took up the practice of law again. But he was not a good lawyer. In his sixties, the toothless old soldier was going to seed, until Georgie Patton gave him a new lease on life with his unbounded hero worship.

Not ten yet, Georgie would go riding near San Gabriel, where the California homestead to which the Pattons had exiled themselves was—he on his palomino pony, his friend on a tall chestnut mare. They would dismount on the beach and sit in the sand, old Mosby regaling the boy with his tales of wars and woes—how he had captured a Union general in bed at Fairfax Courthouse in 1863 and how he had seized a whole train south of Washington with a month's supplies for a regiment from New York. He illustrated his stories with forts built and maps drawn in the sand—and from there, George Patton went on—to the Virginia Military Institute and West Point, to the chase of Pancho Villa as "Black Jack" Pershing's aide in Mexico, to a blazing early career, a cavalry buff turned into a tank zealot in World War I. When it ended, he was a colonel by his temporary rank.

Colonel Patton had been wounded during the closing days of the last campaign, in an accident that was characteristic of him. While a unit of his tanks lumbered against the Hun only forty yards away, he himself was leading them on foot, bellowing useless profanities which his own men could not possibly hear inside the tanks and the Germans in front of them could not understand. He was hit in the buttock by a stray bullet. And though he suffered merely a flesh wound, he would have bled to death if his orderly, an Italian boy named Joe Angelo, and a Jewish boy from Brooklyn, Sergeant Reuben Schemitz, had not rushed him to the nearest evac hospital.

Patton had looked back in anger. Was this the world he had been fighting to save? The roaring twenties? The stock market crash? The Depression? The march of the Bonus Army? Goddamnit, he said. All he got out of that so-called Great War was his captaincy, the Distinguished Service Medal, and that fucking scar in his ass.

The wealthiest officer in the U.S. Army, married to the heiress of one of the big New England fortunes, Patton whiled away the boredom between the two world wars by playing superb polo, riding after the fox, sailing his yachts—with his rich man's pursuits. Everything seemed to be in flux, except the one change that was final in his career. His break with the cavalry was irrevocable. His heart now belonged to armor, but in a courtship that was not easy to bear. The American tank, which could have been the best in the world, was being developed on a shoestring— so much so that when his vehicles broke down and no spare parts were on hand in the Army to repair them, Patton had to mail-order them from Sears Roebuck, and pay for them out of his own purse.

IT WAS the tank in the end that rolled him into World War II. When it first began in Europe in 1939, Patton was fifty-four years old, forty years in uniform. Still only a colonel. But this new war was fought with planes in the air and tanks on the ground. And there was nobody in the U.S. Army better prepared than Patton for the kind of warfare that was making names like Guderian and Rommel household words throughout the world.

On November 11, 1942, less than a year after Pearl Harbor, he had the honor of carrying "Torch," this country's first overseas venture en route to *Festung Europa,* into French Morocco. He went on from there to oust the Germans from Tunisia and conquer Sicily. There he slapped the faces of two battle-fatigued GIs, and it was all over. Suddenly Patton loomed up as the caricature of the goosestepping militarist whom the Allies were fighting to eradicate. In spite of his record in combat, the slapping incident cost him the command of the Seventh Army and delayed his promotion from major general. The scuttlebutt was that he would be cashiered in disgrace.

But no. General Eisenhower was giving him another chance—in *"mutual"* interest," as their good friend Al Wedemeyer would never fail to point out. Ike had written about Patton's fortes in several fitness reports: "Outstanding as a leader of an assault force.... A brilliant fighter and leader.... Aggressive, loyal, energetic. Particularly suited for creating esprit and morale in a force preparing to face great risks."

That was exactly the kind of general Ike needed for his crusade in Europe.

Now, back in England in the spring of 1944, with the prepping and cramming for the crossing of the English Channel going on, suddenly it appeared that, after all, Patton might not be going. It was hopeless. Nobody could save him from himself. Even as he was drilling and exhorting his Third Army for the battles ahead, scheduled as it was to go in with the second wave of the Normandy invasion, he was up to his ears in trouble again.

HIS FIRST CRISIS at this time harked back to Tunisia in 1943. It was the eve of "Husky," the invasion of Sicily scheduled for July, in which Patton was to command the new Seventh Army. General George C. Marshall, his big boss, was in Tunisia, being entertained with last-minute landing exercises. But Patton picked a bad day for the show. He had chosen the 45th Division for Marshall to watch, but it was a green outfit, and nothing was going right. First the Navy was late in disembarking the combat team, then it missed the beach by four miles. And the young GIs, rattled by the mistakes, performed badly.

Patton went out of control. He stormed the beach just as the first men were coming out of the water, and yelled at them in his high-pitched voice that was squeaky in anger. "And just where in hell are your goddamn bayonets?" he shouted, then kept on blistering them, while Marshall, standing with Eisenhower and a bunch of generals nearby, observed the scene in embarrassed silence. "Well," said Major General Harold R. Bull, an officer on Ike's staff, "there goes Georgie's chance for a crack at high command."

That was on June 23, 1943. Now, on March 30, 1944, it seemed, Bull's prediction was about to come true. Returning to Peover Hall from an inspection tour, he was received by Major General Hugh J. Gaffey, his chief of staff, with a piece of grim news. "There is an officer here, sir, from the War Department. He wants to talk with you, General, behind closed doors."

The visitor turned out to be Lieutenant Colonel Joseph B. Williams, sent by the Inspector General of the Army to

investigate a weird aftermath of that prelude to "Husky."
Patton had become implicated in a "war crime" that was
certain to wreck his career unless he had a good excuse.
"General Patton," Colonel Williams told him, "you better
get yourself a lawyer, sir, because you need a good defense
for what I'm going to charge you with. And let me admonish
you, sir. Whatever you say might be used against you."

Back on July 14, 1943, the 45th Division had been fighting bitterly near Scoglitti, a fishing village in southern Sicily, when a company of its 180th Regimental Combat Team
was ambushed. A detachment led by a young captain named
Jerry Compton smoked out the snipers and captured forty-
three of them, thirty-eight in German uniforms, five in civilian clothes. Overwrought by the hardships of the fighting
and by the loss of his men to these bastards, Captain Compton lined up his prisoners against a barn and had them shot.

At about the same time near Gela, a sergeant named
Barry West of C Company was taking thirty-six German
prisoners of war to a cage in the rear. En route, as it was
getting dark, West became apprehensive that this superior
force of bitter Krauts might overpower their armed escort.
He made the Germans halt, and mowed them down on the
side of the road.

When the killings were reported to General Patton, he
brushed them aside as the natural reactions of his men to
a wave of German atrocities. But General Omar N. Bradley,
his corps commander, and Major General Troy H. Middleton, who commanded the 45th Division, persuaded him to
courtmartial Captain Compton and Sergeant West.

Colonel Williams was now in Peover Hall ten months
later to tell Patton that he had become a sort of accessory
to these crimes. At the trial, the defense had argued that
Compton and West were not guilty because they had killed
the Germans on Patton's orders.

"What orders?" the general asked.

"The defense claims you had issued them, sir," Williams
said, "in your address to the division prior to its embarkation
for Sicily. According to the defense, you allegedly had told
the men," and here Williams was reading from the brief,
"that 'if the enemy resisted until we got to within 200 yards,

he had forfeited his right to live.' As far as snipers were concerned, General, you supposedly had told the men that they had to be 'destroyed.'"

Patton did not recall any part of the speech. But he was positive that he had never given such orders. "I could be pretty bloody, Colonel," he told Williams, "trying to get those green troops to the sticking point. But I never— never!—have made any statements from which orders for the killing of prisoners could be construed by the wildest stretch of anybody's imagination."

After being told the details of the case, and after he had refreshed his memory with calls to Bradley and Middleton, Patton was even more emphatic. "Yes," he said, "I remember vaguely the incident. When the question of trying these two men came up, some of my friends advised me not to do it. But it was clearly barefaced murder, and I did not believe then, and I do not believe now, that I can condone murder for my own benefit."

If he was on trial, he would make the most of it. He did not need a lawyer. In an eloquent plea in his own defense, he told Williams: "Naturally, in none of my remarks did I ever contemplate the killing of men who had already surrendered." Apart from any other considerations, he said— like the articles of war, the Geneva Convention, and the matter of simple humanity—the fact that his own son-in-law was a prisoner-of-war in German hands had made him always very careful not to do anything for which there could be retaliation—nothing in the world to jeopardize his son-in-law's survival.

The thorough investigation by Colonel Williams satisfied the Inspector General that the defense had brought General Patton into the case merely to confuse the issue, and was "using quite unethical methods" by trying to "manufacture evidence out of whole cloth." The trial ended with the conviction of Compton and West. But their sentences were suspended and they were returned to their units. Both were killed in action later in the war.

The case was closed. But for Patton it was a close shave. When it was brought to the attention of General Eisenhower, who was to make the final decision on Patton's involvement, he absolved his friend and saved him for another day. But he admonished him. "Georgie," he said, "for Pete's sake. You talk too much."*

IT SEEMED impossible to shut him up. The Sicilian "massacre" was barely out of the way when another incident threatened to remove him from the war, this time for sure and for good. What became known as the Knutsford incident seems ridiculous in hindsight—a crisis so laboriously contrived that it now looks like a conspiracy aimed deliberately at getting Patton out before D-Day. "I am destined to achieve some great things—what, I don't know," was the way Patton himself put it. "But this last incident was so trivial in its nature, but so terrible in its effect, that it is not the result of an accident but the work of God."

The incident got its name from the market town and parish of a few thousand souls in Cheshire near Peover and Toft camps, whose women had come together in a Welcome Club to entertain the growing number of American GIs in their neighborhood. The club invited General Patton to inaugurate the club with a speech, and on April 25, barely six weeks before D-Day, Patton appeared as promised, even if somewhat concerned, for there were reporters at the ceremonies even though he had been told that everything would be off the record.

Patton ad-libbed a little speech on the importance of the Anglo-American alliance. "I believe with Mr. Bernard Shaw," he quipped, "that the British and Americans are two people separated by a common language." Then he added, somewhat ponderously, but harmlessly and off the cuff: "Since it is the evident destiny of the British and Americans to rule the world, the better we know each other the better job we will do."

They played *God Save the King* and *The Star-Spangled Banner,* and the affair was over. Before lunch the next day, however, General Hobart R. Gay, his chief of staff, received

---

*The incident was remarkable for the honesty of its handling, especially by comparison with the U.S. Army's callous indifference to and attempted cover-up of massacres, at My Lai and elsewhere during the war in Vietnam.

a frantic call from the brigadier general at SHAEF's public relations, telling him that Patton's speech was the big story in the morning papers. The trouble was, believe it or not, that he did not mention the Russians among the future rulers of the world.

By then, the fat was in the fire again. In the United States, Patton was pounced upon by liberals and conservatives alike, bringing into question nothing less than "the Third Army commander's fitness for command." Even before Patton could be fully aware of what he had done this time, and that his place in the war was in jeopardy again, Marshall and Eisenhower were burning up the wires debating his future. The violent reaction went far to show that Patton was needed but not wanted. The high command, with the exception of Ike, would have been relieved to get rid of him, even on so trivial a pretext as the Knutsford incident.

Patton was getting fed up. "Certainly," he wrote to General Everett Hughes, his friend, whom Eisenhower had thoughtfully deputized as his sheriff in this case, "my last alleged escapade smells strongly of having been a frame-up." The force of the uproar worried him. On his way to yet another showdown with the Supreme Commander, he told his orderly, Sergeant Meeks, to start packing. "This time, George," he told Meeks, "we're going home."

The incident dissolved in gestures calculated to cement Patton's relations with Eisenhower. At first, their meeting in London plunged him into despair. "I feel like death, but I am not out yet," he said almost ominously. "If they'll let me fight, I will. But if not, I'll resign and will tell the truth, and possibly do my country more good." Back at Peover Hall, he wrote Ike a letter, contrite as usual, but firm between the lines. Before it could arrive, however, Eisenhower called him to say that all was well after all. And yet, the inane scandal left an indelible mark on Patton. It filled him with a bitter taste that was never to leave him. It made something snap in his soul, and question his destiny.

On October 3, 1944, the Third Army began the intricate maneuver that became known as the Saar campaign, leading to the first conquest of the fortress of Metz in 1,301 years.

After a month of relentless fighting, Patton prepared one of his periodic scoresheets, and it showed that he had liberated 1,600 square miles of French soil, had taken more than 30,000 prisoners, and killed or wounded 80,000 Germans. The price he paid was less than one-third of the enemy's losses—23,000 Americans killed, wounded or missing.

Now it was November 11, 1944—the height of the Saar campaign, and everything combined on his birthday to conspire against him. The weather was awful. The rivers were rampaging, trapping man, beast, and equipment either in high water or bottomless mud. The Germans had their spirits up, thanks to the help they were getting from the elements. And Patton was being "screwed as usual" by his own high command. "At the moment," he wrote to General Hughes, the friend on whose shoulder he liked to cry, "I am being attacked on both flanks, but not by the Germans."

General Eisenhower wished him a happy birthday and told him not to worry—"The water will go down," he said, "and you'll go on with your job, as you always have." But when Omar Bradley phoned around five o'clock in the afternoon, he said nothing about many happy returns. Instead, he told Patton he would have to give one of his divisions, the 83rd, to the First Army. "I hope," Patton wrote, "history records his moral cowardice." He recorded it himself in his diary, lest history forget.

His birthdays no longer pleased or elated him. Shall I pretend, he asked, to an unreasonable and prodigious old age? Alexander the Great died at the age of thirty-three when he thought there were no more worlds to conquer. Napoleon and Hannibal were burned out by the time they turned forty. Wellington was forty-four at Waterloo. Wallenstein was forty-eight and through at the time of Luetzen, his last battle.

Now Patton, at fifty-nine, had only to look around to realize that this was not exactly a war of his own generation. His men were in their late teens and early twenties, the officers in their twenties and thirties. As for the high command, General Marshall was well into his sixties, to be sure, and so was Douglas MacArthur. But they were exceptions to the rule Marshall had laid down. When President

Franklin D. Roosevelt named Marshall Chief of Staff at the age of fifty-nine, he promptly purged the Army of the old fogies. Patton was kept. But sometimes he felt like a fossil among all the whippersnappers Marshall had promoted to high command.

Even the man he called "Old" Hodges—General Courtney Hicks Hodges of the First Army—was three years his junior. His friend Jake Devers, who now headed an Army Group like Bradley, was not yet fifty-five. Omar Bradley was fifty-one, Mark Clark forty-eight, Al Wedemeyer forty-seven. And hell, the Supreme Commander was not yet fifty!

While Patton was thinking of these oddities, he was bemused rather than despondent. He was not doing badly for a fusty old soldier. In the wake of his birthday, he saved Ike's neck in the Bulge and crossed the Rhine ahead of Field Marshal Bernard Law Montgomery, entirely on his own, between Oppenheim and Nackenheim, near the spot where Napoleon had crossed it in 1806. Even before that tour de force, after overrunning the Palatinate despite all sorts of obstacles, Patton boasted, "I really believe this operation is one of the outstanding operations in the history of the war, but I think we will eclipse it when we get across the Rhine." On March 23, 1945, while Bradley was finishing his second cup of coffee at breakfast, he took Patton's call and almost dropped the cup. "Brad," he heard Patton say, "don't tell anyone but I'm across."

"Across what?" Bradley asked, and Patton replied, "Across the Rhine, Brad."

"I'll be damned," Bradley just said.

Patton celebrated with General Manton Eddy, whose soldiers had made the Third Army's crossing, and with Major Alexander C. Stiller, the old buddy he kept on his staff to remind him of World War I, then drove to the river, stopped halfway across the pontoon bridge to piss into the Rhine. He had every reason to be exuberant, even adolescent, in his joy. He had broken into Germany with such élan that his Third Army was actually spearheading, like a giant task force, the collective advance of all the Allied armies.

• • •

NOW IT WAS the end of March 1945, less than eight months before his *sixtieth* birthday.

Patton's triumphs had made him increasingly smug. He commended God for favoring him with those victories and ordered Him to keep up the good weather. "The Lord is on my side," he wrote, "but He has a lot of getting even to do for me."

At the same time, his fears were deepening. What would there be for him to do when the war ends? Would he be needed? Or wanted, for that matter? "I will probably be a great nuisance," he wrote to his wife on one of his doubting days.

To steady his nerves, and to keep his sense of history, he was reading *Commentarii de bello Gallico,* the part of Caesar's account that traced the Gallic wars to 50 B.C. It was altogether appropriate for him to identify with Caesar at this stage, for it was across the Rhine, too, that the campaigns in Gaul had fluxed. Much could be learned from the Germans' predicament two thousand years before, crisscrossing the river in forlorn forays and frantic flights.

It was in a twilight mood between the triumphal realities of the recent past and an uncertain future that Patton was asserting himself more and more brashly—opposing the plans, schedules, and wishes of the high command.

His insurrection had begun in February 1945, as soon as the Bulge was over and the Allies could return to the business of delivering the knockout blow to Germany. The Third Army was in the vanguard of these penultimate campaigns, geographically and physically, and, as far as Patton was concerned, emotionally as well. Then, however, he was told to cool it. Washington had decided to take the action away from him in the south and shift the main effort to the north, where Montgomery was plotting, "like a ferocious rabbit," the decisive campaign—to break into the Ruhr across the Rhine and break the Germans' back. Monty was to get nine U.S. infantry and several armored divisions for his drive. In the process, the Third Army would be stripped.

"Whatever it is," Patton said on the record when he heard the news, "we will comply promptly and without argument."

But he had made up his mind to disobey orders. "Personally, I think," he told his staff off the record, "that it would be a foolish and ignoble way for the Americans to end the war by sitting on their asses. And, gentlemen, we aren't going to do anything foolish or ignoble like that—of course."

There is a saying that wars cannot be conducted behind closed doors. But what Patton now set out to do was the nearest thing to that. Even as he was supposed to be sitting tight, he sent the Third Army on a two-pronged drive forward, in the direction of Pruem and Bitburg across the Eifel. It was done in strictest secrecy. "Let the gentlemen up north learn of what we're doing," he said, "when they see it on their maps."

On March 1, he captured Trier on the Moselle in violation of his orders. When Eisenhower signaled posthaste that he must bypass the city because he would need four divisions to take it, Patton signaled back: "Have taken Trier with two divisions. What do you want me to do? Give it back?"

On March 9, Bradley phoned to plead (in that special form of supplication he had adopted in lieu of direct orders) that Patton "coordinate" the Third Army's plans with the arrangements General Patch was making for his Seventh Army, to pick up the offensive in the Palatinate. "Sure, sure, Brad," Patton agreed affably on the line, even when his group commander told him that he was to jump off with Patch in ten days—definitely not before March 19. But no sooner did Bradley hang up than he told his staff: "Get ready to attack, gentlemen." And he did, days ahead of Sandy Patch.

Patton was rolling unchecked. Even before "the gentlemen up north" realized the full magnitude of what he was doing, he had swept across the Eifel and to the Rhine. In the process, the Third Army surrounded twelve armies, one of them our own.

He was summoned to Bastogne, where the Supreme Commander was waiting for him. Patton was convinced that Ike had become wise to his "insubordination" and was calling him in for a dressing down. (A historical precedent always at his fingertips, Patton thought of the crisis at Calvi in 1797, when Horatio Nelson attacked a Spanish armada off Cape St. Vincent behind his superior's back because he feared Admiral Jervis might call off the operation.)

But the rendezvous at Bastogne turned out to be a purely social call. Eisenhower was always willing to gamble on Patton. In the end, it was Ike who received the kudos for the "unauthorized" campaigns west of the Rhine, even as John Jervis was given the peerage and pension for Nelson's victory.

2.

★ ★ ★ ★

Leaps over the Hedges

ON MARCH 27, 1945, Second Lieutenant Hollis Alpert, a young New Yorker serving as the historian of XX Corps in the Third Army, was standing the late watch at a command post in Speyer when he noticed a narrow protrusion on the situation map, stabbing into the enemy's land like a warning index finger. The next morning it vanished without a trace. In no operations plan, nor in any of the orders of battle, could Lieutenant Alpert find an explanation for it. Nowhere had any such operation been planned or authorized, or been even considered—except by General George Patton.

By this time, Patton's place in the esteem of his countrymen was secure. General Eisenhower no longer had to build him up to justify retaining him. The victory in the Saar campaign was followed by Patton's personal triumph in the Battle of the Bulge, by the breaching of the Siegfried Line, and the Third Army's entry into Germany on February 1, 1945. Drives across the Eifel and the Palatinate took them over the Rhine, in almost casual operations, just when the British were set to cross the river on the gigantic pattern of the cross-Channel invasion.

In the House of Representatives in Washington, D.C., Congressman Winfield K. Denton of Indiana moved that Congress send their compliments to General Patton in Germany, but the War Department objected to singling him out. Instead the House adopted a resolution to congratulate General Eisenhower and express the nation's gratitude to his generals for their "magnificent victories." Craving the

33

rewards of conquest, Patton was in no mood to share the glory of his victories. "Congress voted to thank me only," he noted wryly, "and ended up by thanking everyone."

Could he still do wrong? What had appeared on Lieutenant Alpert's map was no mirage. It indicated Patton's private mission to liberate some nine hundred American prisoners-of-war alleged to be held in a stockade near Hammelburg, a fair-sized town on the Saale River in Franken, only sixty miles east from where advance elements of the Third Army stood. It was an urgent mission of mercy, he claimed, for there was reason to believe that the Americans in the camp were in danger of being massacred by the desperate Germans.

Patton's thrust was a stab in almost total darkness, for the presence of American prisoners was but hearsay, the threat to them only a rumor, and intelligence about the place itself was scant. To be sure, there was a P/W camp near Hammelburg called OFLAG XIIIB, a huge compound built in 1941 to confine thousands of Serbs captured when Hitler invaded Yugoslavia. The Serbs were still there, their numbers swelled by inmates from other European armies the Wehrmacht had liquidated. In recent months, according to the scuttlebutt, 1,500 American officers had been added to the camp's inventory, moved from Poland, out of the path of the advancing Red Army.

Patton professed to be interested in *all* the American prisoners in OFLAG XIIIB. Actually he was concerned about only *one* of them—Lieutenant Colonel John Knight Waters, Jr. A scholarly cavalryman who had studied art at Johns Hopkins University before switching to West Point, Johnny Waters was Patton's favorite son-in-law, married to "Little Bea," his eldest daughter Beatrice. This, then, was the setting for an operation that introduced a new Patton to reckon with. It demonstrated most dramatically just how self-reliant and stubborn he had become—how prepared he was to do as he pleased, in defiance of his superiors. Like most of what he was doing these days, in fact, the so-called "Hammelburg incident" caught Eisenhower and Bradley unawares.

• • •

THE PATTON FAMILY had contributed its fullest quota of men to the war. Son George was at West Point, and Jim Totten, husband of Ruth Ellen, the younger daughter, was in the thick of it in Italy, "the best goddamn battalion commander in the army." John Waters was with Patton in Tunisia, a brilliant young officer certain to go far and rise high in the war. It was, therefore, a crushing blow to Patton when Waters was taken prisoner in one of the battles of the Kasserine Pass in late February 1943. Shifted from camp to camp, each time farther to the east, Colonel Waters was sitting out the war behind barbed wire.

From that day on, Patton hoped and prayed that John might somehow escape and make good on the great promise of his career. But it proved increasingly difficult to get even the barest tidings about Waters. Knowing how distraught Patton was, Ike, Bradley and his other friends kept an eye on Waters. A WAC officer, Captain Briggs, had the assignment at SHAEF of monitoring Colonel Waters's movements, to keep Patton posted.

Waters's departure from Szubin became known to SHAEF on February 9. Then Captain Briggs learned that some of the men from Szubin had been taken to the OFLAG near Hammelburg. Since it was in the general area where the Third Army happened to be operating, she wasted no time in informing Patton of the development.

Her message reached Patton on March 23, the day the Third Army was crossing the Rhine. Despite his exhilaration, the news about Waters preoccupied him. He was overcome by an urge to do something, anything, wise or foolish, it did not matter, as long as it yielded Johnny. He could not be certain that Colonel Waters was actually in Hammelburg, and he knew nothing of the place except that it was not too far from where Combat Command B of the 4th Armored Division was positioned. Yet he decided then and there to rescue Waters even if he had to change the set plans of the high command and divert some of his own forces in the process.

By nightfall of March 23, Patton had his decision firm in his mind—he would go for Johnny, no matter what. He sent for Major Alexander C. Stiller, his buddy from World War I, because old Al's derring-do came in handy where

others balked. He would "send," he told Stiller, "a combat
command for Johnny Waters," and wanted Stiller to go
along to take care of Waters. "We are headed right for
John," he wrote to his wife that same night—at a time when
he barely knew where Hammelburg was and could not be
sure that his son-in-law was actually there.

ON MARCH 26, Patton met with Eisenhower and
Bradley at General Hodges's command post, and mentioned
casually, "to cover his ass," his idea to General Bradley,
in whose 12th Army Group he served. Bradley was becoming fed up with his friend's harebrained ideas. Only a week
before, Patton had asked him to assemble all Piper Cubs
in the 12th Army Group, and then to use them to drop a
task force of three hundred handpicked men on the east bank
of the Rhine to establish a bridgehead and beat Monty to
the punch.

And now this half-baked scheme about Hammelburg!
Off the beaten path, on the wrong side of the Saale River,
the town did not figure in any of their plans. Moreover, it
was about sixty to eighty miles *behind* enemy lines in an
area where the Germans were suspected of having elements
of a couple of divisions in transit. Bradley tried to talk him
out of it. Patton did not pursue the matter, and they left it
at that.

But when the meeting broke up, Patton flew straight to
General Eddy's headquarters and ordered Brigadier General
Ralph Canine, Eddy's chief of staff: "Pick up the phone and
tell Bill Hoge* to get off his ass and get over to Hammelburg." Canine stunned him with his reply. "General," he
said, "my orders are to tell you we will not carry out this
one of your orders." But Patton, who never tolerated con-
tradiction, now surprised Canine by telling him quietly:
"Okay, Ralph. Get Hoge on the telephone. I'll tell him
myself."

He did. The wheels began to turn. Combat Command
B of the 4th Armored Division was alerted, but it was no
longer designated to move out in force. When Bradley ob-

---

*Major General William Hoge, commanding 4th Armored.

jected, he settled for a task force—a handful of tanks, a few assault guns, and maybe a couple of companies commanded by a captain.

Picked to lead the raid was Abraham Jacob Baum of the Bronx, a former blouse-pattern cutter in Manhattan's garment district, now a captain at twenty, six foot two, rangy, with crew-cut hair and a fierce mustache.

Crossing streams, climbing hills, Task Force Baum did make it to the P/W camp on a saucer-shaped plateau atop a steep hill, three miles south of the city of Hammelburg. But the mission was a failure. The task force was virtually wiped out—by German reinforcements and by an assault gun battalion that had unexpectedly rolled in from the east just when Baum's force entered from the west.

The first light of day on March 28 revealed a hill littered with wrecked, smoldering tanks and half-tracks. Captain Baum, shot in the leg (his third wound in two days), and Al Stiller tried to hide in a pine grove, but were quickly found by hounds the Germans sent after them. John Waters had tried to escape but was wounded by a sentry just when he was making his way through the barbed wire. His condition was grave but not critical. The camp was liberated a week later, on April 5, by a unit of General Alexander Patch's Seventh Army, and Colonel Waters was flown out in a plane Patton had sent for him, aboard which was the deputy surgeon of the Third Army. When he had his first chance to see his son-in-law since early 1943, it was in the 34th Evacuation Hospital in Frankfurt. Waters had been shot in the left groin, the bullet going through his rectum and injuring his spine. But he was coherent and curious. The first thing he asked his father-in-law was, "Did you know that I was at Hammelburg?"

"No," said Patton, "not for sure."

It was left to General Eisenhower to explain the incident to General Marshall. Though shocked when he heard of Patton's arbitrary action, Ike was not prepared to make an issue of this latest escapade. The war was in its final, decisive stage, and Patton was indispensable to it.

Eisenhower managed to inform Marshall without aggravating him. His report of April 25 endures as the most lucid account of the raid: "[Patton] sent off a little expedition on a wild goose chase in an effort to liberate some American prisoners. The upshot was that he got 25 prisoners back and lost a full company of medium tanks and a platoon of light tanks. Foolishly, he then imposed censorship on the movement, meaning to lift it later, which he forgot to do. The story has now been released, and I hope the newspapers do not make too much of it. One bad, though Patton says accidental, feature of the affair was that his own son-in-law was one of the 25 released. Patton is a problem child, but he is a great fighting leader in pursuit and exploitation."

Patton later described the raid on Hammelburg as "one of the two mistakes" he had made during the war.

ON THE DAY the Germans broadcast that Task Force Baum had been destroyed, which was the only victory they could honestly claim in four months, General Patton busied himself with myriad other chores to take his mind off the "incident." As soon as he was assured that Colonel Waters would not be paralyzed, the raid was forgotten. "What a war!" he exclaimed, obviously back in the old groove.

When asked which way he would be going next, Patton just grinned and said he didn't know. "It has gotten to the point," he said, "where we can go where we damn well please." He did not seem concerned about what awaited him beyond the next ten or fifty miles. He was full of misgivings about the road beyond the war. On April 7, a lazy Saturday, he was brooding more than usual. "I'll go anywhere," he said, "when this thing here ends. But I hope I can go to China." He had visitors, some of whom he welcomed—like Colonel William Orlando Darby, who had commanded the Ranger Battalion when Patton landed in Sicily in 1943. Others he suffered quietly, like Elmer Davis, the director of the Office of War Information, who came with a contingent of prominent newspapermen from the States. To impress them, he took the Davis party to the area of the XII Corps and showed them the 71st Infantry Division in action.

When he returned at noon, General Gay received him with the news that the Third Army had captured its four-hundred-thousandth prisoner of the war. The man had been brought to "Lucky Forward," his headquarters in Frankfurt, where the PR people had assembled newsmen, photographers, and cameramen to record his arrival for tomorrow's newspapers and posterity. Among the other prisoners in the day's bag was Lieutenant General Karl-Heinz Hahn, who had commanded the German LXXXII Corps, and was captured with the remnants of his staff by a handful of men from a quartermaster detachment.

As was his custom whenever a general officer was brought in, Patton sent for Hahn and asked him what he thought was going to happen. The war was over, Hahn said. He was tired of the fighting and saw no purpose in further resistance.

General Hahn was echoed by General Kurt Bolzen, commandant of a defunct Panzer division. When Patton asked him whether every "goddamn Panzer would have to be killed before the Germans threw in the sponge," Bolzen replied: "I don't think so, Herr General. I believe the speedy advance of your forces is ending the war." Patton persisted: "Do you think that there will be an underground movement, fighting from ambushes, and all that crap?"

"Maybe a handful of fanatics will fight on for a while," Bolzen said. "But no . . . the German people are tired of the war."

IT WAS ALL in a day's work, the fighting, the questioning, the fretting—until suddenly the day lit up with a piece of incredible news. At three o'clock in the afternoon, General Eddy called from a place called Werra in Thuringia. "General," he said, almost breathless, "I've just come from a village called Merkers behind God's back, looking over a salt mine which General Earnest's boys had captured a couple of days ago. Believe it or not, there's over a billion bucks in paper money in the mine—mind you, a billion d-o-l-dollars in American greenbacks."

Eddy was talking too much, Patton thought. Why the hell isn't he coming to the point? "Goddamnit, Matt," he said, "did you see any gold in that fucking mine?"

It was by now only a thin secret that the Germans had been shipping all the valuables that could be moved out of

Berlin. Rumors were spreading that much of their gold hoard, if not all of it, had gone to caves in the Thuringian Forest and was hidden in the path of the Third Army's advance.

As a matter of fact, Patton had been alerted by the finance chief of SHAEF to look for the treasure. So, maybe, this was *it*. He was sizzling with impatience. But Eddy was taking it in his stride. "No, sir," he said. "The gold is supposed to be sealed up in a safe behind a big steel door somewhere down there."

"Goddamnit, General Eddy," Patton cried in that squeaky voice of his whose pitch was getting higher the more excited he became. "What the hell is keeping you from opening the safe?"

"Sir," Eddy said, "I don't think we can open it. We've picked up two officials of the Reichsbank. But they swear they don't have the keys and haven't the faintest idea how one could get in unless we blow it open."

"General Eddy," Patton roared, "go and blow it open, goddamnit, and on the double, if you know what's good for you."

He swallowed the rest of his anger and hung up. But General Gay, who knew how high Eddy's blood pressure was, picked up the telephone to bring it down. "Okay, Matt," he told Eddy, "call us when you have the gold." Then he added, for what he regarded as comic relief: "But don't you break your back trying to carry it out yourself."

Patton's notes of those days did not reflect his excitement. But an entry in the diary of the usually unflappable General Gay showed clearly how the news was regarded at Lucky 5—*"If true,"* it read; *"this is probably the most strategic incident in the war with the German nation."*

THE WAR in Europe had less than a month to go, and one of its biggest stories was breaking fast. As it so often happened in Patton's bailiwick, where big stories had a tendency to grow bigger, it was in danger of getting out of control. Wild rumors that the German gold reserves worth billions of dollars had been captured in toto were simmering in the European theater of operations ever since it had become known that the Americans had come upon a salt mine of mystery. Gold has a romance and lure all of its own. The chimerical pot o' gold captured the imagination of the GIs.

What actually happened was that on April 4, 1945, in the area of XII Corps, as the 90th Division of Major General Herbert K. Earnest was surging eastward against sporadic resistance, its 357th Infantry Regiment took Marksuhl and Moehra, and the 358th seized Merkers, a village located between the Buchenwald and Ohrdruf concentration camps. This whole advance through this part of central Germany was developing into a march of mercy. Wherever elements of the XII Corps moved, they found scenes of the Nazis' crimes. They liberated thousands of slave laborers in arms factories, British prisoners-of-war in several Stalags, stragglers who had managed to escape from the concentration camps.

After Merkers had been secured on the fourth, PFC Clyde Harmon and PFC Anthony Kline, a pair of military policemen on their first sweep to enforce the regulation that no German must travel more than six kilometers out of the village, stopped two women on a road at some distance from Merkers. But when they explained that they were on their way to fetch the midwife for a relative who was in labor, the MPs let them proceed. Then, in a sudden fit of chivalry, Harmon and Kline volunteered to escort them to the midwife and back. As they were passing a massive oak door at the foot of a hill, at the entrance to the vast Kaiseroda Salt Mine, one of the women let a cat out of the bag.

"That's where the gold is," she mumbled.

Kline, who spoke German, asked her: "What did you say? What gold?"

Probably moved by the gallantry of these American soldiers, the woman told them what she knew. "They brought the gold here from Berlin," she said, "to this safe place, when everything was about to be lost."

"How much gold?" Kline asked.

"Very much," the woman said. "There was so much of it, Herr Amerikaner, that it took us local people, the foreign workers in the factories, and the prisoners-of-war from the Stalag three days just to unload it."

Harmon and Kline forgot about the midwife. They rushed back to their post, then reported their find to Lieutenant Colonel William Russell, the civil-affairs officer of the 90th Division. Russell managed to get confirmation from a British sergeant who was one of the prisoners-of-war who had helped with the unloading. Then a man claiming to be an assistant director of the National Gallery in Berlin was found, and he told Colonel Russell he was in Merkers to care for an invaluable collection of paintings which was also hidden in the mine.

A check in the village then produced the two Reichsbank officials Eddy had mentioned. They not only confirmed the presence of the hoard but gave a description of the interior of the mine; it had five separate entrances, they said, and some thirty miles of tunnels! By then the case was handled on General Earnest's echelon. He himself detailed the 712th Tank Battalion to guard the main entrance at Merkers, and the entire 357th Infantry Regiment to surround the mine and secure the four other entrances.

On the morning of April 5, after work had gone on through the night to get the steam boilers going to generate electricity for lifts and ventilators, a group of officers had the main door forced open and entered the mine. Near the entrance they found 550 bags containing—not American greenbacks, as Eddy had told Patton in the first flush of the excitement—but 2.2 billion Reichsmarks.

It was at this stage that Colonel Russell notified XII Corps of the windfall. He told Brigadier General Canine, the chief of staff, that he and his officers had been down a shaft which he estimated was two thousand feet below the ground, and found priceless art treasures and a collection of old uniforms stored in the mine, in addition to all that paper money in the bags.

The significance of the division's unexpected good fortune needed a day to sink in. It was, therefore, only on the afternoon of April 6 that General Eddy saw fit to authorize his chief of staff to let Third Army headquarters in on the big secret. Canine phoned Gay, who then, on Patton's instructions, ordered XII Corps to clamp a tight lid on the story—"until," he said, "full confirmation was had." The fortuitous finding of the Nazis' gold hoard was, as he put it, "a piece of startling news that would electrify the world." But should it prove a hoax, he warned, "the reaction would not be favorable."

Then a crisis developed. The 90th Division's chief of staff leaked the story to a couple of newsmen, and the censor at XII Corps passed their dispatches, in violation of General Gay's order. When Patton was told that the story had leaked, his fury knew no bounds. The censor was from SHAEF, a stranger—and, as Gay recorded it, he "was directed [by Patton] to leave the area of the Third Army this date." It was the 8th of April by then.

On the same day, a Sunday, General Eddy called Patton again, but was still not sure whether the gold was there. "Goddamnit, General Eddy," Patton swore, for he already had visions of what to do with all that treasure. "You blow open that fuckin' vault and see what's in it." Eddy called back a few hours later. Engineers of the 90th Division had been sent down with orders to blast an entrance to the vault. The steel door to the vault was open.

What was then found in this robbers' cave was straight out of the Arabian Nights. The vault turned out to be an immense hall, seventy-five feet wide and one hundred fifty feet deep. The floor, as far as they could see, was covered with rows of numbered bags—seven thousand of them by actual count—each containing gold coins or gold bars weighing twenty-five pounds each. Baled paper money was stacked along one wall. At the far end of the enormous treasure trove was the Nazis' most abhorrent loot—valises chock-full of gold and silver fillings from teeth, gold and silver eyeglass frames, watch cases, wedding rings, and strings and strings of pearls. It was the yield of the extermination camps.

The gold, between 55 and 81 pounds to a bag, amounted to nearly 250 tons. All European currencies were represented in the paper money. The largest amounts were 98 million French francs and 2.7 billion Reichsmarks. Then there were the works of art—400 tons in weight—stacked in the other passages inside the vault.

•   •   •

IN THE MIDDLE of all the euphoria, Third Army moved "Lucky Forward" still more forward—to its sixth echelon location since D-Day—to a place called Hersfeld, which the 4th Armored Division had overrun on March 31. In spite of the premature revelation of the windfall, Patton still hoped that he could somehow make the treasure vanish again. He succeeded in keeping the lid on. But then the whole thing blew up in his face—curiously enough, over his eviction of the SHAEF censor. On April 12, lured by the gold and the commotion, Eisenhower and Bradley flew in, bringing with them their own mixture of euphoria and concern.

Patton greeted them at the Cub airfield at eight-fifty in the morning and took them to Hersfeld, where he treated them to a short briefing of the tactical situation. When it was time for a visit to the mine, Patton escorted them to Merkers, where General Eddy took them to the hoard. Down they went, 1,600 feet, in what must have been the world's oldest and most rickety elevator. Patton was in one of his more flamboyant moods. He enjoyed his vicarious wealth like a latter-day Croesus. As the antique lift was descending with them by its single cable, he kept up a barrage of quips. Counting the stars on the shoulder patches of his guests, he remarked with a poker face: "If that clothesline should break, promotions in the United States would be considerably stimulated."

Ike apparently did not entertain fondly the prospect of getting killed in action while on a sightseeing tour in a German salt mine, inspecting a hoard of Nazi gold. "Stop it, Georgie. We don't think your remarks are funny at all." When they arrived in the vault, however, the sight that greeted them was one they would not have wanted to miss.

"Well, I'll be damned," Ike marveled. "But why keep it secret, George? What would you do with all that money?"

"Hell, Ike," Patton said with a nervous little smile, "I'd have some of it melted down, cut up in medallions, one for every sonuvabitch in the Third Army." But most of it, he said, he'd keep for a rainy day, when the Congress of the United States would again curtail the military budget. "Then," he told Ike, "whenever funds got particularly tight, we could dig down into this cave for the money we néeded for new weapons."

Eisenhower just shook his head, looked at Bradley, and laughed. "You bastard," he said to Patton, "you always have an answer."

AFTER the Supreme Commander's inspection tour no margin was left for any scheming. Ike ordered Colonel Bernstein, the deputy chief of the financial branch of his G-5, to make an exact inventory of the treasure and have it hauled away. Bernstein picked up Lieutenant Colonel Barrett, his opposite number at General Bradley's headquarters, and the two of them went looking for a safe depository further back in the SHAEF Zone. They finally settled on the Reichsbank building in Frankfurt, close to Ike's mushrooming new headquarters at Hoechst.

The moving began at 9:00 A.M. on April 14. In twenty hours, the gold, currency, and a few cases of art were loaded on thirty ten-ton trucks, each with a ten percent overload. Down in the mine, jeeps and trailers hauled the treasure from the vault to the shaft, where the loaded trailers were put aboard lifts and brought to the surface.

At the surface, an officer registered each bag or item on a load slip. Then an officer and an enlisted man checked the load slip to verify that each item from the vault was loaded on a truck. Another officer recorded the name and serial number of each driver, assistant driver, and guard.

The convoy left Merkers April 15 for the 85-mile drive to Frankfurt. It was escorted by five rifle platoons, two machine gun platoons, ten multiple-mount anti-aircraft vehicles, and a flock of Piper Cubs and a fighter squadron for air cover.

In the early afternoon of that same Sunday the convoy arrived in Frankfurt, and the trucks were unloaded—the job lasted the rest of the day and the whole night. Each item was checked against the load list and was checked again as it was taken into the bank. Two infantry companies cordoned off the area. Although rumors floated around for some time afterward that one of the trucks had "disappeared" on the way to Frankfurt, the Army insisted that the thirty trucks that began the journey also ended it exactly as planned and scheduled.*

By then Patton had lost interest in the venture—easy come, easy go. All that gold had ceased to glisten for him. He was gone again—far from the scene—the treasure expelled from his mind. Even as the precious convoy was rolling toward Frankfurt, he was at Mainz to attend the inauguration of the Rhine Bridge. When invited to cut the ceremonial ribbon, he scornfully refused the pair of oversize scissors Major General Ewart G. Plank, his host from Com Z, had handed him for the ritual.

"What are you taking me for, Plank," he grunted, "a tailor? Goddamnit, General, give me a bayonet."

---

*The gold remained in the Reichsbank vault in Frankfurt under Army control until January 24, 1946, when responsibility for it passed to the International Reparation Agency. It returned the gold on a pro-rated basis to the various governments from which the Nazis had looted part of it and which had, therefore, legitimate claims. A considerable part of what was left went to compensate and resettle Jewish victims of Nazism. Although under the terms of the Yalta agreement, Thuringia later passed to Soviet control and became part of Communist East Germany, the Soviet Union was not included in the distribution, since it had relinquished all claims to captured gold in the Potsdam agreement. In addition to the gold and art objects, the salt mine also contained the records of the German Patent Office, Luftwaffe material and ammunition, records of the German High Command, libraries and municipal archives, including two million books from Berlin and the entire Goethe collection from Weimar, as well as the files of Krupp, Henschel, and other major German industrial concerns.

3.

Sloughs of Despond

If the trumpet give an uncertain sound, who shall prepare himself for battle?

—I CORINTHIANS

BACK AT Lucky Forward with Eisenhower and Bradley the morning after their inspection of the Nazi treasure, the big story of the gold was overtaken by bigger news. President Franklin Delano Roosevelt had died suddenly from a massive stroke at his cottage in Warm Springs, Georgia.

Patton was not a man who knew how to hide his feelings. He held strong—sometimes extreme—opinions about men, things, and events, and had his ingrained views on many topics—Italian food and Arabian horses, the usage of tanks and the use of the saber, the old Normans and the new Russians.

His likes and dislikes were not always congruous. He liked Roosevelt. He would take time after the battles to send the Commander in Chief souvenirs he had captured with the President's interests in mind—ship's models, rare books, postage stamps, old maps, a painting here, a bust there. He forwarded them directly to the White House, each with a charming little note that never failed to enchant Roosevelt.

As security-minded as Patton was indiscreet in this correspondence, F.D.R. sent his letters to Grace Tully, his confidential secretary, for safekeeping. "Keep these communications from George Patton under wraps," he wrote on a slip. "He is our greatest fighting general, and sheer

47

joy." With such strong links as their wealth and aristocracy, they were close friends. Roosevelt's passing on April 12, 1945, moved him deeply.

Psychologically, Patton was adrift. He was beginning to view the world darkly in the shadow cast on it by the Russians, and to see the Nazis in the light of that threat. His doubts were becoming more cruel than the worst truth.

In what turned out to be the final hurricane of the war, the question of what to do with Czechoslovakia intruded on all the fancy plans and commitments Teheran and Yalta had produced. Patton all of a sudden found himself in the eye of that hurricane. The decisions on this score, reached during the last four weeks of the war, became the hinge of modern history. And Patton's moves would impact on the future of a continent in the balance between freedom and servitude. A Russian deserter who had managed to make his way to the Third Army from a unit of General Andrei Vlasov, a former Stalinist general now fighting with the Germans in Czechoslovakia, hit upon the theme.

"How fortunate you are, you lucky Americans!" he said with tearful eyes. "You are rid of Hitler. But we, your companions in victory, still have our Stalin."

Patton's historic mission was as far-reaching as it was simple. He was to push forward as fast and as far as the Third Army could go until it met the Red Army. This broad sweep would take Patton deep into Czechoslovakia—to Prague and maybe beyond—and into Austria, and would give the West control of the greater part of the European heartland, the geopolitical pivot of the continent.

The Third Army's penetration of territory the Soviet Union was craving was possible because the Red Army was falling behind in its timetable. On April 11, however, General Bradley outlined a stop line for Patton, restricting the advance of the Third Army to a line slightly to the west of the Czechoslovak border. But Bradley and Patton had a tacit agreement that the stop line was tentative. As a matter of fact, a few weeks later Bradley issued explicit orders to the Third Army to "cross the Czechoslovak border and advance to a line running north and south through Budweis-Pilsen-Karlsbad." More important, he told Patton to be prepared to advance farther eastward.

The intoxicating prospect of final victory was in the air. It did not seem too late to forestall the Russians. On May 2, the Red Army captured Berlin, and the Second White Russian Front met the British forces along the Wismar-Wittenberge line. Troops of the First White Russian Front linked up with the Americans southeast on the Elbe. But in Czechoslovakia the Ukrainian armies were still held up, fighting for every inch. And the Red Army troops earmarked to take Prague were still busy at Dresden and Görlitz in Germany.

On May 4, Patton sought permission to resume the Czechoslovak phase of his last campaign. He sweated it out at his command post all day until 7:30 P.M., when Bradley called him with the good word. "Ike has just called," he said exuberantly. "You have the green light for Czechoslovakia, George. When can you move?"

"Tomorrow morning," Patton whooped back. His friend's eagerness kept puzzling Bradley, so he asked, "Why does everyone in the Third Army want to liberate the Czechs?"

"Oh, Brad," he answered, "can't you see? The Czechs are our *allies* and consequently their women aren't off limits. *On to Czechoslovakia and fraternization!*" he yelled into the telephone. "How in hell can you stop an army with a battle cry like that?" Patton said nothing about the Russians.

ON MAY 5, after a three-man OSS team had reconnoitered the Czechoslovak capital, Patton called Bradley, told him that Prague was ripe for the picking, and asked, "Is this stop line through Pilsen really mandatory? Can't you let me go into Prague? For God's sake, Brad, those patriots in the city need our help! We have no time to lose!"

He suggested that he would "get lost" on May 6, and while he was incommunicado, his troops would enter the Czech capital. He would then come out of hiding and report to Bradley—from a phone booth in Prague.

Bradley sounded as if he liked the idea. But he refused to let Patton go all the way to that phone booth in Prague without clearing it with Ike. He put in the call to Eisenhower. It was imperative, for he could not afford to be just half safe in a situation as extremely delicate as the liberation of Prague, which had important political ramifications.

The Supreme Commander was at his sternest when he told Bradley to stop Patton. He had compelling reasons to be so firm. The day before, General Eisenhower had suggested to General Alexei Antonov, the Red Army Chief of Staff, that after the occupation of the line through Pilsen, the Third Army be allowed to move to the Moldau and the western suburbs of Prague. Antonov dissented strongly. He urged Eisenhower "not to move the Allied forces in Czechoslovakia east of the originally intended line"—to avoid, as he put it, "a possible confusion of forces."

Antonov then added ominously: "The Red Army had stopped its advance to the lower Elbe east of the Wismar-Schwerin-Dömitz line at the Supreme Commander's request. I hope, General Eisenhower, that you will comply with our wishes relative to the advance of U.S. forces in Czechoslovakia."

Ike had no choice. He assured Antonov that he would halt the Third Army on the prearranged line. Now he ordered Bradley to find Patton wherever he was and tell him that under no circumstances was he to go beyond the Budweis-Pilsen-Karlsbad line. Moreover, the city of Prague was out of bounds.

On the morning of May 6, returning from church, Patton was called to the phone. It was Bradley, calling to convey Ike's orders. "The halt line through Pilsen *is* mandatory, George, for V and XII Corps," he said with the utmost emphasis. "Moreover, you must not—I repeat, *not*—reconnoiter to a greater depth than five miles northeast of Pilsen. Ike does not want any international complications at this late date."

"For God's sake, Brad," Patton protested, "it seems to me that a great nation like America should let others worry about complications."

But Bradley was off the phone. And Prague was off the Third Army's shopping list. On May 7, Patton was busy the whole day guiding Judge Patterson, the Undersecretary of War, on a sightseeing tour through his sector. It was 8:00 P.M. when he got back to his headquarters. A top secret message from SHAEF was waiting for him:

"Final German surrender fixed for 0001 May 9."

Patton was in no mood to celebrate. For the first time in the war he felt lonely and tired.

His DOUBTS about the Russians were getting resolved. But he was hazy about the Nazis. The Nazi theorist Alfred Rosenberg's fancy "myth of the twentieth century" was just a lot of esoteric garbage to him. And the official line of the U.S. Army, that the Nazis were the new Hun who had to be erased from the face of the earth, was either too simplistic or too complicated for his taste. A pragmatist at heart, he was always uneasy with "theories," no matter how plausible, preferring "facts," no matter how fallacious.

Patton entertained a nebulous philosophy of the problem that this war was supposed to solve. In its frame of reference, Hitler was just a crackpot and the Nazis were a wild bunch of punks who terrorized the neighborhood. Around this time, a unit of his Third Army picked up a fine bust that the noted German sculptor Arno Breker had made of Adolf Hitler. Patton sent it to General Marshall as a souvenir, suggesting that he have a hole knocked through the top of the Führer's head and use it as a spittoon.

He did distinguish between soldiers and civilians, and between Germans and Nazis, but vaguely, and only when it did not slow down his advances. Just then, John J. McCloy, Assistant Secretary of War, was visiting the ETO, and Patton took him on drives up and down the ravaged countryside. Going through one of the badly bombed big cities, he called McCloy's attention to "the wanton and unnecessary bombing" of civilians, adding the professional plea: "We all feel that indiscriminate bombing has no military value, and is cruel and wasteful." But whenever the Third Army was slowed by German resistance or, indeed, by "civilian" roadblocks, he did not hesitate to call for more support from Air, or to complain, sometimes all the way to General "Hap" Arnold, when it was not forthcoming.

The first branded Nazi—actually so marked by the SS with a hot iron under the man's armpit—that he met face to face was a bully with a ruddy, round face, broad, red neck, and a stocky, fatty frame—one Brigadeführer Anton Dunckern, with the rank of major general of the Waffen-

SS. Dunckern surrendered in the Metz area in November 1944, even as the German general of the Regular Army sent out word from his beleaguered fortress that he would fight to the death. "We are going to oblige him," Patton quipped when told of the officer's heroic stand, but he respected the man and loathed the Nazi.

Confronted by Patton, Dunckern tried to explain his decision to give up, claiming that he had obeyed his orders to the bitter end, and had not perished by his own hand only because, as he put it, he could not find a gun. Afterward, when he had completed his interrogation of the "Gestapo general," Patton described him as "the most vicious-looking human being I have ever seen, and who, after I got through talking with him, was unquestionably one of the worst scared."

No sooner had he finished with Dunckern than he sent for Colonel Constantin Meyer of the German Regular Army, who had also been captured near Metz. He received him with a chair, a friendly smile, and a cigar. "Tell the colonel," he instructed the interpreter, "that this SS general I had in here stood up, but I am having him sit down because he is a professional soldier and I have respect for him." Then he began to overdo it. "I have great respect for the German soldier," he went on in a vein that contrasted totally with what he was telling his soldiers. "I know the colonel has been a gallant soldier and has shown courage and has fought for his country and army. He is not a Party man, and has fought for Germany because it is Germany."

When he dismissed Meyer, he told the guard, "I want this colonel treated much differently from the other man." Up to this point, Colonel Meyer personified to Patton the good German and Dunckern the bad Nazi. Beyond that he did not go, for he did not know yet how bad, indeed, the bad Nazis had been. But his education was continuing. In a letter to General Charles L. Scott, his old mentor from his early tank days preparing for World War II, he now wrote: "We have lately been liberating the slave camps and honestly, words are inadequate to express the horrors of those institutions."

Ohrdurf Nord was the first camp the Third Army had the

honor, as Patton described it, of liberating. It was in the throes of chaos and confusion. Since April 3, when the Americans were only forty miles away, the so-called base camps had undergone an immense and frantic evacuation, in the course of which nearly thirty thousand emaciated inmates had been entrained for other camps off the beaten path. Ohrdurf was one of them. But evacuation, during the collapse of Hitler's Reich which was being squeezed like a lemon between two invasions, was nothing but delayed death sentence by hunger and suffocation in sealed prison trains that vanished without a trace.

Its population swelled by thousands of newcomers, many of whom died soon after arrival, Ohrdurf was a frightful and frightening sight. It so upset Patton that he became sick to his stomach. On April 12 he took Eisenhower and Bradley on a tour of the camp. There was no time yet to tidy it up, none even to bury the dead, and the stench was unbearable. Hundreds of bodies were left to rot on the ground. Some two hundred corpses had been dug up, apparently by the SS guards just before they fled, with the idea of burning them to destroy the evidence of their atrocities. But the advance of the Americans had been so rapid that they had had to leave the corpses smoldering on the embers of a huge pyre.

General Walton H. Walker, commanding XX Corps, whose troops had liberated the camp, now ordered as many of his soldiers as he could spare to see this scene of depravity. He arranged the tours partly to show what his men could expect should they be captured by the Germans, but mainly to give them an "inkling of what treatment should be afforded to people of such sadistic temperaments."

General Eisenhower was stunned. "This evidence of inhuman treatment, starvation, beating, and killing," he said, "is beyond the American mind to comprehend." When Weimar fell on April 15, with it fell Buchenwald, one of the oldest and, next to Auschwitz and Treblinka, the most notorious of extermination camps. "[Ohrdurf] was quite gruesome," wrote General Gay after he toured Buchenwald with Colonel Frank McCarthy, General Marshall's military assistant and secretary of the General Staff. "But in comparison to the sights witnessed in the internment camp near Weimar, it was of a minor nature." From Patton, it elicited the horrified cry: "This is yet another evidence as to the unbelievable brutality of the Germans."

BUCHENWALD in particular became a tourist attraction—every visiting VIP was taken on a tour of the chambers with the iron hooks on the wall and the "six furnaces much like a baker's oven" in which the Nazis had cremated their victims. Its gruesome memory receded, however, as another "villain" entered Patton's world to take over from the Nazi as a "person" to be feared and loathed. He was the Displaced Person, a generic name that covered a vast multitude of the homeless, the stateless, the rootless, and the shiftless.

The first time the problem cropped up in Patton's experience was on the day of his exhilarating crossing of the Rhine, when it was the last thing he needed to spoil his fun. In the midst of elation and gratification, Patton took time out nevertheless to commiserate. In a warm moment of humane concern, he sympathized and, indeed, empathized with the people who were clogging the roads, filling the camps, manning the black markets—the thousands streaming back in seemingly endless columns, utterly forlorn.

Patton was shaken by their sight, if only because he blamed himself for their plight. He saw one woman with a perambulator filled with all her worldly goods, sitting on a hill and crying. An old man with a wheelbarrow, followed by three little children, was wringing his hands. A woman was handing around a small tin cup to feed her five children—she was crying, too. "Am I getting soft?" Patton posed the rhetorical question. "I did most of it!"

Although the situation deteriorated quickly, nothing more was said about the problem for almost three weeks. On April 10, however, after noting the visit of financier Bernard Baruch to Lucky Forward, General Gay recorded what was by then preoccupying Patton. "The situation reference displaced persons continued to be aggravated," he wrote. "Most of them are like animals, or worse, and unless force can be used on them to insure reasonable sanitary measures, it would appear that disease, perhaps something bordering on plague, is in the offing." He concluded: "It [is] felt that the front line troops had defeated the Germans on the battlefield, but if something was not done reference this matter, we would probably lose the victory—at least the fruits of victory—behind the battle lines."

Nowhere in this record so impressively recorded by Patton and Gay were the camps described by their true names, as *Vernichtungslager*, or extermination camps, but rather as camps for political prisoners or slave-labor camps. There were thousands of slave laborers among their inmates, even a sprinkling of political prisoners the Nazis had put to this slow death. But more than half of the outcasts were Jews, doomed in the camps and burned in the furnaces—solely because they were Jews.

Yet never was a single explicit reference made to the Jewish victims of the holocaust—not until later, when General Patton equated them with the people General Gay had described as animals.

THE WAR had only a few days to go. Then on May 7, 1945, the day before it ended, General Patton—he had been made a full general on April 18—received word that another group of "displaced persons" had shown up in XX Corps area. The famous Imperial Spanish Riding Academy of the Hapsburgs had been moved out of the path of the Red Army, going from Vienna in great secrecy to Schloss Arco at St. Martin in western Austria. It was found there, horses and men living in luxury, by a unit of XX Corps.

Much has been made (including a full-length Walt Disney film) of Patton's generous interest in the proud Lippizaner horses, how he saved and pampered those highly bred, exquisitely trained animals amid the ravages and vagaries of the war. Actually, they disgusted him. On May 6, Robert Patterson, the Undersecretary of War, arrived at his headquarters, and Patton thought he might be entertained by watching the Lippizaners perform. They motored to Schloss Arco in the morning, were given an imperial reception (whose stilted anachronism appalled both Patton and Patterson), and were then treated to a "show"—after which

Colonel Podhajsky, custodian of the Academy and chief trainer of the horses, pleaded from the rostrum amid the splendor of the world's most elegant stables:

"I ask you, General Patton," he said, "and the representatives of the U.S. government, to take under your protecting hand this old Austrian Academy, a cultural institution of the noble art of riding, unique in Europe, and perhaps unique in the world. This school demonstrates the development of culture of the sixteenth century and it represents the era of the Baroque almost kept intact."

Patton was unimpressed. "It was rather peculiar to realize," he wrote, "that with a world tearing itself apart in war, about twenty middle-aged men in perfect physical condition and about an equal number of grooms had spent their time teaching horses tricks. As much as I like horses, it seems to me there is a place for everything."

It was obvious—the world was turning upside down.

4.

★ ★ ★ ★

From "Overlord" to "Eclipse"

Western Europe—All hostilities in the European Theater of Operations are officially terminated at 0001, as surrender act becomes effective.

—ALLIED COMMUNIQUÉ, *May 9, 1945*

CALLED "LUCKY" by its cocky inmates, the bustling, sprawling encampment in trailers and under tents in Regensburg was the Third Army's sixth forward echelon headquarters since it had become operational in Europe in August 1944. The capital of the Upper Palatinate on the Danube in Eastern Bavaria, one of the oldest German cities, had surrendered to Major General Willard G. Wyman's 71st Infantry Division on April 27 without putting up a fight. It was there that General Patton experienced the first pangs of the misery and grandeur of the end of the war.

The word came a few minutes after four o'clock in the morning on May 7, 1945, when General Bradley buzzed "Lucky Forward," got Patton out of bed in his caravan and told him: "Ike just called me, George. The Germans have surrendered. It takes effect at midnight, May 8. We're to hold in place everywhere up and down the line. There's no sense in taking any more casualties now."

The announcement so stunned Patton that he could not decide right away whether it was good news or bad. When he hung up, he stepped to the window and ripped off the

blackout blinds. It was still dark outside. But where the V
Corps was spread out in Czechoslovakia, the first rays of
the sun lit up a thin line on the horizon. It was to be a busy
day, this seventh day of May, and Patton's diary crowded
up with the brief record of the events:

A German colonel general had come from Norway to
explain to his adamant colleague, Field Marshal Ferdinand
Schoerner, the diehard Nazi holding out somewhere near
Prague, that the jig was up and that he, too, had to surrender
like the rest of them.

The redoubtable 99th Infantry Division of Major General
Walter E. Lauer had reached the Isar on April 26, and took
the town of Moosburg, where they found a Stalag chock-
full of Allied prisoners of war. (Patton was sending Colonel
Charles B. Odom, the surgeon of the Third Army, to the
camp to assure himself that the freed P/Ws were getting the
best medical care.)

He had a distinguished visitor that day, Robert Porter
Patterson, the Undersecretary of War. Patton treated him
to a show of the Lippizaners at Donaukirchen, then spent
the rest of the day with him. Flying from one headquarters
to another, they wound up late in the evening at the command post of General Walton H. Walker, whose XX Corps
had just captured the gold, art treasures, and crown jewels
of the Hungarians.

All this was duly recorded in the diary, but there was
not a word about the most momentous event of the day. All
wars must come to an end sooner or later. But this war
ended for Patton too soon.

THE THIRD ARMY had its last days of fighting on
May 5 and 6, in a truncated campaign. It was so vast in
concept and so hazardous in its implications that it quickly
outran the new realities of this fading war and had to be
"restrained," which was the official word for what happened. On May 4, at 7:30 P.M., General Bradley had phoned
and instructed General Patton to take two corps, the XII and
the V, and attack northeast into Czechoslovakia. It was
music to Patton's ears, but he heard more of it than Bradley
was playing. The Army Group Commander was giving him

a "restraining line" on which the attack was to halt—it ran from Karlsbad through Pilsen to Budweis, its pivot fifty miles west of Prague. That plum was reserved for the Red Army. But giving its mission to the V Corps, Patton told Major General Clarence R. Huebner unequivocally: *"Destroy the enemy in zone and advance on Prague."*

By the sixth, a Sunday, the Third Army's attack was so obviously aimed at Prague that Bradley called, frantically at this time, to convey to Patton Eisenhower's order—"You hear me, George, goddamnit, *halt!*" Patton waited till eleven o'clock in the morning. When word was received from Huebner that Pilsen had been taken by the 16th Armored Division, he ordered the advance to halt. It was the last campaign. "We will probably never do this again," he told General Gay, adding cryptically, "at least not in Germany."

General Gay knew what Patton meant. Then those five little words were spelled out in the evening of that same May 6, when Patton's frustration was freshest and the disappointment rankled him most acutely. The Undersecretary of War was Patton's houseguest. They stayed up and talked long into the night—this was the threshold of a brand new era, and these men carried some of the burden of shaping it. It was then, probably for the first time outside his own circle, that Patton verbalized clearly what he had weighing on his mind.

"Mr. Secretary," he said, "let's keep our boots polished, bayonets sharpened, and present a picture of force and strength to the Russians. This is the only language they understand. If you fail to do this, then I would like to say to you that we have had a victory over the Germans and have disarmed them but we have lost the war."

"What would you have us do, George?" the Undersecretary asked.

"Tell them where their border is, and give them a limited time to get back across. Warn them that if they fail to do so, we will push them back across."

Patterson recoiled. "You don't realize the strength of these people," he said.

"Yes," Patton said, "I have seen them. They have chickens in their coops and cattle on the hoof—that's their supply system. They could probably maintain themselves in the type of fighting I could give them for five days. After that it would make no difference how many million men they have, and if you wanted Moscow, I could give it to you."

Was this the inspired vision of a *cold* war? Or was he going berserk with his cravings for another *hot* war? "In my opinion," he wrote on May 18, in the privacy of the diary, "the American Army as it now exists could beat the Russians with the greatest of ease, because while the Russians have good infantry, they are lacking in artillery, air and in tanks, and in knowledge of the use of combined arms, whereas we excel in all three of these. If it should be necessary to fight the Russians, the sooner we do it the better.

"General Eisenhower and General Bradley were somewhat worried about the attitude of the soldiers. Personally, I don't think the soldier cares. The present American soldier is so well disciplined and so patriotic he will fight anywhere he is told to fight and do a good job. I believe that by taking a strong attitude, the Russians will back down. So far we have yielded too much to their Mongolian nature."

Two days later, even as Patton was embarrassing Undersecretary Patterson with his vision of the future, the 4th Armored Division closed to the Enns River and found the Russians somewhere in the darkness. "Our signal lights," it signaled back, "were answered by the Russians, using the prearranged signals."

"Operation Overlord," which had begun on June 6, 1944, was essentially accomplished. "Operation Eclipse" was now on. But as Patton saw it, it was all over. "I hope I don't stay here long," he wrote home. "I want to go home for a while on my way to China."

ON MAY 10, 1945, General George S. Patton, Jr., had issued General Order No. 98, terminating the war also insofar as the Third Army was concerned. Then, accompanied by Brigadier General Otto P. ("Opie") Weyland, who commanded the XIX Tactical Air Command in support of the Third Army, he flew to Wiesbaden to attend a conference General Eisenhower had called in great secrecy, to draw the lessons of the past and to plot the course of the future. They met over lunch, ten of the U.S. Army's topmost generals—Ike and Bradley, the four Army Commanders—Patton, Alexander M. Patch, Courtney H. Hodges, and William H. Simpson—and their air officers.

After lunch, General Eisenhower addressed them in a thoughtful speech, obviously designed to coordinate their postwar accounts and assure that none of them would be talking out of turn. The Supreme Commander spoke very confidentially of "the need for solidarity"—in the event, he said, that any of them might be called before Congressional committees probing the conduct of the war. He went on to outline, in so many words, what he would say when quizzed, then suggested that the others pattern their responses on that model.

"He made a speech," Patton noted afterward, "which had to me the symptoms of political aspirations, on cooperating with the British, Russians, and the Chinese, but particularly with the British. It is my opinion that this talking cooperation is for the purpose of covering up probable criticism of strategic blunders which he unquestionably committed during the campaign."

Three days later, on May 13, Patton recorded in his diary: "Nothing of importance happened." It was not possible to see it then, but it was, in fact, a day that produced a turning point in his career—indeed, in his life. On that day began the preparation of the Third Army for its future as one of the American forces designated for what was then called "the efficient policing of a devastated Reich."

A huge plan was floating around, not unknown to the Germans, whose secret service had succeeded in procuring an early draft, outlining in massive detail the management of the Reich after Hitler. Called "Eclipse," it presented a reasonably fair and hopeful design for the American share in the occupation of Germany.

The plan created two districts, east and west, in the so-called American Zone of conquered Germany that would be governed by the Army of Occupation. The western district, with headquarters in beautiful Bad Homburg (an old resort in the Taunus Mountains, seat of the romantic prin-

cipality that produced the famous hero of Heinrich von
Kleist's immortal play about the dilemma of insubordination
in battle, *The Prince of Homburg)*, was assigned to the
custody of Lieutenant General Geoffrey Keyes, Patton's
friend and protégé. The eastern district consisted of Bavaria,
and the Third Army was to govern it. When no other job
could be found for Patton, he was left in command of the
Third Army in Europe, and thus became the Military Governor
of the Eastern District.

On the day when supposedly nothing of importance happened, the redeployment of the Third Army began in earnest. The 474th Infantry Regiment was the first unit to go
home, followed by the 97th Infantry Division. But it absorbed four hundred separate units from other major commands. By May 21, for example, the four elite divisions
and the famed cavalry group of the XV Corps passed from
General Patch's to General Patton's command. The Third
Army was growing by leaps and bounds, even as the Ninth
and Fifteenth Armies were liquidating themselves.

The job that fell to the Third Army was staggering. Its
basic policy had been agreed upon by the four powers.
"During the period of occupation," their declaration read,
"Germany shall be treated as an economic unit"—for the
purpose of carrying out "the reparations and demilitarization
and denazification and other policies agreed upon." The
Potsdam agreement stipulated that Allied control "shall be
imposed on Germany only to the extent necessary"—but
this was not how far the Third Army was expected to go.

The term "assumption of occupational duties," under
which it was to function henceforth, encompassed an enormous field that was filled with problems and complexities.
It included the task of providing subsistence for the vast
assortment of people in the so-called "Eclipse" area—seven
million Germans and two million others—refugees, fugitives, prisoners-of-war, displaced persons, former inmates
of the extermination camps, drifters, stringers, stragglers,
and transients. Also, of liquidating the last vestiges of Nazism and its pernicious ideology; of helping the Germans to
pave their way back into the family of nations.

IN LESS THAN a fortnight, regrouping was so far advanced that the fantastic experiment of restoring Germany could begin. Nobody could know and no one dared to guess whether the plan, which seemed so pat on paper, would work in practice, in a land that had been totally spoiled for even a semblance of democracy.

As for the immediate task, "Eclipse" spelled it out in three words—demilitarization, denazification, and deindustrialization. "Demilitarization" implied "the complete disarmament of Germany"—a seemingly hopeless mission in a land whose Prussian spirit had become the people's way of life.

"Denazification" was both a challenge and a necessity— all members of the Nazi Party and its various formations, who have been "more than nominal participants in their activities," and all other persons "hostile to Allied purposes," were supposed to be "removed from public and semi-public office and from positions of responsibility in important private undertakings." The archives of the Nazi Party, which the Third Army had captured intact when the Brown House was occupied in Munich, showed that over forty-five million Germans, out of a population of sixty million, had been members of the Party in one capacity or another. The question was, would it be possible to rule the land with seventy-five percent of its population blackballed?

"Deindustrialization" was not as sweeping as the word sounded. The old Morgenthau Plan, which would have erased all industries and turned Germany into a rural wasteland, was long dead. By now, the contours of an industrial Germany had become vaguely visible, and "deindustrialization" merely meant "the elimination of control of all German industry that could be used for military production."

Superimposed on the "three Ds of Potsdam" was yet another ban, both portentous and frivolous. It was called non-fraternization. The idea was to humble and humiliate the Germans, to drive home to them that they were not the Master Race after all. Patton, for one, never thought that non-fraternization was a good idea, or, for that matter, that it would ever work. The ban had only been on a few days, while he was still in Regensburg, when he passed a forbidden scene enlivening the shattered countryside. There in a ditch but barely shielded by a row of skimpy bushes were two obviously virile American soldiers engaged in vigorous fraternization with two women. Patton stopped and called out to the GIs. They promptly abandoned their pleasure at the sight of the general and became all business, as they stood stiffly at attention, caught literally with their pants down.

One of them was a sergeant, and Patton addressed him as was becoming his rank. "Well, sergeant," he said in his squeaky voice. "Don't just stand there like a prick on the wedding night. Don't you think you owe me an explanation?"

"Yes, sir," the sergeant said briskly, saluting with one hand, the other pointing to a couple of frightened women in the ditch. "These are two *Yugoslav* ladies, sir, who don't know their way around in Germany and we were just giving them directions."

Patton burst into laughter. "That's a new one," he said. "All right, sergeant! Carry on!" After the incident, he wrote to Frederick Ayer in Boston: "I think that this non-fraternization is very stupid. If we are going to keep American soldiers in a country, they have to have some civilians to talk to. Furthermore, I think we could do a lot for the German civilians by letting our soldiers talk to their young people."

The tenet that was to inspire his concept of the occupation was already firmly formulated in his mind. What actually became the motto of his rule was expressed in ten simple words: "All Nazis are bad. But all Germans are not Nazis."

On MAY 23, 1945, a Wednesday but two weeks after V-E Day, the Third Army was ready to disband "Lucky Forward" at Regensburg and move General Patton's new seat of power about a hundred miles due south, to a place called Bad Toelz. Originally, the plan was to transfer to Munich, the capital of Bavaria. But when General Gay inspected it he found that the beautiful city of the Wittels-bachs was too badly destroyed for comfort. Bad Toelz was then chosen partly because it housed the ultimate in military accommodations and a number of villas to lodge the officers.

Almost hidden in a nook of the Isar just twenty miles from Munich, and surrounded by gentle sloping mountains rising to snow-capped heights in the distance, Toelz began as a Celtic settlement in antiquity and gained fame as a resort in the twentieth century, when its many springs were found to have healing qualities. The beautiful old town on both sides of the river had seen occupation by alien armies often before, and had learned how to take them in stride. The local populace barely paid attention to the newcomers, and the latter hardly interfered with the town. Toelz was not one of the rabid Nazi outposts in Bavaria and needed no drastic measures of purification.

As it was, the presence of the Allies was confined to a string of handsome villas on the outskirts of the town and to that formidable enclave on the hill—a fantastic com-pound covering forty acres on which stood a single enor-mous quadrangle building. Erected around a courtyard that was so big that it could serve as the parade ground for two entire divisions, it was the former *Junkerschule* of the Waf-fen-SS. There the handpicked cadets of Himmler's officers corps were trained, in an installation that was considered the finest military post in all Bavaria.

The main building consisted of nine hundred rooms, af-fording such facilities as offices, barracks, messes, a chapel, a theater, and a post exchange, all under a single roof. Other facilities included a laundry, a gymnasium, and a swimming pool, surrounded by an athletic field, stables, a riding hall, and the motor pool. Uncharacteristically under the Nazis, who named all their installations for one or another of their heroes or martyrs, the *Junkerschule* was called simply that. But Patton changed that on his first day. He named the place the "Flint Kaserne" or Flint Barracks, in memory of Colonel Harry Albert Flint.

"Paddy" Flint, an eccentric soldier in Patton's own mold, was one of his closest friends, godfather of his only son. "Probably," he wrote in a special tribute when the gallant

Vermonter was killed in Normandy in July 1944, "his death was fortunate because he had been fired at too much and it had gotten to the point where he was [becoming] timid, not particularly for himself but for his men."

Now it gave him great pleasure to name this enormous place, still teeming with the memories of the Nazis they had just evicted, for the old soldier he admired most and loved best.

Patton occupied a light and spacious but not too large suite on the second floor, the former office of the *Junker-schule's* last commandant, a blond giant, Richard Schulze by name, who had been Hitler's personal adjutant before taking over the school when everything was lost.

In May 1945, Colonel Schulze had just been captured and was kept apart with the other elite of the Waffen-SS, under heavy guard in a special cage reserved for the "most dangerous" remnants of armed Nazis. His office was occupied by the man who had had a lion's share in liquidating his beloved Führer.

General Patton liked Schulze's cozy little office on the second floor of the cavernous Kaserne, this stronghold of the young Junkers, Himmler's idea of a new feudal nobility patterned on Prussian cavaliers and Japanese samurai. But he had Schulze's spartan furnishings thrown out, because he had word of a certain find that struck him as eminently fitting as a decoration for what he expected would be his last command post in Germany. Scouts at large searching for such precious Nazi memorabilia as Hitler's eyeglasses and the diamond-encrusted baton of Reichsmarschall Goering reported from Stuttgart that they had come upon a desk that supposedly had belonged to Erwin Rommel, the famed leader of the Afrika Korps forced to commit suicide on Hitler's orders for his alleged participation in the plot of July 20, 1944.

Patton became flushed with excitement. He sent Colonel Codman to Stuttgart to secure the desk for him, and Codman returned in triumph with the precious loot. But Patton was appalled when he had his first glimpse of it. It turned out to be a dainty piece, a lacy study table, rather small, suited more for a vicar's wife than a victorious American general.

It had come complete with an upholstered highback chair whose fabric was going to pieces and a battered rug of obscure oriental pedigree. Codman warned that it was by no means certain that the pieces were ever actually owned by Rommel. But Patton eagerly appropriated them.

At one point in the campaigns in North Africa, Patton had proposed that he and Rommel meet face to face, each in his own tank, in a tournament of armor, in a clash unto death. This way, he suggested, the issue could be decided man to man, without the sacrifices of an omnivorous war. Nothing, of course, ever came of the idea, and Patton never had the chance to take on Rommel.

But these relics appeared to be the next best thing—and so it passed that General Patton settled down in the former *Junkerschule* to the task of punishing the Germans, from behind the orphaned desk of Feldmarschall Rommel.

5.

$$\star \star \star \star$$

Keegan's Heroes

ON MAY 25, 1945, General Patton had a visitor in the Flint Kaserne—so ebullient that he filled the small office with an exuberance that belied his fiftyish appearance. He was Charles Edward Keegan, the New York politico—*Colonel* Keegan now. The silver chickens were new and shiny on his shoulder straps and color patches.

Patton had never heard of the man, but Keegan saw to it that he would never forget him. The first thing the general spotted on the colonel's freshly tailored Eisenhower jacket was the Bronze Star and a couple of clusters on his Purple Heart, and that mellowed him. A mere captain in the reserve, and in his late forties already when he rejoined the Army for his second world war, Keegan had seen action in both the Pacific and Europe, and had been made major and lieutenant colonel in battlefield promotions.

An authentic hero, to be sure—but Charley Keegan was not on another combat mission. He came to Bad Toelz in style to report to the general and ask his blessing, because he had just been named Military Governor of Bavaria under him. That in itself ruined Patton's day.

THE RAVAGED LAND under Patton's aegis was a tortured place. And it was not easy to grope one's way through the moral ruins that the Nazis had left in their wake.

Resorting to a mixture of contrition and arrogance, the Germans found myriad ways to trip up the conquerors. Their favorite trick was illustrated by a yarn making the rounds, more than just a joke. During the night, so the story went, when Munich was under siege and its fall was imminent, a man, defying gunfire and curfew, streaked through the streets to Schwabing where a well-known language teacher had his house. The man banged on the door and drummed on the windows, until the frightened professor appeared. "What do you want?" he asked.

"I want to take an English lesson," the man said.

The teacher was nonplussed. "At midnight?" he asked. "When the city is about to be captured by the enemy?"

"But I want to learn only five simple words," the man pleaded.

"Five words?" the teacher said. "What five words?"

"Ich bin nie Nazi gewesen," the man said. "I've never been a Nazi."

Governing foreign people on such a scale, in the aftermath of defeat and holocaust, was an entirely new experience for Americans abroad. It was also a perplexing challenge. The magnitude of the problem surpassed any the Romans faced in Gaul, the Turks in Hungary, the Moors in Spain or the British in India. The management of this unprecedented enterprise was now entrusted to the Third Army, one of the world's greatest machines to make war, expecting it to become abracadabra an occupation army to make peace.

At its head, General Patton was thrust into the task, sink or swim. Watching him making the plunge, Colonel George Fisher, his chemical-warfare officer, put it best. "Instead of killing Germans, what he knew best," he said, "Patton is asked to govern them, what he knows least." He shook his head. "It won't work," he said sadly.

It was, then, to run Bavaria within Patton's domain that Charley Keegan was chosen, in line with the Army's policy to name reserve officers with experience in municipal administration to the military government jobs in major areas. This was how politicians like Charles Poletti and William O'Dwyer had been made governors in Italy. And this was, too, how Keegan got his job. Unless, however, it was pressure from Edward T. Flynn, the powerful Democratic boss he had served faithfully in the Bronx, and word from Archbishop Francis J. Spellman of New York, the two great mentors his wife had asked to get "a good job for Charley" in Germany, it was difficult to find rational explanation for Keegan's selection. A former crime reporter on the old New York *Evening World,* as was his better-known brother "Wee" Willie Keegan, Charley was pure Mr. Dooley with a parish school education. A jowly, smiling, dapper Irishman, his greatest assets were his glad hand and glib gab.

In spite of his popularity and visibility, however, he never made it into the big time. Elected an alderman in 1935, he was but a $5000-a-year councilman in New York when his country called in 1942. The closest qualification he now had for the assignment in Bavaria was that he was born in Yorkville on the east side of Manhattan, where most of the Germans in New York City lived.

"My job here," Charley wrote to his friend Louis Cohn of the Bronx, who had replaced him as councilman for the duration, "is to show these Krauts what a cad their Great Führer was, and I intend to make the most of it. Incidentally, Lou, I've just been made full colonel, and mark my word, you boys will be proud of me yet."

At an early session of the City Council, Lou Cohn then duly moved and his colleagues unanimously adopted a resolution extending congratulations to their distinguished former member. In New York City, indubitably, Colonel Charles E. Keegan was a great success.

It did not work out in Bavaria. Charley Keegan was not a bad guy by any means. There was nothing wicked about him or sinister about his ways. He had lived and worked in the New York melting pot all his life, and loathed the Nazis with the fervor of his innate decency as well as the smart reckoning of the political pro. But it was his experience in New York that entrapped Keegan in Munich. Back home it was the rule to "clear things" with the Powerhouse—with the archdiocese, that is, at whose modest redbrick building on Madison Avenue the city's politics were made.

Archbishop Spellman wielded enormous influence as the primate of New York, traditionally the power at the Powerhouse. And now, in 1945, he not only recommended

Keegan for the job, but personally introduced him to the Munich equivalent of his seat of power, headed by Michael Cardinal von Faulhaber, his good friend from their days in Rome.

Colonel Keegan lost no time in Munich in presenting his credentials—Archbishop Spellman's letter of introduction—to Cardinal von Faulhaber, the seventy-six-year-old archbishop of Munich and Freysing. During most of World War II, when all opposition was muffled, the cardinal was the only primate in Germany who attacked the Hitler regime for restricting religious freedom and persecuting the Jews. He was, therefore, the logical person among the Germans to be contacted by the new military governor.

Received in the old palace of the archdiocese by Auxiliary Bishop Johannes Neuhaeusler with all the pomp and deference due the conqueror, Charley was taken to the famed prelate for what became a historic audience. Colonel Keegan thus embarked on his rule of Bavaria by kissing the cardinal's ring.

CHARLEY KEEGAN was overwhelmed, and no wonder. Imposing in appearance, with aristocratic hauteur, his voice booming, his presence felt like that of a swarm of wasps in a room, Michael Ritter von Faulhaber, scion of an old Franconian clan of hereditary knights, was an almost medieval figure as a prince of the Church. He was sturdy and steady like the mountains of his native highland, his head as strong and clear as Alpine air. A theologian of world renown and a man of noble character and deep religious conviction, the old cardinal had great personal charm, unfailing good humor and piercing wit. But he had iron in his will and steel in his spine, and great personal courage—his famous *Zivilcourage* that emboldened him to scold Hitler to his face. He regarded his struggle with the Nazis as a passion play—the classic bout of the faithful with the Devil.

Cardinal von Faulhaber emerged from these soul-searing days an international hero and the uncontested spiritual leader in Bavaria.

But the cardinal was no liberal by any means, and his goal was not the establishment of true democracy in Ger-

many. A strong ultraconservative and monarchist during his
entire episcopate, he was an unceasing critic of the old
Weimar Republic and of the new democratic forces that
struggled for recognition. Mere rumors that the occupying
powers intended to "democratize" certain features of the
German educational system proved enough to elicit from
him violent objections. And he branded the Allies' early
liberalizing measures in Bavaria as "but another form of
dictatorship."

Keegan was drawn into the formation of an administration in Munich that could become a government by the
Church. Prominent Catholic laymen closely connected with
the archdiocese, the monasteries, and the clergy at large—
politicians, lawyers, doctors, financiers, and industrialists—who helped with the management of the vast holdings
of the Church in Bavaria and protected them from all com-
ers, suddenly appeared as the white hopes of a new democracy in Germany.

As Colonel Keegan interpreted his orders, a civilian government had to be formed locally with all possible dispatch.
And it was critical for the future of the area as, indeed, for
the success of denazification in general, that a German head
of a new "civilian government" be found for Bavaria.

Cardinal von Faulhaber let Charley Keegan know that
he had the man he was looking for. He was Dr. Fritz Schaeffer, the cardinal's lawyer and friend, a fifty-seven-year-old
politician in excellent standing and a former inmate of the
Dachau concentration camp. The combination was impressive, the recommendation irresistible.

On May 27, 1945, only sixteen days after V-E Day,
Colonel Charles E. Keegan named Herr Schaeffer Minister
President of the former Kingdom of Bavaria. It was the
largest chunk of conquered land to be put under a single
German. Charging Schaeffer with responsibility for estab-
lishing a government of his own down to the lowest level,
exclusively of German nationals, Keegan wrote: "You will
act in all matters of administration without reference to race,
creed, or political influence. In particular you will admin-
ister faithfully to eliminate all influences of the Nazional

Sozialistische Deutsche Arbeiter Partei from the Bavarian Government and administration."

Herr Schaeffer's record as a husband of thirty-three years and the father of four sons was excellent. His standing as a Bavarian politician was unimpeachable—he had been in politics since 1918, as a member of the archconservative, ultra-Catholic Bavarian People's Party. But his record as a victim of the Nazis was spotty. Schaeffer had been arrested in March 1933 and held in the Brown House—for a single night. He was arrested again in May and held for two weeks at Stadelheim. In 1944, when the persecution of members of the pre-Nazi political parties had become rampant, he spent forty-six days in Dachau. But he was freed soon and remained at large for the rest of the Nazi regime.

Sworn in by Keegan, Fritz Schaeffer thus became what the headline in *The New York Times* described as "the ruler for Bavaria." Five days later, General Patton, who was supposed to be the overlord of the zone in which Bavaria was situated, left for the United States—without as much as laying an eye on Herr Schaeffer. Did it matter?

The situation cast an ominous shadow on Patton's future as the proconsul, not because Bavaria had a German "ruler" again, and so soon, but because it had no American ruler, and would have none during the whole month of June, while the new Minister President was broken in. Did Patton know who Dr. Schaeffer was or realize the implications of his appointment? If he did, he gave no sign that he knew or cared.

General Patton had only twelve days to spend in Bad Toelz at this time. He was scheduled to go on what he described as "a goddamn bond-raising tour in the United States." Actually, he was going home to receive the homage of a grateful nation due one of its most colorful heroes.

At 9 A.M. on June 4, Patton flew to Paris en route to the States. He was leaving behind the load of his new and complex job.

Patton was barely gone a couple of hours when the problems began to pile up. A telephone call from the Army Group announced the coming of a General Bonesteel to "conduct an investigation," as it was put, of conditions in the camps where the displaced persons were kept in the care of the Third Army. Then Army Group called again, ordering Third Army to relieve the British of German prisoners they were holding in their cages. General Gay was baffled by the Bonesteel mission and incensed about the order to help the British. The Third Army was in the process of discharging its own prisoners-of-war, not in taking in more, especially not just to ease the burden of the British. "The earmarks of the General Staff," Gay wrote in his diary, "which is preponderantly British in SHAEF, seem to loom up in the distance." Had he been there, General Patton could not have put it better.

Everything was in flux. Nobody knew how things would work out. But Patton was going home, not as the proconsul of Bavaria, but as the conquering hero.

6.

★★★★

Conquering Hero
with Foot in Mouth

THE WAR in Europe ended before the Japanese were defeated
or the schools were out in the United States. These two
factors somewhat restrained the celebrations—but not the
jubilation. The British in particular, to whom the war in the
Pacific was but a sideshow, pulled out all stops after V-E
Day. In the feudal tradition of the Plantagenets and the
Tudors, and in the grand manner of the Victorian era, when
their conquering heroes were given dukedoms and wealth,
the declining empire raised its victorious generals and ad-
mirals to the peerage and voted them enormous cash awards.

Things were quite different in the United States. This
country had no titles to bestow, no stipends to disburse, not
even additional ranks to dispense. The cupboard of such
honors, nearly bare anyway, had been emptied altogether
before the war ended. Full general with four stars was the
highest statutory rank in the U.S. Army. At one point,
creation of the rank of marshal in the U.S. Army was seriously considered in Washington. But the idea was abandoned when it dawned upon the powers that it would have
sounded silly to address the Chief of Staff as Marshal Marshall.

Another exalted rank, that of "General of the Armies,"
had been pre-empted by George Washington and John J.
Pershing, and Public Law 415 stipulated that it was to lapse
upon Black Jack's death. All that was left was "General of
the Army," the five-star rank Congress gave Ulysses Simp-

son Grant in 1866. It was revived in 1944 for Marshall, MacArthur, and Eisenhower.

RANK in the Army titillated or grated, and though advancement in wartime was much quicker, it was mostly on a temporary basis. The shuffle of ranks was a scramble in which seniority was often ignored and valor came to be measured by bureaucratic standards or the rules of protocol. Thus Ike, who had been a major for sixteen years, had six promotions—one about every six months, rising from lieutenant colonel to full general in less than three years. He was given a fifth star on December 16, 1944, ironically the day the Germans handed him his greatest setback by unleashing the counteroffensive in the Ardennes. Mark Clark graduated from West Point eight years after Patton and was still a lieutenant colonel in 1941, when Patton was a major general. Then, however, he pulled away and became a full general—ahead of Patton.

It was not the best way to raise what Patton called the fallen arches of his self-respect. Made a lieutenant general only on March 12, 1943, after two years as a major general, he wore his three stars for two more years in spite of his victories. And he was uncertain whether he would retain his temporary rank after the war, because he was still only a colonel in the Regular Army.

In March 1945, he had been overtaken again, not only by Ike, but by Bradley, Devers, Clark, and Spaatz—who were promoted to full generals. Neither Patton nor Hodges nor Simpson nor, for that matter, Sandy Patch was included in the promotion list.

Knowing how rank-conscious Patton was, and how he resented such rebuffs, Eisenhower pleaded for him and for Hodges in Washington. But General Marshall vetoed their promotion on the ground that, as he put it, it would have been a slight to Bradley and Devers who by then were commanding army groups. Patton grinned a little more grimly than usual when he was told he had been passed over, but bore the snub surprisingly well. Just then, he was compensated by a sudden avalanche of other rewards. Luxembourg awarded him its coveted Croix de Guerre, France made him a Grand Officer of the Legion of Honor, and the

City of Metz had a huge medallion minted for him. And besides, he said, "I am having so much fun fighting that I don't give a damn what my rank is."

But he did care, of course. When, four months after Ike's promotion, and four weeks after the others had been given their fourth stars, he also was made a full general, he was less than elated. "Sometimes I feel," Patton wrote on the eve of his last promotion, "that I may be nearing the end of this life." And more characteristically, in a less macabre mood, "I sometimes think that it is disadvantageous to do too well."

Patton would never catch up to Ike in rank. But it did not matter. When the nation had its first good look at General Patton in full regalia after the war, he was agleam with twenty-eight stars, all glittering from polish freshly applied by Sergeant George Meeks, his devoted orderly. He wore four on his shiny helmet, four on each shoulder loop, four on each collar tab, and four each on the butts of his two pistols.

BY THIS TIME in the summer of 1945 the country was getting around to paying tribute to its heroes on the installment plan—with a series of homemade parades. On his way to the Pacific Courtney Hodges became the first so honored, in Atlanta, Georgia. General Eisenhower was scheduled to be the last, with mammoth celebrations in New York, Washington, Kansas City, and his boyhood home at Abilene, Kansas.

In between, Omar Bradley had his homecoming parades in Philadelphia and Moberly, in his native Missouri, and Jake Devers was welcomed both in York, Pennsylvania, and in Fayetteville, North Carolina. The others had to be satisfied with lesser celebrations—General Patch, for instance, with being cheered at a baseball game in Washington, D.C., and General Simpson with a party on his mother's porch in Connecticut.

Patton's turn came on June 7, a month after V-E Day. Landing in Boston, he was welcomed with a reception that dwarfed the memory of the tea party. "New England had rarely seen anything like it," an observer noted. "But, after all, the world had rarely seen anything like General George

S. Patton, Jr." Massachusetts was his home state by marriage only, but the people of the Old Colony (whose proud motto had been *Ense petit placidam sub libertate quietem* for 167 years*) considered him as native as the chickadee. To the deafening tune of "All Hail to Massachusetts" and under blue-and-gold state flags fluttering in the light breeze in the sun, he was greeted by at least a million people who jammed the twenty-five-mile parade route.

Patton did not disappoint the immense crowd. Aglitter with two dozen stars on his attire, three big rings on his fingers, an automatic pistol at his hip, and a silver-handled riding crop in his gloved hand, he was the personification of the conquering hero. His hair was white and his face was lined. The war had taken its visible toll. But he was erect and turkey-cock, listening with a knowing smile when Governor Maurice J. Tobin compared him to Washington, Sheridan, Grant, Forrest, and Stonewall Jackson.

At the state dinner that night in the Copley Plaza Hotel, he blew kisses and beamed happily at his wife and children, until he choked up, with tears rolling down his cheeks, and sat down, apparently all spent, after a four-minute speech. But then, after putting a big handkerchief to his face, he pulled in his belt, straightened out the big automatic which he still wore, lit a huge cigar—and Old Blood and Guts was back in business. "That's my Pop," said his son, a cadet on leave from West Point, and the crowd cheered.

PATTON'S homecoming was fantastic and, as usual, not without mishaps—portents of a new crop of indiscretions. During the tour, he mixed corn with substance, bombast with humility, bravado with modesty—homilies at Sunday schools with brash statements at mass meetings. He could not have been humbler and sweeter than he was in a class of children at the Episcopal church in San Gabriel, which his pioneer ancestors had founded, or more eloquent than at his parents' grave, on which he placed a wreath and did not say a word.

But obviously tired from the three days it took to get him from Paris to Boston, and carried away by the incredible

---

*"By the sword we seek peace, but peace only under liberty."

crowd awaiting him at the Hatch Shell on the Charles River, Patton talked out of turn at times, as if trying to confirm Walter Bedell Smith's *mot* that "George's mouth doesn't always carry out the orders of his brain."

Talking to four hundred wounded veterans of the Third Army lined up on the Esplanade, Patton said warmly that it was with their blood and bones that the Germans had been crushed. But then he went on to say something about the men who died in the war: "It is a popular idea that a man is a hero just because he was killed in action. Rather I think a man is frequently a fool when he gets killed."

The remark, featured by the Associated Press, provoked instant reaction from coast to coast. A father complained to General Marshall that it was "heartbreaking for my son to lie in his grave in France and for Patton to be alive and telling who the heroes were." Much blunter, another father wrote to Senator Arthur Vandenberg of Michigan, blasting "the face-slapping, gun-toting general" and demanding "an apology to the gold-star fathers and mothers of the United States."

Americans' voiced abhorrence of Patton's image of those foolish dead was so bad that General James Ulio, the Adjutant General, had to clarify in personal letters to Alfred C. Stoddard of Arizona, G. W. Nicholson of Michigan, and scores of others, what Patton himself supposedly had in mind. He did not mean to be contemptuous of the honored dead by any means, General Ulio wrote. What he meant was that some men were killed by the tragic mischance of war.

When this last of his tempests in yet another teapot did not subside, Secretary of War Henry L. Stimson personally intervened to defend Patton. Confronting head-on the shock and dismay, he insisted that the general had deep respect for those killed in action and was saddened by the misinterpretation of his words. Then Patton himself chimed in to offer his own clarification. "In Boston I said that some men were wounded or killed," he told one of his audiences, "because they were damn fools. What I meant was that a man wasn't necessarily a hero just because he got killed or wounded, as too many get wounded or killed for trivial reasons."

It was not a very good clarification. But, then, it was not a very good controversy either. The storm blew out as usual. "Patton acts on the theory," General Bedell Smith summed up, "that it is better to be damned than say nothing—that some publicity is better than none."

PATTON'S performances baffled his countrymen. In their bewilderment, they were blowing either hot or cold. To his critics, who saw in him the dreaded man on horseback, there was little right he could do. Dwight Macdonald, probably his most articulate critic, thought that he was "brutal and hysterical, coarse and affected, violent and empty." To be sure, Macdonald warned, "Old Blood and Guts" had a fine presence. For all his bathos and bombast, he could be paternal and a bit diffident. But the warm smile on his face was belied by the message of his speeches. "These utterances of Patton are atrocities of the mind," Macdonald wrote, "atrocious in being communicated not to a psychoanalyst but to a great number of soldiers, civilians and school children; and atrocious as reflections of what war-making has done to the personality of Patton himself."

To his admirers on the right, who welcomed him as their man on horseback, he could do no wrong. Like George Washington, who felt insulted by the invitation that he become the emperor of America, Patton was appalled by propositions offered by influential political forces that he run for the presidency on the Republican ticket but with an absolutist program. "I am like Sherman," he wrote in some consternation. "I would not run if nominated, nor serve if elected!" There was no politicking in his future! "I intend to remove my insignia and wrist-watch," he told his friend Everett Hughes, "but will continue to wear my short coat so that everyone can kiss my ass."

Political proposals kept pouring in, and since Patton was making light of the propositions politely in public, some assumed that he might be seriously interested in a political future. Patton was now riding the crest of his popularity in the nation. Nothing he was saying or doing on this triumphal tour could make even a dent, no matter what some people were writing or thinking.

During this glorious week on the road—going from Boston to Los Angeles, and home to San Gabriel, California, where the house in which he was born was turned into a shrine—Patton was lionized and cheered by multitudes. It had become evident that Georgie Patton was *the* folk hero of the war—except for Ike.

SOME OF the high points of the trip did not occur in the presence of those thousands. They were reserved for the few private moments he could save for himself. In San Gabriel, he prayed at the graves of his forebears, silently, by himself. And in Pasadena, he stayed with his sister Nita, but two years younger, a great lady in her own right, with a story both romantic and tragic.

There was an uncommon bond between the two—she his only sibling, in whom the frontier spirit of their California origin was unmellowed by any New England fads. When Georgie was a fresh-baked first lieutenant in the cavalry in 1916, Anne or Anita Patton—the popular Nita, who was then twenty-nine years old—visited him at Fort Bliss in El Paso, Texas, and was introduced to the commanding general, John J. Pershing. Old Black Jack, twenty-six years her senior at fifty-five, was smitten by the vivacious young woman. He had just lost his wife and daughter in a fire, and was thinking of marrying again. The romance that blossomed from this chance encounter remained one of the best-kept secrets of the U.S. Army.

By the time Pershing was going off to the war in 1917, George Patton was his aide-de-camp and Nita Patton his "constant companion," seeing him off on March 13 to lead the American Expeditionary Force in Europe. At the time of their departure, her brother played a little game with the reporters, "decoying" them, as he put it, "so they would not bother the general," actually to conceal the presence of Nita at the farewell party.

Miss Patton joined the Red Cross, and while she pulled strings in efforts to join her friend in France, Pershing did not think it was a good idea. "It would make a bad impression at present," was the way he put it. Chaperoned by George and Beatrice Patton, the romance was decorous throughout, George playing *postillon d' amour* with Pershing in France, and Beatrice "sweet-talking" Nita at home out of doing anything rash.

When the war was over, Nita went to England "to settle the matter one way or another." Her plans were indefinite, she said, and so were Pershing's, she found. She returned to the States alone, and when her brother missed her in New York, he wrote a letter instead, to welcome her home. Somehow it marked the end of the romance. He suggested that she go into business, and wrote of many other things: of the state of the Union and of his own state of mind, of his soaring plans and blighted hopes—what he called "songs of the wind in the trees"—and of the lessons of history which his countrymen were notoriously incapable of learning—"the red fate of Carthage" and "the Rome of shame under the Praetorian guards." But there was not a word of Pershing in the long letter.

Apparently, when Pershing had met Nita in London at last, he decided that their relationship had run its course. Nita still thought that the embers might be fanned by their reunion, but Pershing's ardor had cooled. Known for his "fickleness" as the Army's most eligible widower, Pershing had found other romantic interests in France, a coquettish French lady named Michelle, for one, and a young American woman, Elizabeth Hoyt, for another. Others appeared from time to time—but not Nita, ever again.

Now in 1945, Nita was still unmarried, scarred by the one great love of her life. It was not a subject for discussion when she greeted Georgie amidst the pageantry of his return from another war. She celebrated it as her brother's "revenge," as she put it, with the authentic Patton touch, "on all the slimy jealous toads who tried to do you harm."

ON HIS WAY BACK, Patton stopped at Fort Riley, the great encampment of the old cavalry and scene of some of his wildest capers. The memories of those bygone pranks so overwhelmed him that he broke down at the commandant's dinner and could not go on with his speech. But he was his old ribald self again the moment he sat down.

Patton had done what he said he had come home to do—he sold millions of dollars' worth of war bonds, by thundering home the message that "the Japs still had to be licked." His contribution was properly receipted, so to speak, in a delightful little note from the Secretary of the Treasury. Patton was so charmed by it that he was willing to overlook momentarily that the Secretary was also the author of the Morgenthau Plan, which he loathed so violently.

The certificate was given him when he returned to the East Coast to embark on the second leg of his leave. He arrived in Washington on June 13, the doting father and loving grandpa. The picture that appeared in the papers in the morning of June 15 had none of the blood and guts of his popular image. With the caption, "Here the General is Just 'Grandpa,'" it showed him relaxing in a huge armchair at the home of his daughter, Mrs. John K. Waters, with one of his grandsons, George Patton Waters, in his lap. His left arm around John, the other grandson, with their dog Ajax snugly at their feet, the general was obviously enjoying himself.

Then came the press conference. And Patton, who had the distinct talent of switching personalities, was back in his element. The conference had been scheduled somewhat reluctantly, in response to the clamor of the media. Only a few days before, Patton had been in the Coliseum in Los Angeles, which he filled with a hundred thousand cheering, adoring fans. He gave them what they had paid for with those bonds—he wept, swore, and roared for the defeat of Japan. His speech contained so many of his familiar exaggerations and indiscretions that it would have created the usual commotion had it not been—as was his similar performance at the Rose Bowl—delivered in a carnival setting.

General Marshall took up the perils of Patton first with Major General Alexander D. Surles, the Army's seasoned public relations chief, who had handled the Patton crises before, and then with Secretary Henry L. Stimson himself. The issue was not whether to let Patton hold a press conference. The question was how to rein him in. Stimson told the Chief of Staff not to worry.

Stimson knew Patton better than most, had been close to him since 1911, during his own first term as Secretary of War in the Taft Administration. Patton was then Stimson's regular companion on his morning rides at Fort Myer and shared his ideas about the army and war with the much older man. The lasting impression he left benefited him during World War II, when he sorely needed the good will of the man who was again the Secretary of War, now in the administration of Franklin D. Roosevelt.

As a matter of fact, Stimson told Marshall, he had decided to chair the press conference and see to it that Patton would not make a fool of himself.

But General Marshall remained concerned. Even though George might not disgrace himself, he could still embarrass them. Marshall and Eisenhower had concluded at the time of the Knutsford incident that Patton had seizures of a form of dementia, when he would lose control of himself and act out his fantasies in a kind of psychodrama. General Eisenhower had this in mind when he characterized Patton as "this mentally unbalanced officer" in one of his reports to Marshall, as harsh a diagnosis as he could make short of proper psychiatric examination. And this was in effect what Marshall meant when he told Secretary Stimson that one could never tell when Patton might "go off the rocker."

Marshall's idea was bizarre under the circumstances, but showed how seriously the Patton problem was considered by the superiors in whose hands his fate and future rested. They were never, in fact, completely satisfied that George Patton was quite immune from what Maynard Keynes had described as one of "those semi-pathological propensities" which is best handed over to experts in mental disease.

The Chief of Staff thought that it might not be a bad idea to have a competent medical observer in the audience at the press conference, to analyze Patton, so to speak. Marshall consulted the Surgeon General about identifying the psychiatrist best qualified by training and tact to watch the proceedings for any such clues. General Milliken told the Chief of Staff that he knew the perfect specialist for the delicate consultation. He was a captain in the Navy Medical Corps, a psychoanalyst stationed in Bethesda, who had treated several high-ranking officers during the war in incidents of nervous breakdown.

The plan was vetoed by Stimson, and an opportunity was

probably lost to "analyze" Patton—for even without the presence of a psychiatrist in his audience, distinct symptoms of some unbalance in him—such as excessive euphoria or touches of a personality disorder—could have been evident. This time, though, few if any showed, probably because Secretary Stimson knew how to handle his own favorite general. The scenario of the press conference, carefully prepared in advance, left no margin for error. It had none since it was held on Thursday, June 14, in time to generate its own headlines before it would be overshadowed by Ike's homecoming, scheduled for the weekend.

NO SOONER did they sit down in the packed auditorium than Stimson took over, allowing Patton only to comment on such harmless topics as tanks, horses, and combat psychology. Sitting at the left of the general, Mr. Stimson presided as a combination master of ceremonies, interviewer, and censor. He asked almost all the questions, answered several from the floor, and ruled out of order some of the queries that the reporters had a chance to pose.

Patton did not seem to mind. He was at his amusing best, staying cheerfully within the bounds the Secretary was setting for him. He regaled his enchanted audience with colorful anecdotes—like the story of his meeting a soldier on a mule. "The poor kid," he said. "He fell off the goddamn beast because he tried too hard to salute me and stay in the saddle that was slipping off the mule's neck in the meantime."

They loved it.

"If we'd had horse cavalry in Tunisia," he went on, "the bag of Germans would have been much bigger. It was simply a question of mobility and speed in terrain where the tanks couldn't fight. Well, at one time I needed cavalry so badly that I had extemporized some of it, and had nine hundred immortal heroes mounted on anything I could find that moved on four legs from horses to mules to bulls."

Punctuating his remarks with gestures of his hands and arms, Patton said that a battle to him was much like a prize fight. "You keep the enemy rocking back on his heels," he said with a grin, "until you knock him out. In real battle, if you keep up your pressure, the enemy has no chance to revive between rounds. I prefer to hit hard, even if I lose ten thousand men in one day, instead of dawdling along and lose five hundred a day for twenty days."

A reporter asked what magic General Patton had employed to build the morale of the Third Army so high. Patton just smiled and said: "It was simple, ladies and gentlemen. I just had the honor and happiness of commanding some very great men. Thanks to them, we—and by 'we' I mean the Third Army, because I keep forgetting there are any others—well, *we* destroyed 2,300-odd German tanks, including 890 Panzers and Tigers, and we lost half that many."

Summing it up by talking about the ultimate hazards of war, he said: "It isn't particularly smart to take unnecessary chances." Obviously he took none on this particular occasion.

That same afternoon Patton marched into Walter Reed Hospital and took charge for two hours as if it had been one of his own command posts. With a cavalryman's crop under his arm, but minus any of his guns, he walked from ward to ward, patting wounded veterans on the back, shaking their hands, and delivering pep talks. As long as any of the patients were around, the general carried his air of cheer and encouragement through the wards. He broke down only once, when he visited the maimed and mutilated, waiting for their artificial arms and legs. Suddenly he burst into tears and said: "Goddamnit, men! If I had been a better general, most of you wouldn't be here!" Then, outside, still wiping his eyes, he said: "This tears the hell out of me."

Over the public address system of the hospital, General Patton made a little speech, addressing his audience as "fellow soldiers of both sexes." Mindful that the war was still on, he told them: "Your comrades expect you to carry on with the same valor when you leave here that you did on the battlefield. Your duty is never done until you die."

Was he talking about himself?

All this was the sideshow—incidental and immaterial—purest public relations. What really mattered was merely touched upon and was quickly dismissed. Everybody at the press conference wanted to know what Patton had up his sleeve. They remembered how the Germans had been puzzled after D-Day, when he was kept idle in England, saved for the coup de grace in Normandy. But Secretary Stimson ruled out any questions about his future assignments. "General Patton will return to Europe," he said tersely, "to complete all the unfinished business there before he does anything else."

PATTON wound up the tour at an American Legion post reception in Hamilton, a Boston suburb, another of his adopted hometowns. His neighbors gave him a genuine Paul Revere bowl and serenaded him with a song for which he had written the words many, many years before. It was still only the middle of June.

Then he vanished for a couple of weeks in rare privacy, spending the days he had left of his leave with his wife and her family. He was becoming increasingly restless. He could not comprehend what had made the United States change so drastically—all those half-baked civilians running amuck and telling the soldiers how to conduct their wars. When he was ready to get back into harness, Sergeant Meeks remarked: "Well, General, we've sure done our thirty days in the brig."

"In a sense," Patton noted, "I had a similar feeling." He could not understand what made his country so "inimical," as he put it, to the realities in Europe. He was not alone by any means in his perplexity. Most of the soldiers coming home were experiencing the same sense of "dislocation," as it was called, during a period of transition. But while the malaise lasted but a few weeks with others, it became chronic in Patton's case, as he found himself incapable of shedding attitudes and habits not only outré, but taboo in a civilian world.

He spent his days brooding over his fate, in deepening depression, his frustration filling him with hostility and cynicism.

7.

★ ★ ★ ★

Tempest in a
Clouded Crystal Ball

WHILE he was on the road, the powers in Washington were debating in a whisper what to do with General Patton when the cheering stopped. The war was not over by any means. His colleagues in command in Europe were being moved to the Far East one by one. It seemed inconceivable that only Patton would be left behind, the one man who had just licked the Germans singlehanded, as he himself liked to say, albeit with a grin.

Now in the summer of 1945, from the perspective of Washington, D.C.—in the immediate wake of his triumphant homecoming—Patton was moving heaven and earth in the Pentagon to have himself transferred either to General Douglas MacArthur in the Pacific or to General Albert Wedemeyer in China.

He had buttonholed every VIP who had visited him—Undersecretary of War Bob Patterson, General Hap Arnold, Bernard Baruch, the columnist Henry J. Taylor—urging them to promote his transfer. His friend Baruch wrote, "I have not forgotten what you said about your desire to tank around in China." Baruch took up the matter with his good friend, George C. Marshall, but he did not have to prod the Chief of Staff. Marshall was hard at work to find a billet for Patton.

Very soon it became evident, however, that nobody wanted him. Festering memories of old troubles and expectations of new problems were keeping him out in the cold. In Washington he soon learned that it was mostly General W. Mark Clark who lobbied against another "operational" assignment for Patton in what was left of the European theater. Commander in chief now of the Allied forces in the whole of Italy, facing a new foe, Marshal Tito of Yugoslavia, Clark was never enchanted by Patton's antics. "I don't want that sonuvabitch anywhere down here," he signaled to General Eisenhower when somebody proposed that he be sent to fight Tito in Trieste.

Patton had hardly endeared himself to Clark, to whom he referred frequently as an "egomaniac," and whom he described as giving him "the creeps."

At his final briefing on V-E Day, Patton assured his staff that they would be "going to China" very soon. So confident was he that he would be permitted to "earn his pay" a little longer in that other war that he told the correspondents covering the Third Army: "We are heading for the Pacific." He did not care how big a force he would command, as long as he was allowed to take on the Japs. In a letter to General Marshall, pleading to expedite his transfer, he told the Chief of Staff he was prepared to go in any capacity, even "in command of a single division"—that, at a time when he had seventeen divisions under him.

Admiral Mountbatten expressed interest in him for the China-Burma-India Theater, and Patton was raring to go, even though he would have been serving again under superiors who were almost fifteen years his junior. But his hopes to go to the mysterious East were fading fast. "I doubt," he wrote to his wife, "if I will go to China unless something happens to Doug"—General MacArthur, that is.

Then Patton's last hope was crushed. On June 13 he called on President Truman in the White House, and later went to the Pentagon for a conference with General Marshall. He was told categorically that the Pacific was out. A touch of mystery was added when Secretary Stimson, in a press conference the next day, ruled out all questions about Patton's future. There were rumors that Stimson and Marshall had opted for Patton's transfer, but caved in when General MacArthur opposed it.

The decision to leave Patton in Europe was justified with

the explanation that he was too fast for the Japanese. "Patton's sweeping rather than methodical method of fighting Germans," as it was put, "was not applicable to the Japanese." Patton was flabbergasted and hurt. "Such criticism," he said, "is only another example of the great brevity of human memory." Actually it was the charitable way of letting Patton know that MacArthur had categorically rejected him.

"I am still confused," Patton wrote after the stop in Washington, "as to just what one has to do." And more sadly: "I am like a rat without a tail."

HIS YEARNING to fight in the Pacific or to take on the Japanese in China was genuine, of course. He had reached the point in his career when he did not really care where the battlefield might be so long as they would let him go on fighting.

Actually, by now, he would have preferred to remain in Europe to take on the Russians. His crystal ball was working overtime. His vision of a clash with the Russians had little if any political or ideological connotation. Patton was totally apolitical, so much so, in fact, that he had neither patience for nor, indeed, a perception of ideologies per se, nor any interest in the processes that produced them.

For a long time, Patton had been largely indifferent to the Russian presence in the war. On the day the Germans invaded the Soviet Union in 1941, for instance, when the Russians changed abruptly before our eyes like an ugly frog turning into a handsome prince, Patton had been happily engaged in what he described as "a very pleasant maneuver in Tennessee" in which his new division, the 2nd Armored, "established so high a standard that we will have difficulty in maintaining it."

In the wake of Pearl Harbor and the German declaration of war on December 11, 1941, the Russians and the Americans found themselves fighting the same enemy. Patton continued to ignore the Russians, but as he was advancing eastward in Europe in 1945, the Red Army was moving westward. All of a sudden, the Russians were in his way. The problems they posed became acute. The Russians succeeded in preventing him from gaining for the United States a vantage point from which better to rule the world after the war. Eisenhower had vetoed the march into Prague and the liberation of Czechoslovakia by Patton's Third Army.

After that, his admiration of Ike sagged and the Russians ceased to be his allies. They became in his eyes "a scurvy race and simple savages." If we had to fight them, as we would have to sooner or later, this was the time! Even before the war had ended, Patton anticipated the cold war in what in hindsight appears to have been an uncanny strategic prognosis. It was, in fact, a self-serving forecast inspired by his regrets to see the fighting end.

The heady excitement and the glamor of war, which had propelled him to unexpected heights of exhilaration and acclaim, were receding rapidly. He abhorred a vacuum. Fifty years earlier he had written to his future father-in-law, an obstinate pacifist, to justify his profession: "It is as natural for me to be a soldier as it is to breathe." To be a soldier in times of peace was unsatisfactory then. It was intolerable now when he was perceiving a new peril—the Soviet menace.

Though the Russians loomed largest, they were not alone among his bêtes noires. There were the British also, especially Field Marshal Montgomery. He used to call him "the ferocious rabbit." Now he became "that little fart." His xenophobia was acute, but it was not all-inclusive by any means. He continued to like the French with reservations. And in the deepest recesses of his heart, he was developing a special feeling of good will for the Germans.

Patton was totally exhausted and badly in need of rest, but he was not granting himself any respite. In his fatigue aggravated by a nervousness that he could not bridle, he was becoming of little use to anyone. It seemed that his great value in war did not necessarily preordain him for comparable services in peace.

His confusion and frustration were showing in regrettable slips—of both omission and commission—all of which were casting an ominous shadow on his usefulness. In a moment of reckless indiscretion, he expressed regret for Mussolini, who had just been put to death by the Partisans;

they had left the Duce's corpse hanging on a hook like a side of beef. "I had great admiration for the man," said Patton. Then maligning the whole nation for the dictator's gruesome end, he added: "It was a typically Italian stunt to murder him."

Notoriously impatient with many people, Patton had an excellent record of tolerance in the Army. His liberal attitude to the black soldier, for example, harked back to his early cavalry days when the horses and their black grooms were an officer's best friends. Once when he was stationed in Fort Riley, Kansas, the white trash of nearby Junction City's honky-tonk row threatened to lynch one of his black noncoms. Patton ordered a squad of the cavalry to mount, borrowed a cannon, and moved against sin city, warning that he would level it unless his man was released—and he promptly was. William George Meeks, his black orderly ("about the only man who can find anything"), and Meeks's wife Virginia were among his closest intimates.

Although he had no doubts about the prowess of the black sergeants in the cavalry, he was not so sure that the black soldier of World War II was the equal of the white GIs. Yet in England, preparing the Third Army for the invasion, he promoted integration of combat troops more vigorously than any of the other commanding generals.

There was not much opportunity in his social set and in the Army to meet many Jews. But he did come upon a few, and he invariably liked them. The man who could sound off like a bigot but had no trace of bigotry was devoid of the fashionable social anti-Semitism of his caste. As a young man in 1912, when he dreamed of being sent to Sweden as a military attaché, the Congressman who aided him in his quest (in vain, as it turned out) was a Jew, Julius Kahn. So was Jacob Silverman, an eminent New York educator, who tutored Patton's son for his West Point entrance examination and again for his reexamination when young George failed in math during his plebe year and was turned back. Among other kudos, General Patton praised in particular Dr. Silverman's "psychological influence" on the cadet.

In 1918 it was a Jewish soldier who saved his life, and

he remained so grateful that he was still in touch with him twenty-three years later—trying, in fact, to get Sergeant Schemitz into his World War II outfit in spite of his age. During the assembly of his long-serving staff, initially for "Torch" in 1942, no bias excluded a candidate. As a result, Patton had a considerable number of Jews on his staff. Among them the most prominent was Colonel Oscar Koch of Carbondale, Illinois, his G-2, who had joined him in North Africa and stayed with him all the way to Bad Toelz. Major Martin Blumenson, the Third Army historian, was also Jewish, handpicked by Patton when others, fearful of Patton's alleged anti-Semitism, tried to get another detail for Blumenson. He was chosen by the family in 1966 and 1968 to publish Patton's outspoken papers, after decades of suppression following his death.

The limited assembly of his favorite soldiers—a very small group, indeed—included two Jewish officers at the top of the short roster. They were Colonel Harold L. Cohen from Chicago and Captain Abraham J. Baum from the Bronx. It was to Abe Baum, the Army's second most decorated officer, that he eventually entrusted the operation to rescue his son-in-law from a German P/W camp.

And yet, as if contaminated by the plague with which Hitler infected Germany, Patton suddenly broke out into gratuitous bigotry. His growing intolerance was not confined to foreigners. When Senator James O. Eastland of Mississippi made racist charges against black soldiers, an indignant black man wrote Patton from Philadelphia asking that he correct the impression. Patton marked the letter to be filed without a reply.

He referred to American newspapers collectively as "the non-Aryan press," and amidst other outbursts of flagrant anti-Semitism, the wandering Jew had come to bear the brunt of Patton's creeping neurosis. The survivors of the Holocaust, just emerging from utter degradation, many of them still waiting to be deloused and scrubbed, became the subjects of his most rampant impatience and intolerance. "The Jewish type of DP," he wrote in the privacy of his diary, "in the majority of cases, is a sub-human species without any of the cultural or social refinements of our time." This was patently the language of Nazism. He was adopting it for his own brand of ism—what he himself called "Anglo-Saxonism."

Yet the strange metamorphosis in Patton passed unrecognized by those who had custody of his future. Neither Secretary Stimson nor General Marshall—nor, for that matter, Ike, who was closest to him—recognized anything in Patton's new outlook and swagger that should have called for caution. When all efforts had failed to find a berth for him elsewhere, his friends decided to send him back to Germany as a military governor. They gave him Bavaria, where Nazism was born.

His friends meant well. They acted with compassion on the principle that there is not a more unhappy being than a superannuated hero. But just when they hoped to salvage his pride, bolster his self-respect, and save him from deadening idleness, they doomed him.

★ ★ ★ ★

Book Two

The
Lord
of St. Querin

War, he sung, is toil and trouble; Honour but an empty bubble; Never ending, still beginning, Fighting still . . .

—JOHN DRYDEN, *"Alexander's Feast"*

8.

⭐ ⭐ ⭐ ⭐

Return of the Proconsul

*In the nightmare of the dark, All the dogs of Europe bark,
And the living nations wait, Each sequestered in its hate . . .*

—W. H. AUDEN, *"In memory of W. B. Yeats,"* 1939

Now that the war was won and the big decisions had been
made, General Patton's absence was felt by his staff, but
mostly socially, so to speak. Invitations were pouring in
from all the friendly allies in the neighboring occupation
zones, and from the Russians, whose celebrations were assuming bacchanalian proportions. Settled comfortably in the
stately homes of Germany and Austria, the victorious generals gave glittering parties to commemorate their splendor
while it lasted. Parades, investitures, galas, farewell parties,
and reunions were held everywhere, topped by enormous
banquets and the generous flow of French and German
wines, Scotch whisky, and Russian vodka. The great captains were constantly on the road, calling on one another
or visiting famous cities whose grateful burghers vied to
honor them.

General Patton was in no hurry to return to Bad Toelz,
the clearest indication, if nothing else, of his interest, or the
lack of it, in his new job. Paris was his favorite city, and
the Georges V was his favorite hotel. Holed up in his regular
suite on the third floor, doted upon by the management and
the room service staff, he was having a wonderful time. It
was Independence Day, and he was the guest of honor at
the American Embassy.

Robed for the occasion by Sergeant Meeks in his tightly tailored combat jacket with four rows of ribbons on his breast, and wearing his pink gabardine breeches with Mr. Faulkner's masterpiece of a pair of Argentine leather boots, the general did not let down the crowd. He clutched his silver-topped swagger stick with apparent diffidence as he accepted the plaudits that became quite boisterous—he was kissed and patted and mobbed. "It was somewhat reassuring to find," he wrote afterward, "that I was still a fairly good size lion."

ALTHOUGH HE WAS on the eve of immersing himself in the enormously complicated new task awaiting him, the problems of the job were absent from his thoughts. Neither by experience nor by training, neither by philosophy nor by temperament was he the man who could possibly perform the miracle of reforming the part of Germany where the stench of the Hitler regime was polluting the air most. And he was burned out, showing, in fact, alarming signs of fatigue and imbalance. In his truculent frame of mind, his mission in Germany made him more restive and reckless. It made him more than usually insecure, and he suffered from all the ravages of his insecurity. As usual in such a frame of mind, he was blaming others for woes of his own making, and Germany for the awful challenge. "It is," he wrote at this time, "a very depressing place."

But Hap Gay knew how to cheer him up. There was, in fact, only a single gift he could not get for Patton as a homecoming present. On June 29, he had asked General Bradley to award an oak-leaf cluster to the general's Bronze Star for the capture of Pilsen in the part of Czechoslovakia from which the Third Army had not been banned. But General Allen called back two days later to say that his boss was sorry, he could not see how he could grant the request.

But otherwise, nothing was missing. The weather was perfect, the seasonal warmth of this July day tempered by a light breeze blowing in from the mountains to the south. And the setting was superb. In Bad Toelz the *Junkerschule* commanded the hill—it had been, just a few weeks before, a Teutonic West Point where the cream of the crop of the

Waffen-SS officers were trained. According to local legend, it was put there by the Führer in a fit of spite. He was supposedly so displeased with the lukewarm reception he once received from these townspeople, whose ardor for Nazism left much to be desired, that he planted this most Nazi of all institutions on their necks to punish them.

Those same townspeople showed the same indifference for the new rulers, now that the *Junkerschule* was called the Flint Kaserne. But up on the hill they were ready for Patton as never before. His plane had already been flown to Paris by Colonel Bob Cummings, his general factotum in the Third Army, a couple of days before, and was waiting to take him to Bad Toelz. They left Paris at 9:15 in the morning of this July 5, and were flying over Strasbourg when Sergeant Meeks, who was sitting up front with him, tugged at his sleeve. "Look, General," he said, pointing at the sky outside the window. Patton suddenly saw a flock of planes swarming around him. They were P-51 fighters, twenty-four of them, from the XIX Tactical Air Command, to escort him to Hoelzkirchen, the airfield nearest to Toelz. They were Gay's first installment of the pageant to come.

Upon alighting on the airstrip at 12:15 P.M., Patton found an armored infantry battalion lined up as his honor guard with a division band. Then, flanked by a bevy of motorcycle outriders with their sirens blaring, and covered by an umbrella of fifty fighter planes, his limousine passed row after row of tanks, their crews lining the road and saluting smartly, and men of an antiaircraft battalion, deployed along the route, presenting arms.

A company of armored infantry and a company of black soldiers stood guard on each side of the road at intervals of fifty yards. Patton made it to the commanding general's sallyport entrance at the Kaserne, where he was greeted by Major General Louis A. Craig, probably the man happiest to see him, because he could now relinquish his acting command of the Third Army, to which he had been temporarily assigned in Patton's absence. Also assembled were his corps commanders—Generals Keyes, Harmon, and John W. Leonard—and as many division commanders as could be spared.

It was an unforgettable scene, unmatched by any the Waffen-SS, with its remarkable flair for pageantry, had ever produced on these same premises. The march music of the massed band filled the air, as a battalion of artillery was firing the salute. The honor guard, supplied by two companies of MPs, was standing at stiff attention in front of rows and rows of soldiers lined up in the huge plaza.

Craig and Gay escorted Patton to a platform for the review, after which, with moist eyes and a voice breaking in its high pitch, he greeted his men with what he later called "a few well-chosen words." The big parade over, he proceeded to the Officers' Mess for cocktails and lunch. He was the proconsul again.

THE LUNCH OVER, the Annsbach Uralt, the heady German brandy, sipped to the last drop, and his exquisite cigars smoked, it was time to go home. General Gay and Colonel Harkins escorted Patton to the house that was to be his next to last residence in Germany. It had been quite a change on May 23, when the general was moved from his trailer at "Lucky Forward" in Regensburg to the big house on the edge of St. Querin, the village named for the patron saint of all Upper Bavarians; the house was still warm with the comforts of the Nazis. It was, until then, the villa of the man Patton called "Mr. Emann"—Max Amann, that is, Hitler's sergeant in World War I.

During the halcyon days of Nazism, Amann had been the director general of Eher Verlag, Hitler's publishing empire. "As a result," Patton wrote, "he has one of the best houses I have ever seen." It had a bowling alley, a swimming pool, a large number of rooms, a boat house, and two boats on the Tegernsee. "If one has to occupy Germany," Patton added, "this is a good place to do it from."

From the large window of his bedroom on the second floor, the countryside could be seen at its best—the beautiful lake glittering with the rays of the summer sun, blue ripples and coquettish little circles of fresh white foam in the water. Neat chalets and sturdy old churches dotted the shores in a kaleidoscope of bright colors—red, white, blue, green, and yellow flowers were everywhere. "It is the prettiest country," Patton wrote. "War has not touched it to any extent."

Until a few weeks before his arrival, it had been a sort of hallowed ground. Next door was the villa of Heinrich Himmler, and farther down, the house of Franz X. Schwarz, treasurer of the Nazi party—territory that, one would have thought, was mortgaged irrevocably to history. Wild rumors were abroad that the Nazi treasure, vast and mysterious like the gold of the Nibelungen, was buried somewhere in or near St. Querin; and that Himmler had concealed the loot of the SS in a huge steel vault built secretly at the bottom of the lake.

But this was no lane of memories. The ghosts were gone, their haunts already forgotten. As far as the Amann villa was concerned, its Nazi owner had fled so helter-skelter that the beds were unmade and the dishes unwashed when the Americans arrived.

The millionaire tsar of the Nazi publishing empire did not get far. Found hiding in the underbrush behind a neighbor's house, he had surrendered with a sigh and a shrug to men from a regimental combat team of the 36th Division passing through St. Querin. It had been May 3—just three days before all hostilities ceased in the area, with the surrender of the German army group to the Seventh U.S. Army at the nearby village of Haar.

Amann had been at home in this neighborhood on the Tegernsee, one of the most enchanting of the many Bavarian lakes, and had chosen a spot in 1936 that gave him several stunning views of the lake and the dark hills on the western shore. The grounds were just large enough to assure privacy off a much-traveled road winding along the lake. And though the three-story main house with a two-story wing for the servants was huge, it managed to look neither ostentatious nor oppressive, because Herr Degano, the architect, knew how to abide by the local lines and colors. When Amann owned it, he had to drive sixty miles to get to it from Munich. For Patton it was only a fifteen-minute ride from the Flint Kaserne, barely ten miles away on a low hill in Bad Toelz astride the road leading from Munich to the Tegernsee.

The villa had been one of more than three hundred fifty such country homes of *nouveau élégance* which the Americans confiscated peremptorily because of their Nazi ownership. At this time the decision was already in the making to erase from the surface of the earth Hitler's enormous compound in the sky, which succeeded in being breathtaking and *petit bourgeois* at the same time. But nobody in SHAEF ever thought of demolishing any of these delightful houses that showed more taste and had more of the native touch than the Führer's haven held in bogus baroque.

There were in this collection of precious real estate more grandiose palaces to house a conquering hero. But none was more soothing in its quiet refinement than the villa Max Amann had occupied for only nine of the thousand years Hitler had promised the Germans. Remembering Patton's violent reaction to his perfumed, mirrored flat in Mayfair on his arrival in England in 1944 to get ready for D-Day, and how he never forgave Lieutenant General John C. H. Lee, who had picked it for him, the advance men who chose the villa for him showed good judgment and taste in selecting it. Patton approved the choice. "It is the prettiest country," he wrote to his wife, "with snow mountains, forests of all shades of green, and green fields."

Yet somehow, the place unsettled the general. The beauty of the mountains and the magic of the lake had no message for him. He gained neither joy nor solace from their charm and serenity.

For one thing, perhaps, they came into his life at too hectic a juncture to fill him and becalm him with the tranquillity that comes from nature at its best. For another thing, he found no escape even in this environment from the problems, troubles, worries, and controversies confronting him. "The villa," he wrote to a friend in Boston on his second day in St. Querin, "is the handsomest house I have ever seen except the one I had in Morocco." But this was Germany. The issues that were soon confronting him dwarfed anything he had had to face in Casablanca.

"IT GAVE ME a very warm feeling," Patton said, "to be back among soldiers." But that was about all. "It seems to me," he said in the same breath, "that there is nothing more of interest in the world now that the war is over."

It was thus not in any special surge of eagerness to embark on his job, but rather because he could not possibly evade his responsibilities any longer, that he spent July 6, the day after his return, "reviewing the activities," as General Gay put it, "which had taken place during his month's absence in the United States." The record does not show that those "activities" included anything directly affecting the Eastern District of Occupation which he was supposed to govern. Except for a brief synopsis of what Colonel Roy L. Dalferes, his new G-5, called "the displaced persons situation"—inspiring Patton to a bit of punning, calling them "displeased persons"—there was no reference to any of the "three Ds" he had been ordered to promote and enforce.

In particular, he did not bother to hear about the changes Colonel Keegan was making in Bavaria, and did not seem to care how the experiment with the Schaeffer government was working out.

What interested him now as before was the *military* situation—in the flux of regrouping, repatriating, and reassessing, the whole Third Army apparently hanging in the balance. Brigadier General Halley G. Maddox, his G-3, presented him with lists of the units still in the Third Army, the units that had been moved out, and the units that had orders to move. Maddox told him, with a pride shared by all, that as of that moment, the Third Army was the largest military organization of its kind in history—comprising the unprecedented number of twenty-seven divisions under one commanding general.

That was the gist of the briefings, except for a report by the Provost Marshal. Reading from a status sheet, Colonel Philip C. Clayton told Patton that out of the total of prisoners-of-war the Third Army had been holding on V-E Day, a million had been discharged. Half a million Germans were still on hand for future disposition.

Nothing more exciting developed until Patton dismissed the staff and remained alone with General Gay, for the confidential briefing he regularly reserved for just the two of them. As it turned out, a number of major problems had surfaced during his absence.

Two of them concerned the 11th Armored Division, whose commander, Major General Holmes E. Dager, one of the Third Army's most dashing combat team leaders during the war, was among Patton's top favorites. The heat was on at Army Group headquarters, Gay now told him, because Dager, troubled by a sudden increase of VD cases in his division, had ordered that whenever one or another of his soldiers contracted gonorrhea or syphilis, his next of kin be notified.

Actually, Dager had cleared the order with Patton, and Gay was cognizant of it. But it scandalized the Army Group, and when Gay now related how upset General Bradley was on this score, Patton sadly said: "It's a bloody shame, Hap, because it's a damned good idea. But tell Dager to cancel the order."

Far more serious was an investigation by the Inspector General that now threatened to cost General Dager his command. It developed that in the heat of the Battle of the Bulge, soldiers from the 11th Armored Division had allegedly killed a number of Germans who had surrendered to them. It was not a nice story, as it emerged from a report of the Inspector General of the VIII Corps.

Released for the Bastogne campaign from SHAEF reserve to the Third Army on December 24, 1944, the division had undergone its baptism of fire on December 30 in the drive on Houffalize. The fighting was intense and the progress was slow at exceptionally heavy cost. On January 14, 1945, on the Longchamps-Compogne road and at Noville, where the division had come under withering fire, the high casualties unnerved the young soldiers of Major General Charles S. Kilburn. And when they succeeded in taking prisoners at last, some men, and even a few officers, vented their frustration and wrath by mowing them down in cold blood. The incident was investigated by the VIII Corps, and it was found that Brigadier General Dager, then leading Combat Command B of the 4th Armored Division, had been somehow involved in the "massacre."

In February, when the first probe was concluded, General Bradley took up the matter with General Patton, and—remembering what happened to Compton and West in the "massacre" in Sicily—they decided to take no action. They were apprehensive that any intervention on their part would give the case publicity. "In turn," Bradley explained, "the German forces would learn about it and probably would bring forth acts of retribution." For his part, General Gay pigeonholed the report, concluding that the "fewer people who knew about it, the better."

But the case was not closed. On June 10, and again on June 13, the Inspector General revived it, now recommending that General Dager be relieved of his command, to which he had been named in March 1945 at the head of the 11th Armored Division.

As soon as Gay laid before him the report, placing Dager's neck in the noose, Patton called Bradley and said, "I thought we had put the lid on this case."

Bradley agreed that they had.

"Then, for Pete's sake, Brad," Patton said, "why don't you tell Lev Allen to put the hiatus on the bastard who keeps throwing this goddamn report at us?"

The Army Group commander thought that that was a good idea. This time he feared that any publicity might inspire the Japanese, who did not need any incentive to commit their own atrocities.

The case is still open, marked "pending," in the patient files of the Inspector General.

9.

★ ★ ★ ★

More Gold, More Mysteries

ON THE AFTERNOON of June 28, Colonel Philip C. Clayton, the Provost Marshal, called General Gay in some excitement and demanded that the chief of staff see him right away. Gay told him to come over, and at 4:00 P.M., Clayton came in, accompanied by a young officer from the military police detachment at the Third Army. He turned out to be Major Richard G. Allgeier, and he had "an interesting story" to tell.

"Early yesterday morning," Allgeier said, "a couple of civilians accosted one of my lieutenants—Jack Murphy, to be exact—and told him that they were privy to an important secret. Since they wished to be in our good graces, they told Lieutenant Murphy they would divulge it, provided Lieutenant Murphy guaranteed that the Third Army would take care of them."

Murphy had told them he could not give any such guarantees. But, he said, if they had important information, he would like them to tell it to his superior officer, Captain Arthur Neubauer, which they agreed to do. "They told Neubauer," Allgeier said, "that they happened to find out, how they did not say, where a large part of the German gold reserve was hidden, together with a mass of foreign currencies. The treasure was in a cave, they claimed, not far from Toelz. If they were given transportation, they said, they would take *certain people*, as well as a person or persons Captain Neubauer would designate, to the spot."

On his own authority, then, Neubauer turned over a couple of cars to these civilians, and detailed Lieutenant Murphy with a few of his men to accompany them. They returned to the headquarters of the MP company at dawn of June 29, bringing with them what Allgeier estimated amounted to $700,000 in various currencies—U.S. dollars, British pounds sterling, Dutch guilders, French francs, and "a few other types."

But not bringing any gold. They had found about a ton of it—all that was left, the civilians insisted. The bulk had been looted, they said, before they had found out about the hoard. Even a ton proved too heavy to be transported in the cars, and Captain Neubauer asked Major Allgeier to assign a detail and a truck to bring in the gold. Allgeier sent forty men under three officers to return to the treasure trove.

The chief of staff was scandalized. "I hope you realize, Major," he told Allgeier, "that your procedure was quite *unusual,* to say the least. What you should have done, was to go yourself, Major, inventory this alleged $700,000 worth of currency right where it was and bring it, *together with the gold,* to this headquarters where it could have been put under heavy guard."

Gay then directed the Provost Marshal to impound the currency and move it "at once" from Allgeier's office at the military police to Clayton's office and place it under guard there, day and night. "And remember, Phil," Gay said. "Nobody must be allowed into the room except as approved by you or MacDonald"—Colonel John MacDonald, that is, the Deputy Provost Marshal. Gay ordered Clayton to be personally present when the detail Major Allgeier had sent for the gold returned with the bullion.

"Now listen, Phil," Gay said, "listen carefully, and you, too, Major. I don't care if anybody tells you otherwise— the newspaper people must not be notified of this. No leaks, hear me, or you'll be dead! This is an incident that has serious international implications. It's a *delicate* matter and it's got to be handled on the *highest* echelon."

Gay then called in Colonel Oscar W. Koch, the veteran G-2 of the Third Army, and directed him to have Colonel Charles E. Milliken, the finance officer, inventory the currency. "But Oscar," Gay said, "don't let Milliken's people know what they are coming here for. And you, Phil," he told the Provost Marshal, "you see to it that enough of your men are detailed to the place where the caches are," and added, somewhat melodramatically, "to protect them from whatever assault may be mounted by superior numbers."

As they were leaving, he warned them: "I want the gold, when it gets here, brought to this office, and nowhere else, and nobody is to find out about it. Am I making myself clear?"

General Gay had made up his mind to sit on the trove until Patton returned, not even letting the acting Army commander know what was going on. Then, he figured, it would be up to General Patton to dispose of the hoard through channels or decide who should be notified. Or to do as he pleased.

COLONEL CLAYTON called General Gay at 9:31 P.M. to say that "Albatross" had returned, using the code word the chief of staff had coined for the mission, probably to show how heavily this gold business was weighing around his neck. "Is *it* there?" Gay asked, accentuating the word "it" for "gold." But Clayton did not get it. "What do you mean?" he asked, and Gay, in his impatience, threw caution to the wind. "Damnit, Phil, the gold!" he said. "Have they brought it with them?"

"Well," the Provost Marshal said, "I really don't know. The currency has been brought over, as you ordered, and it's now in my office. And Neubauer did bring back a number of boxes which are quite heavy. But I don't know what's in them. I've seen to it, though, that everything was put in a room under guard."

"Is the guard heavy?" Gay asked.

"Well," Clayton said, "it depends on what you regard as heavy. I consider it adequate." Gay was not amused.

"Make sure," he said with a touch of irony, "that your orders to them are also adequate."

The next morning, accompanied by Colonel Clayton, Brigadier General Halley G. Maddox, the Third Army G-3, and Lieutenant Colonel John J. Edwards, representing the finance officer, General Gay went to the room on the third floor of the Flint Kaserne in which the Provost Marshal

was storing the currency and the crates. At first, the sentry
would not let them in, and they had to send for the officer
of the day to clear them. In the room, they found the bags
and the boxes, and Gay asked Edwards to open some of
them. The bags contained bundles of currencies, neatly tied,
including U.S. and British, and even Swedish, Swiss, and
Turkish banknotes.

Other bags, which were so heavy that Colonel Edwards
needed help to lift them on a table, contained gold coins
of twenty Reichsmarks each. When the boxes were opened
at last, they also contained gold coins rather than bullion.
"I was unable to estimate the value of this paper money and
gold coins," Gay recalled. "My rough guess was that it
amounted to something over a million bucks."

THE BIG STORY behind General Gay's report, and
the background of Allgeier's gold, was as interesting as was
the mystery of the treasure's end—an open end, to be sure,
for its odyssey is not over by any means. In this fateful
spring of 1945, neither the Allied nor the Russian intelligence was any good inside Berlin. They did not even know
that Hitler had holed up in the capital. And they were ig-
norant of the very existence of the *Führerbunker*. But they
had a smattering of knowledge of what General Eisenhower
called "the movement of valuables." Anti-Nazis had tipped
off Allen W. Dulles, the OSS director in Switzerland, when
the art treasures began to move. And there were rumors that
the Nazis' gold reserve had vanished from its vaults in the
Reichsbank.

The dispositions the Germans had made to protect these
treasures were hampered by Hitler, who regarded any such
measures as signs of defeatism punishable by instant death.
It was only on January 7, 1945, in one of his directives
about "evacuation and concealment," that Reichsminister
Albert Speer referred first to these troves, but so vaguely
that nobody could or dared to interpret it as a definitive
order or as urgent.

Hitler himself showed no great concern for these hoards.
But in a *Führerbefehl* (executive order) on April 2, after
the Third Army had begun its march into Thuringia, he
ordered an Alpine division, and a hastily assembled unit of

over-age men suffering from stomach ulcers and other illnesses, to stem Patton's advance "at all cost." Although some of the treasures had been moved into the path of the Third Army's advance in the meantime, Hitler issued the order to protect the ball-bearing production concentrated in that area, still dreaming of a fight to the finish if not ultimate victory.

The valuables were moved out of Berlin in the end because Hitler had decided to make his last stand in the capital. On April 20, he celebrated his fifty-sixth birthday deep underground in his cement palace, brooding and fuming. He exited ten days later by blowing his brains out.

ACTUALLY it was Martin Bormann, Hitler's deputy, who conceived the master plan to move those "valuables" to presumably safe places, and then supervised the transfers. The Party functionary who represented him in these delicate transactions was a mystery man named Melmer, who then vanished without a trace, most probably with part of the treasure he was supposed to safeguard. The officials in actual charge were the two Reichsbank officials the Americans had captured at Merkers—an inspector named Albert Thoms who had been in charge of the vaults, and Emil Johann Rudolf Puhl, the senior vice-president of the Reichsbank, who had responsibility for the whole treasure trove. The crating, bagging, and loading were supervised by Thoms. When the last shipment was ready to leave, Puhl joined him and together they accompanied the priceless cargo in Herr Puhl's car.

It was at this stage that the Third Army entered the melodrama, because most of the treasures had been shipped into hiding places that happened to be in the path of its advance. The major hoard had been found on April 4 at Merkers, and was safely back in the Reichsbank vaults in Frankfurt, in the custody of the Americans this time. Fragments showed up here and there, and were duly accounted for. But what came to be known as "Allgeier's gold" had come from another trove.

On April 13, two heavily guarded special trains—code-named "Adler" and "Dohle"—had left Berlin for Munich, carrying 520 million Reichsmarks. The next day, another

part of the treasure left the capital in a convoy of five Opel
Blitz trucks, consisting of 365 bags, each containing two
bars of gold.

Its destination was a mine at Preissenberg, fifty kilometers southwest of Munich; also in the shipment were
ninety-four bags of foreign currencies, six cases of Danish
gold coins, two bags of German gold coins, and four boxes
of gold bullion. And last but not least, a load of jewelry
was flown out of Berlin by an SS general named Joseph
Spacil, with destination unknown.

The train "Dohle" and the convoy of the five Opel trucks
arrived safely in Bavaria, and their cargoes were accounted
for during the postwar gold rush. Spacil's hoard, flown to
Salzburg and buried on a hillside near Taxenbach, was
unearthed by the Counter Intelligence Corps of the U.S.
Army in June 1945, was properly inventoried and taken to
Frankfurt.

Apparently the "Adler" was lost en route. But the gold
the Opel trucks were taking to Preissenberg could be tracked
part of the way, only to wind up in confusion and mystery.
By the time the Third Army had broken into Thuringia,
Herr Puhl had received orders to take his loot farther south
and disperse it, hiding some in various mines in Upper
Bavaria, burying some in the Austrian Alps, or sinking part
of it in the mountain lakes. It was, then, from these telltale
clues in the wake of the windfall at Merkers that Colonel
Milliken, Patton's finance chief, was able to establish that
the bulk of the fugitive treasure had been moved into "Patton
country," and would be recovered—if and when found.
Considerable quantities of art treasures and other valuables
were discovered after Merkers. But no gold showed up, nor
any foreign currencies—until those civilians in Bad Toelz
betrayed the final resting place of some Nazi gold.

Now it developed that it was, in fact, part of the hoard
that had gone farther south by Puhl's arrangements. When
he found that the Preissenberg hiding place was flooded,
Puhl had sent the entire load of 461 bags and ten boxes to
the vicinity of the secluded monastery of St. Nicholas near
Mittenwald on the Austrian border. They stashed it there
in a huge cave in Einsiedel mountain where the Nazis pre-

viously had kept some stolen treasures of the Roman Catholic Church.

NOW PATTON was back in Bavaria and asking questions. "Okay, Hap," he said grimly. "Gimmee the sta-*goddamn*-tistics." From spitting his words and splicing them with his cusses, the chief of staff knew instantly that the general was upset or excited.

When the gold of Merkers had slipped through his fingers and gone "down the drain," Patton professed that he could not care less. In a press conference on V-E Day, when the lid was back on the scoop, a reporter asked: "Do you have any objection about releasing the story about the gold?"

"I have no objection to anything," Patton said.

"There is a question, General," another reporter said, "as to who owns the gold."

Now Patton replied gruffly: "I don't give a damn."

But it did ignite his imagination. Another treasure had turned up in his own backyard, and General Gay's astute handling of the incident assured greater discretion.

"The facts, Doctor Watson," he said to Gay. "How much is this hoard worth all told?"

"Milliken had figured it out, sir," Gay said, then read from a piece of paper. "The gold we're holding is valued at $1,387,560 and change. The currencies could be worth a little over eight hundred thousand bucks if they're real. But we think most of it is counterfeit."

"Does the press know about this?" Patton asked, and Gay said: "No, sir, not even Deane and Gauthier know anything about it." (They were the Third Army's own press officers.)

"How many people do?" Patton asked.

"Well, sir," Gay said. "Major Allgeier is cognizant, of course, as is Lieutenant Murphy, and Captain Neuhauser, and the..."

Patton broke into his figuring. "Don't ackack, Hap." It was his word for stammering when a straight answer was forthcoming in fragments. "Your esti-*goddamn*-mate, General Gay! *How many people know about this fuckin' hoard?*"

"I'd say a hundred, maybe more," Gay said.

"You mean the entire Third Army," Patton shot back.

He paused for a moment, obviously thinking. Then the man who usually got rid of his temptations by yielding to them, told Gay: "That's about a hundred too many, Hap. Tell Milliken to pack up this fuckin' find, all of it, and order Conway to send it to Frankfurt, right away. I want the padre to go along to pray all the way that it gets there safely, and Colonel Cheever should also go to see to it that the receipt we get is legal."

Suddenly he seemed relaxed. He sounded almost cheerful. He was joking again. "And hear this, Hap. I want those stupid civilian bastards handed over to the Criminal Investigation Division, and see to it, Hap, that an investigation is started to find out what happened to the rest of the hoard. I don't want anybody ever to say that that sonuvabitch Patton had stolen any part of it."

He broke out in a grin. "Peanuts, Hap. A million bucks won't buy thirty seconds of war in the black market."

NOTHING WAS HEARD of the Mittenwald loot, estimated at millions already thirty years ago, until it showed up, so to speak, as an item in the *Guinness Book of World Records*. It read in part:

> The greatest robbery on record was that of the German National Bank's (Reichsbank's) reserves by a combine of U.S. military personnel and Germans. Gold bars, 728 in number, valued at $9,878,400 were removed from a cache on Klausenkopf mountainside, near Einsiedel, Bavaria, on June 7, 1945, together with six sacks containing $404,840 in dollar bills and 400 pound notes (possibly forged) from a garden in Oberaer.

The romantic story of the heist did not attract the public attention it would have deserved, probably because it brought prompt rebuttal from Washington. Using as a peg the Scottish-sounding name of the McWhirter brothers, editors of the Guinness book, a Pentagon spokesman dismissed the item with a quip. "You have your Loch Ness monster," he said. "We have our Great Gold Robbery."

Actually, the Army was not taking the matter quite that lightly. That the treasure had existed to begin with was proven beyond the shadow of a doubt. That it had vanished from Mittenwald had been established from evidence that the Army had come to regard as reliable. More than three hundred investigators were assigned to the case—tracking down every lead, checking out every rumor, probing every charge, acting on every tip, looking into every clue. The Army clammed up only when nothing was found—not enough hard evidence, that is, that would have closed the case.

To this day, the Pentagon denies categorically that anything resembling the robbery mentioned in the *Guinness Book of World Records* had ever really occurred, or that any part of the German gold or Nazi treasure, which the Americans had succeeded in finding, is unaccounted for.

BUT THE OFFICIAL history of the Third Army tells a different story. It records bluntly that some gold of an unspecified nature had been found near Mittenwald, 728 bars of it by actual count. It featured a grinning GI holding up one of the bars. And years later Colonel Milliken added a cryptic footnote when he told me: "I am convinced that some of the gold the Germans had shipped south disappeared in the commotion. I think it's even possible that part of this particular hoard also vanished in some unauthorized hands."

Anything seemed "possible" in the dirty backwash of the war. The enormous Nazi treasure, much of which had been looted, begot a new crop of looters. Huge chunks of the various hoards were vanishing right and left. A GI from Cicero, Illinois, literally walked out of Bavaria with a Rembrandt, then, unmolested, smuggled it into the States. The WAC major who managed an American officers' club in Kronberg Castle, former residence of the Dowager Empress Frederick of Germany, stole the crown jewels of the Hessian royal family that she had found in a secret alcove in the cellar behind a bricked-up door. A colonel, holding the negotiable assets of a Nazi tycoon he was supposed to defend in court, pending the disposition of his case as a war criminal, vanished with the man's liquid fortune—which the industrialist had succeeded in keeping out of the covetous hands of the Nazi looters.

The Army's probe of the missing gold generated its own melodrama. Each time the American investigators came up with a promising lead, some setback returned them to scratch. Once, when a whole team of army gumshoes, led by a Captain Weisner from California, had gone in for the kill, with the evidence apparently on hand to clinch the case, it met with disaster. The house in which they spent the night before the strike next morning burned down, trapping all its sleeping residents. No member of the Weisner team survived. But part of their evidence did.

The ill-fated expedition of investigators under Captain Weisner had succeeded in piecing together the mystery. What they found, dooming them as it did, was the true story of a missing trove that was replacing the Rheingold in folklore.

According to their findings, accepted as plausible if not actually as true by the U.S. Army, the gold had already been spirited away, if that is the phrase, in June 1945, as soon as the search team had found it near Mittenwald, a picturesque Alpine village that, until then, was famed solely for the skill of its violin makers. The theft was reminiscent of the coup immortalized in *Brass Target*, a British motion picture of a historic heist masterminded by a former commando officer.

The part played by Jack Hawkins was in the real-life drama played by Robert MacKenzie of the Third Army, the American mayor of Garmisch-Partenkirchen, a famed mountain resort near Mittenwald. But the real virtuoso of the coup was another captain, one Martin Borg, who was the local military governor. Their search team had come upon the hoard in a cave on the Klausenkopf—actually tipped off by the civilians who would later tell about the hoard to the Americans, after they had been gypped out of their share by MacKenzie and Borg. They loaded on the trucks as many of the bags as they could take, and turned around in triumph to deliver their find to their headquarters at Garmisch-Partenkirchen. But on the way, Captain Borg was suddenly struck by a better idea. He ordered the truck to stop, made the driver get out, and shot him in cold blood at the roadside. Then he jumped into the cab of the lead truck, seized the wheel, and, accompanied by MacKenzie and the other members of the search team, raced the few miles to the Austrian border, where he crashed through the barrier at the checkpoint—and sped away.

Their trail was picked up in a day or two in Switzerland and elsewhere, and Robert MacKenzie, using the alias "Ben F. Harpman," was eventually found by the FBI in the United States. But after a while the chase slackened and the trail petered out. The story was that Martin Borg, using the alias of "Neal" or "Neil," holed up in a place called Vitznau in Switzerland, and hid there until March 1946, when he escaped to South America with a couple of million dollars of the loot. When last seen or heard of, he was said to have been enjoying the fruits of his coup unmolested on a secluded ranch in Argentina.

The "civilians" who lost out to MacKenzie and Borg hoped to recoup some of their share by tipping off Lieutenant Murphy to part of the loot (and, indeed, part of the story), but they vanished by the time the CID started looking for them on Patton's orders. Actually, the case remains open on the books, and the mystery of the "Allgeier gold" lingers on. And General Patton continues to be part of the legend, because of attempts at connecting him with the mystery, to give it glamour in lieu of its sordid dénouement.

The source regarded as "the authority" on the Mittenwald/Einsiedel gold is W. Stanley Moss, a British journalist and author of a book called *Gold's Where You Hide It*, where, in fact, the Guinness people found the yarn for the item in their *Book of World Records*. Moss's book was so unconvincing on the face of it that no American publisher ever bought it. Having vanished down the drain, it was resurrected years later by Frederick Nolan, a British writer who borrowed Moss's story for his novel *The Algonquin Project*.

According to Nolan's thinly disguised plot, "the Einsiedel treasure was partially plundered by a combination of U.S. Military Government personnel and German civilians."

The Patton connection was tenuous. "If the Mittenwald

gold was stolen by U.S. officers in association with German civilians," Nolan wrote, "it is conceivable that Patton would have known them; and once an investigation started, it was possibly only a matter of time before he made the connection in his own mind." By hovering over the secret, it seemed, Patton signed his own death warrant. Others marked him for death as the man who blocked their way to the treasure. One way or another, Patton was doomed by the Mittenwald gold, whether he himself misappropriated it or had stumbled upon others who had embezzled it.

Nolan was described as very articulate and convincing. "Listening to him," a young lady who had researched the incident for Metro-Goldwyn-Mayer wrote, "one is able to make the link between the gold and the possible assassination of Patton."

It was, however, not the *missing* link. The evidence is now conclusive that the gold had no connection with General Patton's end and that Patton had nothing to do with its disappearance. "No part of the cache," Colonel Milliken told me, years after the event, "which Major Allgeier's MPs recovered fell into any unauthorized hands. Whatever there was of it in our custody was inventoried by me and my officers, and was then sent under heavy guard to the Reichsbank in Frankfurt. It was deposited there in the vault, with the rest of the gold recovered by the Third Army."

Those close to Patton during these days banish the thought that he might have had anything to do with the disappearance of the gold—some do it angrily, others with a tolerant smile, but all do it. General Gay had closed the book on the whole case. He remembers it only from what he had recorded in his diary (on which much of this present account is based). General Paul D. Harkins, who stood in for Patton in the final disposition of the gold, considers the insinuations preposterous. And Major Deane, the press officer who handled the lid on the story, regards them as ridiculous.

10.

★ ★ ★ ★

The Specter of Streicher

"The more I see of people [the more] I regret that I survived the war."

—*In a letter on July 27, 1945*

GENERAL PATTON tried to settle down to some sort of peaceful coexistence with the "wrong enemy" he had just defeated. But he found it difficult to adjust. There was something in the air, like a miasma, that was imperceptibly but unmistakably exercising its power over him.

Upper Bavaria's scenic splendor—its mist in the morning, its fog at night, both filled with spirits, quaint and mischievous—always had a strange effect on the beholder. It inspired verses of recondite chauvinism and Hitler's Wotan-like views. This mystical land produced demented poets and moody painters, mad kings and statesmen who were among the most reactionary in German politics.

It was not, it seemed, what was manifest to the eye, but what was beneath the surface, that left its lasting impression—a depressing haze that enshrouded the mind and darkened one's mood. It bewitched all who settled even temporarily in this region of true Wagnerian bathos.

General Patton, apparently, was neither immune to this spell nor capable of liberating himself from it.

LIFE IN St. Querin was pleasant but dull. The Amann villa was a sumptuous place, and it was undamaged, exactly as Amann had left it. Priceless Persian rugs covered the shiny parquet floors made of imported Brazilian wood.

Enormous sets of Rosenthal and Hutschenreuther china were stored in the pantries. Silk sheets were on the beds.

Yet its new tenant, who could have lived in viceregal pomp, suddenly opted for the simple life. Though this gregarious man wilted quickly without company, he nevertheless decided to withdraw into his shell. He lived with General Gay in the big house; the household staff—all new except for Sergeant Meeks, was put up in the wing. His aide-de-camp was also new—Major Van S. Merle Smith, a relative of his stepgrandfather's, for whose sake Patton's father had changed his middle name from William to Smith.

A tall, handsome young officer with much of Patton's snap and polish, Major Smith had replaced Colonel Charles Codman, who had gone home on a holiday and was then prevented from coming back by illness in his family. Patton's relations with Codman had been unorthodox in the Army. The debonair, publicity-wise Bostonian wine merchant was more of a kind of maitre d' than the usual ADC on his staff. Patton had sent for young Smith because, for one thing, the major's mother had asked him to rescue her boy from a humdrum post in Italy. For another thing, and surely more important, Patton was looking for an aide he could trust implicitly. And last but not least, he wanted someone who could play a mean game of badminton with him. "He is a gentleman," was the only reference to Merle Smith in his letters home.

During happier days, Major Smith would have made the perfect ADC, what with his elegance and savvy, and his efficient ways in a job that mixed secretarial and social chores. Now the most important contribution he could make was to help the general in whiling away the monotony of his empty hours.

The Amann villa did provide the facilities for relaxation within its own walls—the bowling alley, the swimming pool, the tennis court, and a new squash court that Patton had added. "I think I'd go mad without this squash," he wrote home, and also: "Hap Gay and myself go riding here every day on two captured animals, whose only virtue is that they do not run on gasoline." Actually, they were a couple of magnificent French horses that the Third Army had "liberated." The deluxe stables were filling up with other fine horses handpicked for Patton.

After dark, the routine was deadening. Patton spent most of his evenings reading—both the current nonfiction that Beatrice was picking for him, and rereading the volumes of military history that he had carried with him in a portable library throughout the war. He was the only general in the U.S. Army who had such an excess baggage in his gear, even as Admiral Spruance was the only admiral in the U.S. Navy who had a collection of classical records in every one of his assignments afloat. Patton's vices were few and moderate—a couple of cocktails a day, at the most, and, on and off, his cigars. He had a couple of very dry Martinis before dinner or a Manhattan—he liked them both. He was also reconciled to the dry sherry that the British preferred and Paul Harkins had come to like. But otherwise he was almost abstemious.

Cigars had been Patton's best friend since his plebe days, when he had smoked them surreptitiously at the Point. He was rarely seen without them after that. Frugal in his personal habits, he smoked Elroi Tens, a moderately priced cigar that sold for ten cents each in 1945, and it was the long version he liked. He rarely had to buy them, for he had the habit of "borrowing" or stealing cigars, and was the recipient of generous gifts of some of the best of them from friends and admirers. They kept coming, the Dunhills and the Upmans from England, the Montecristos from the United States—a huge specimen which Patton did not just smoke with obvious relish, but brandished with the ostentation he otherwise reserved only for his two pistols.

He was not supposed to smoke at all. He had a spot on his lips from time to time, and Dr. Odom would caution him that he might develop cancer there if he did not stop smoking. So he stopped, but mostly to fool his doctors. At this time in St. Querin the sore had flared up. Patton packed up the cigars he had in his drawer, marched across the corridor in the Kaserne to Harkins's office, dropped the box on his desk and shouted: "Goddamnit, Paul, I'm stopping smo-*goddamn*-king for good. You keep these ci-*fuckin'*-gars." He must have been truly upset, because he swore

between the syllables of words only when he was really
angry.

Harkins put the box into his drawer and saw that Patton
had eleven Upmans left in it. Then as the days passed and
Patton seemed to be sticking to his vow, Harkins happened
to look into the box and found that seven of the cigars were
gone. Patton would sneak over from time to time and steal
one of his own cigars when he had the urge.

FOR ALL the activities embroiling him, for all the
beauty surrounding him, for all the challenges confronting
him, General Patton was lonely and bored. To his neighbors
in St. Querin and to the people of the village he was merely
a fast-moving apparition, an earsplitting sound shattering
the silence of this solemn countryside twice a day with the
cry of a hundred tipple flutes—the strident blast of the
foghorns on his limousine.

There was no "fraternization," of course, with any of the
Germans, and none with the handful of *Prominente* among
the liberated foreigners, like Leopold III, King of the Bel-
gians. One distinguished transient in town was the venerable
Gerd von Rundstedt, decrepit dean of Hitler's field marshals.
Rundstedt had got back into harness from retirement in the
fall of 1944 to lead the Nazis' last offensive in the Ardennes—and was rather expeditiously retired again.

Assuming that he would be welcomed by soldiers as an
old soldier, Rundstedt had made himself comfortable in Bad
Toelz, with a court of his own, waiting for the Americans
to pay him homage. Patton ignored him. Then word was
received from SHAEF that the field marshal was to be taken
into custody like any prisoner-of-war and removed to the
VIP cage in Luxembourg. That deprived Toelz of the only
dignitary who, under different circumstances, might have
interested Proconsul Patton.

The only friend he made in Bad Toelz was his stable
boy, who took excellent care of his horses. No ordinary
groom, he was Baron von Wangenheim, Germany's premier
horseman, captain of the equestrian team that won the gold
medal at the 1936 Olympic Games. A colonel in the SS
cavalry, he had been paroled to serve as Patton's stable

sergeant. Colonel von Wagenheim was also an unreformed Nazi who was of the opinion as well that even though the Americans had fought the wrong enemy, it was not too late to make up for the mistake.

This was the official Nazi line, conceived by General Alfred Jodl the morning after he had signed the instrument of unconditional surrender. It did not take long for the idea to take root. These Nazis, still infatuated with the Führer rather than his philosophy, based their expectation of a comeback on "the inevitable split" between the Americans and the Russians. And from the outset, by some osmosis, they spotted Patton as a potential ally.

Colonel von Wangenheim was not in St. Querin by accident. His mission as Patton's groom had been slyly arranged by the Sicherheitsdienst, the security service of the Nazi party, partly to spy on the proconsul, and partly to stimulate his anti-Russian slant. Patton rated his English-speaking, debonair stable sergeant "a very good man." And the baron was, indeed, a delightful companion on long rides when General Gay was prevented from accompanying him. In spite of the vast differences in their ranks and status, the general and the groom were becoming friends. "I have never had any animus," Patton said, "against the professional soldiers who fought against me. That was what they were hired to do."

HE HAD occasional visitors in his office at the Kaserne or in the privacy of his residence at St. Querin, like-minded people handpicked to cater to his mood and partake in his pungent views. Patton was not oblivious to the danger those opinions held for him, and of the possibility of some surveillance "by the ubiquitous Communists and Jews." Quite early in the game he assumed that his quarters might be bugged and his telephone tapped, and saw to it that his office was regularly swept. Whenever he noticed that one or another of his visitors behaved nervously and cautiously, looking around or over his shoulder, as if trying to detect some hidden listening devices, Patton laughed and reassured him: "Don't worry, there is no Dictaphone here. You can speak freely with me."

Patton had little physical contact with people in the world outside, and was having few opportunities to come face to face with the realities of that world. Patton was, therefore, dependent on whatever information he could procure even second or third hand.

At this time, either confronting at last the abject truth or trying to mask it still with a strained joke, Patton conceded to himself in so many words that he did not really know what the score was, who was who, and what was going on in his protectorate. What he did record as his understanding of the situation showed how profound his ignorance was. "There is," he wrote, "a very apparent Semitic influence in the press. They are trying to do two things: First, implement Communism, and second, see that all businessmen of German ancestry and non-Jewish antecedents are thrown out of their jobs. . . .

"Another point which the press harped on was the fact that we were doing too much for the Germans to the detriment of the DPs, most of whom are Jews. I could not give the answer to that one because the answer is that in my opinion and that of most non-political officers, it is vitally necessary for us to build Germany up now as a buffer state against Russia."

It was obvious, under the circumstances, that he needed a very special type of person who agreed with him. Bishop Govlina, chaplain general of the Polish army, was one of them, and Patton gave him high marks both for his intelligence and his prejudices. An old acquaintance, G. A. Kemper, was another—a German-American who had repatriated from Hawaii in 1936 and managed Woolworth in Germany under the Nazis. And Father Bernard Hubbard, the famous arctic explorer also known as the "Glacier Priest," who interrupted a lecture tour in postwar Europe to drop in and pay his respects.

These visitors catered to his rationalizations and caressed his prejudices—the bishop calling eloquently for a holy war against the Russians and the Woolworth executive warning that Germany must not be delivered into the hands of Communists and Jews. Father Hubbard, fresh from honors

awarded him in New York by the Anti-Defamation League
of the B'nai B'rith, joined Patton in his favorite new pastime
of blasting the Russians and abusing the Jews.

THERE WAS something else. The Patton who had
come back from America was not the man who left Germany
in early June. The month he had spent in the United States
became a catalyst. As the cheering faded and the flags were
rolled up again, as his fate was catching up with him, the
uncertainty of his future was unnerving him. What was still
there to look forward to? And who was to blame for this
dismal turn?

In America, the question was answered eagerly in the
homes of his wife's relatives. One of his in-laws, Charles
F. Ayer, Beatrice's half-brother, was an arch-conservative
of the old school, saddled with more than the Beacon Street
regulars' usual quota of ingrained prejudice. His anti-Semitism in particular, honed and deepened by Nazi propaganda,
was inaccessible to feelings of Christian charity. Though
Patton was much closer to Frederick Junior, Beatrice's
brother, he suffered her half-brother gladly. The older man
had insinuated himself into his good graces with fulsome
flattery, never missing an opportunity to tell him how great
a historic figure he was.

During the two weeks he had spent with the family (his
anti-Semitism abetted also by Beatrice's half-sister, and her
husband, William Wood) Patton confided to Charles his
misgivings about the Jews, and Charles responded with his
own bigotry. It was, in fact, Charles Ayer who planted in
his mind the idea that he should have fought and licked the
Russians. From there it was but a step to the Jews. Were
not the Jews and the Communists the same? Was not the
duty of every Communist to give aid and comfort to the
Soviet Union? Ergo, was it not the "execrable Jew" whose
insidious influence and propaganda dragged America into
the war against the Germans?

In Patton's mind, the Jew was no longer just a scapegoat.
Now he made the Jews responsible for all the troubles of
the world and, more significantly, for the downturn in his

own fortunes. As his hatred and contempt for them were
growing, so mounted his love and admiration for the Germans.

What produced in him this dramatic shift? The provo-
cations were profound and violent— the end of the war,
the feeling that he was no longer needed and, even worse,
no longer wanted, the enormous burden of responsibility
in his complex proconsular job. They were enough to make
even a more stable person restive, impair his judgment, and
lower his ability to adjust to his environment. Not usually
willing to abide by the opinions or to acquiesce in the conclusions of others, he had become wide open to such influences. He was filled with bitter, violent, and completely
irrational anti-Jewish sentiments—provoked in equal measure by his aesthetic indignation at the sight of that "stinking
bunch" of Jews in the DP camps and by his new political
and social views. He now hated the Jews—all Jews—personified by those his armies had saved from certain death.

HE HIMSELF had seen few of the surviving Jews at
close quarters. But those he was hearing about—mostly in
unflattering terms from irate G-5 officers—were "less than
exquisite." They were in fact the survivors of the extermination camps, the products of the Nazi hell—still too
dazed by their experience to summon the will to recover.
If anybody still said, he remarked, that the Displaced
Jew was a human being, he did not know what he was
talking about. "These Jews," he wrote, using the vocabulary
of the defunct *Der Stürmer,* the Nazi newspaper in which
Julius Streicher published his anti-Semitic diatribes, "are
lower than animals." Then projecting them onto a screen of
the future, Patton committed to writing one of the most
savage thoughts this period of his bigotry produced. "Should
the German people ever rise from the state of utter degradation to which they have now been reduced," he wrote,
"there will be the greatest pogrom of the Jews in the history
of the world."

Now in his domain in Germany and Bohemia, he sought
to spend whatever time he was giving over to socializing
with the fossils of Austrian aristocracy, like the Schwar-

zenbergs and the Hohenlohes. It did not take them long to return to their empty lives of pleasure and indolence. Patton joined them eagerly in their pastimes.

But it was sheer escapism. The impression he had brought back from America—the absurd picture of a nation decadent and defenseless—was gnawing at his innards. He did not dare to parade his suspicions for fear, as he put it, that his "frank views might be misunderstood." But to his wife he wrote: "I can't see how Americans can sink so low. It's semitic, and I'm sure of it."

11.

★ ★ ★ ★

The Month of the Stag

ON JUNE 13, while Patton had been in the States, a TWX was received from Twelfth Army, so critical in its long-range implications that it warrants reproduction in full.

"INQUIRY INDICATES CONCLUSIVELY," it read, "THAT THIRD ARMY IS DISREGARDING THE INSTRUCTIONS ISSUED BY THIS HEADQUARTERS REFERENCE CATEGORY DISCHARGE AND DOCUMENTATION FOR DISBANDMENT OF GERMAN DISARMED FORCES. YOU WILL INSTITUTE IMMEDIATELY ADEQUATE MEASURES TO CARRY OUT THE PRESCRIBED INSTRUCTIONS FOR DISBANDMENT AND FURTHER TO BRING UP TO DATE THE DOCUMENTATION OF THOSE ALREADY DISCHARGED WITHOUT DELAY. ADEQUATE INSTRUCTIONS ON THESE MATTERS HAVE BEEN ISSUED YOUR HEADQUARTERS."

The message was marked, "Personal, General Craig," in his capacity as the acting Army commander. But Craig did not know what it meant or portended. When he asked General Gay for an explanation, the chief of staff sought to dismiss the matter. "This TWX is highly unjust," he told General Craig. Then, stressing form rather than substance—by emphasizing the "documentation" part of the message instead of its accent on "disbandment"—he said indignantly: "We did ask Twelfth Army Group some time ago to rescind the order concerning all the paperwork on these P/Ws, inasmuch," he added cryptically, "as it does not apply to most of the cases."

That, however, was not the issue bothering Army Group. What troubled General Bradley was that the Third Army appeared to be delaying the release of *certain* German prisoners of war, taking refuge behind the subterfuge of heavy paperwork. The controversy had reached Bradley when the Russians, who had begun to suspect Patton's pro-German sentiments, flooded his district with spies to find out what he was up to. They protested what appeared to be Patton's deliberate and selective husbanding of German units. They went so far as to suggest that Patton might be trying to put together a private army for some weird adventure of his own.

The Russians charged that elements of elite divisions of the Waffen-SS that had surrendered in Czechoslovakia in May had neither been accounted for in the roster of the Nazi troops the Third Army had captured nor had been dispersed—nor had been disarmed! At first the complaint struck General Bradley as so outrageous that he dismissed it as not deserving serious consideration. But when the Russians followed up their charges with pinpointed data they had procured through their spies, and mentioned Garmisch-Partenkirchen and Pullach, for instance, as two of the cages where Patton was supposedly "hoarding his SS-men," Bradley gave orders to look into the matter.

Several times before, General Bradley had demanded that the disbandment of *all* German units be expedited, and that the Third Army should be "most liberal in their interpretation of the categories of prisoners" eligible for immediate discharge. Patton kept mum, and Gay hoped to keep the lid on during Patton's absence. But when the message arrived, marked clearly for the acting Army commander, General Craig could not ignore it. He accompanied General Gay to Army Group headquarters, supposedly to clarify things. But he wound up helping Gay to minimize the problem and obfuscate the issue.

General Bradley had insisted that whatever German troops the Third Army was still holding back be released. Back on June 17, then, even as Patton was in Washington discussing his future in the war, SHAEF also joined the controversy. In response to increasingly urgent Russian protestations, a special delegation of four senior G-3 officers led by Colonel Anton De Rohan arrived in Bad Toelz to investigate not only the case of the German P/Ws, but a whole set of similar problems. SHAEF was by now seriously concerned that the Third Army was either reluctant to face up to or incapable of coping with its responsibilities as the American Army of Occupation in Germany. To find out, a secret investigation was sent to the cage in Pullach, and still another to Garmisch-Partenkirchen.

Nothing developed for the rest of Patton's leave of absence—and then the whole issue was put on the back burner. Now that he was back, and taking the bull brazenly by the horns, he called Bradley first and Eisenhower next, protesting indignantly about the "harassment." And that, he said, in the face of what he called the best goddamn record any army had in liquidating a war.

Instead of putting an end to their concern, Patton's righteous indignation merely whetted their suspicion. A task force of officers—consisting of one colonel, two lieutenant colonels, and three majors—was assembled sub rosa at SHAEF to keep the situation under surveillance. Its members were told to convey their findings directly and secretly to Major General Walter Bedell Smith, Ike's own chief of staff.

Behind Patton's sudden abhorrence of the Jews was a much more complicated emotion, for some anti-Semitism was endemic in his world. But the infatuation of a victorious general with the enemy he had just defeated was rare. To be sure, there is a hoary tradition in professional chivalry to honor the foe, even to exaggerate his qualities once he has been defeated. Both Napoleon and Wellington had been guilty of such modesty. But neither had shown such a high degree of sudden admiration for the vanquished enemy as Patton now evinced at the expense of the Jews.

"Actually," said Patton, "the Germans are the only decent people left in Europe. It's a choice between them and the Russians. I prefer the Germans."

The German was no longer the Hun in his eyes. Not even the Kraut. That nickname had become taboo in Bad Toelz. Patton had come to regard the German as his ally in a joint crusade against the Bolsheviks.

In the vast new "army" he was assembling in his mind, any German was welcome. The Nazis? Oh, they were just members of a political party, "like the Democrats or the Republicans in the States." And the SS? More of the same: "SS means no more in Germany than being a Democrat in America." He made these statements on May 8, 1945, at a press conference on V-E Day, according to the typescript. If they were not printed until nearly five months later, it was because Patton, though careless in blurting out these innermost thoughts, was still capable of controlling his public relations. "That's not to be quoted," he said quickly as an afterthought. And the censor had strict instructions not to pass them.

The incongruity reflected strange and rebellious traits hidden in this man. In May, his statements were foolish notions and indiscretions, but still nothing but words. After his return to Bad Toelz from the United States, they had become deeds. On July 28, for example, he toured his part of Czechoslovakia in triumph, to the vociferous acclaim of the grateful populace. At Susice, the town near Pilsen liberated by the troops of Brigadier General Milton B. Halsey's 97th Division on May 5, the people greeted him with gifts, and Patton kissed a little girl with an enthusiasm that seemed to symbolize his collective embrace of the whole community. At the conclusion of his trip, he was given Czechoslovakia's highest decoration, the Order of the White Lion and War Cross. Yet only a few days later he provoked the wrath of the Czechs by ordering the removal of some 1,500 Polish Fascists the Nazis had foisted upon them, to protect the Poles from the retribution the Prague government was preparing to mete out.

By late August, Patton was in deep trouble. His employment of a German whose record clearly showed that he had been a member of the SS was publicly criticized. And he was censured for a statement questioning the wisdom of getting rid of a group of Bavarian bankers and industrialists with the stain of Nazism in their past. Many of them had been employers of slave laborers, whose death camp Patton had described in such moving words only five months before.

His thoughts and actions were now colored by his apprehension about the Soviet menace. He equated everything in Germany with the prospect of a war with the Russians. He was determined not to become a party to the destruction of "a good race," only to "replace" it with "Mongolian savages." On V-E Day he had bet Field Marshal Montgomery one thousand pounds that before long the Western Allies of World War II would be fighting the Soviet hordes.

"It may well be," he said, "that V-E Day is misnamed and simply marked the beginning of a relatively short armistice." Monty, who thought otherwise, gave him a ten-year limit on his bet. Now it was but a few months after victory in Europe, but Patton already had his expectancy up. "I fear," he wrote, "that his Scotch soul is worrying. I hope it is."

The Germans were quick to sense that they had a friend in General George S. Patton. They greeted him in his rare public appearances with cheers and threw flowers from the windows, shouting, "He is our savior. He has saved us from the Russian mob."

AFTER a promising start, complaints multiplied that the denazification program was bogging down in Patton Country, that deindustrialization was a farce, and demilitarization a shambles. Unbeknown to Patton, and behind the back of Colonel Keegan, the military governor, a probe was conducted of charges that the Schaeffer government, which Keegan had put together as a favor to Cardinal von Faulhaber, was not working out. G-5 investigators from Wiesbaden found that the Minister President had rigged the administration by naming militarists, ultranationalists, and former Nazi intimates to all the high offices. It also developed that Schaeffer himself was involved in a ridiculous intrigue to return the Wittelbachs, the old ruling house of Bavaria, to the throne from which the Weimar Republic had ousted them in 1918.

The regime of Dr. Schaeffer, the investigators concluded, "was only a little better than the Nazis it replaced." His Minister of Economics was a war profiteer who had enriched himself under the Nazis, thanks to his close friendship with the Gauleiter of Bavaria. The acting head of the Interior Ministry turned out to have been chief of the VDA (Verein des Deutschtums im Ausland), a notorious pan-German propaganda front which the Nazis turned into a global web of spies. His second in command, a Nazi Party member since 1927, had been a *Brigadeführer* (major general) in the Nation Socialist Motor Corps and the personal adjutant of the Gauleiter until 1942. The Minister of Education may not have been a Nazi himself, but now he sabotaged as best he could the denazification of the Bavarian educational system.

The Third Reich's railroad tsar, Julius Dorpmueller, who had seen to it that the trains ran on time to Auschwitz, Treblinka, Mauthausen, Bergen-Belsen, and the other extermination camps, was freed to serve Colonel Keegan as a consultant on transportation, although he was wanted as a war criminal by Poland, Czechoslovakia, and Belgium. Professor Ernst Rudin, the scholar, so called, who devised the "scientific" foundation of the Nazis' intricate system of mass murder, was found teaching race hygiene in Munich.

THE BOMBSHELL hit on August 21. The man whose advice had been instrumental in securing the jobs for these incumbents, by screening them for Keegan, was exposed by the American investigators as an ex-convict. When Keegan had first arrived in Munich in May, a stranger among strangers, Erich Schulze appeared at his side from nowhere to guide him through this typically Bavarian labyrinth. Keegan liked him instantly, and soon trusted him. After he read the forty reports Schulze had written for him on political, financial, and other matters, including the personalities under scrutiny for responsible jobs in the Schaeffer administration, Keegan exclaimed: "This is the first German I've encountered who makes sense. He's my man."

But Schulze fooled Keegan. He was a professional con man with a long criminal record for fraud, forgery, and other white-collar crimes extending back to 1907. When he was arrested at his comfortable home stocked with U.S. Army packages of coffee, cigarettes, sugar, canned milk, and tobacco—a private PX in the black market—fifty-nine-year-old Erich Schulze produced credentials attesting that he was employed as a "confidential adviser" to the military government. They were signed by Colonel Keegan and by Lieutenant Colonel Sam R. Long, chief legal officer of the military government in Bavaria.

Although Schulze was a mere pebble, he started the avalanche. Suddenly the house of cards Keegan had erected began to fall apart. He panicked. His cushy place in Munich became a hot seat. Where he hoped that his governorship in Bavaria would lead to greater things at home, he now found that his inept stewardship might jeopardize his political future in New York. When Patton abolished the governorship on September 4 Keegan flew to New York without bidding farewell to his many friends in Bavaria. Back home, he resumed his seat on the City Council, and was in that chamber on October 1.

In New York, Keegan wrote to Newbold Morris, president of the City Council, that he had *resigned* the job in Munich: "How happy I will be to resume my seat at a time when so many grave problems are arising in the affairs of the city and in preparation of the city's part in readjusting the great number of women and men who so nobly represented our city in the great conflict just terminated."

But in Munich, everybody knew that Charley had been fired. General Adcock put it more bluntly: "I kicked him out on his bloody ass. He was the worst mistake we've made in this goddamn job." The political confusion that held Bavaria in its grip was all Keegan's doing. Now Keegan was gone. But his sacking was not doing anybody any good. He was leaving behind a legacy of problems for General Patton to solve, and Patton was only compounding them.

KEEGAN'S DEPARTURE only focused further attention on General Patton as the man actually responsible for the failure of the denazification and demilitarization programs.

Up to this time, General Patton was not yet the chief target. The image of the hero Patton still outshone the new picture of the villain Patton. Even as leftist a newspaper as New York's *PM* paid a straightforward tribute. "General Patton," it said on the eve of the upheaval, "has probably done as much to win this war in the field as any American;

certainly as much as any army commanding officer." Even in the wake of the Keegan imbroglio, the criticism that had begun to concentrate on him was still gentle. "The business of the present and of the future," *PM* now reported in a dispatch from Munich, "is not to kill men on the battlefield, but to see that men never again be so killed. This is not the kind of job General Patton is prepared to tackle." The solution was then proposed in the most considerate terms: "He ought, for the good of his country and for his own, to be brought home, before his reputation as a warrior is tarnished by an ignominious failure as a man of peace."

The situation had become so bad that Ike had to caution Patton several times, lastly on August 27, during a special conference called to discuss the control of Germany. "I demand," Ike told him, "that you get off your bloody ass and carry out the denazification program as you're told instead of molly-coddling the goddamn Nazis." The following day, back in his office in the Flint Kaserne, Patton asked Frank Mason, a former newspaper executive in Germany at the behest of Herbert Hoover, "What do you think of the progress we are making denazifying Germany? We are doing pretty well, aren't we?"

"General," the man replied, "I think denazification is a lot of bullshit."

"There is no Dictaphone here," Patton said with a grin. "So do I."

ACTUALLY, Patton was indifferent to the problem. "I had never heard," he wrote, just when the Keegan affair was bringing the issue into sharp relief, "that we fought [the war] to de-nazify Germany—live and learn." If he paid attention to these matters, or was even aware of them, he gave little evidence of it, except for an occasional snide or flippant remark about the folly of denazification. They showed his disdain for the whole system and, more than that, his scorn for its purpose and ignorance of its techniques.

At the very moment when Charley Keegan was getting the boot, Patton was standing in for Ike at a victory parade with Marshal Zhukov and others in Berlin. When in St.

Querin, he was going on long outings on horseback with
General Hap Gay, or, when his chief of staff was prevented
from accompanying him, with Baron von Wangenheim. His
admiration of the German equestrian star was in full bloom.

He traveled up and down to visit the friends he had made
during the war, like General Alphonse-Pierre Juin in Paris.
To Juin he attributed sentiments surprisingly similar to his
own about the Germans and the Russians, but startling for
a loyal Frenchman whose country had just been freed from
the Nazi yoke. He also called on old friends, like the aged
General Houdemon. He had met him in 1912, when de-
touring from the Olympic Games in Stockholm to take épée
lessons from the adjutant at the famed cavalry school at
Saumur. Patton motored to Salzburg to be entertained by
General Mark Clark (whom he detested); to Bad Homburg
to visit Lieutenant General Geoffrey Keyes (of whom he
was very fond); and to St. Martin to watch another exhibition
of the famous Lippizaners.

Above all, he busied himself inspecting his soldiers in
the process of redeployment, regrouping, and repatriation—
bidding the departing units emotional farewell with a set
speech he had memorized. It was an excellent speech, even
if it seemed to be different when one read it and one heard
it. When read, his remarks were reasonable and peaceful.
"Let me say," he had written, "that it is my profound hope
that we shall never again be engaged in war." But it had
all the old brimstone stuff, too, especially when one listened
to it. "Also," he said, raising his squeaky voice to its highest
pitch, "let me remind you of the words of George Washington: 'In time of peace, prepare for war.' That advice still
holds." He left it at that. "I am in no way trying to pro-
pagandize you," he told the GIs, and probably he meant it,
too.

In between, Patton was working on a book. It was published posthumously as a kind of military testament. It consisted of diary extracts and bits and pieces of the writings
he had done over many years, summing up his experience
in war. And looking to the future, he was plotting "the war"
with the Russians in the sandbox of his imagination. "In my
opinion," he wrote Colonel Hugh G. McGee in New York

on August 23, "and strictly for your private ear, we never had a better chance of producing another war than we have in Europe now."

But if Patton's last September in Germany had been given a name to remember it by, in the manner of the Chinese tradition of naming the years, it should have been called the Month of the Stag. For under the clouds of the gathering storm, and ignoring the warning of distant thunder, Patton was spending much less time at his desk governing Germany than in the field hunting ducks in the Sudetenland, Hungarian partridges in Baden, wild geese in Bavaria, and fallow deer in the Bohemian Forest.

12.

★ ★ ★ ★

The Crisis at Camp Number 8

ON SEPTEMBER 5, 1945, General Patton stopped en route to another shoot to inspect the huge prisoners' cage in Garmisch-Partenkirchen. It was Camp Number 8, notorious because it held the "cream" of the interned Germans—the SS from Buchenwald and Dachau, for instance, and the most unrepentant of Nazi bigwigs—those the "Eclipse" plan had singled out for "automatic arrest" and as "security threats," and blacklisted as "war criminals."

The visit to the camp had been planned merely as a whistle stop. He had squeezed it in between a parade of the 16th Armored Division in Pilsen and a deer hunt in the huge wild-game preserve of the Princes zu Schwarzenberg in the Sudetenland.*

Patton's coming had been confided to the Germans in the camp by Major Emmett W. McCrary through Hauptmann Carl Vogel. "On the impression you fellows will make

---

*Patton was fond of Karl Philipp Prince zu Schwarzenberg, the Austrian field marshal (1771–1820), because he was the only general who succeeded in defeating Napoleon before Waterloo. The Schwarzenbergs were arch-reactionaries at the imperial court of Vienna, instrumental in suppressing the liberal reforms of 1848 in Austria and Hungary. At the time of Patton's visit at their château in Bohemia, Adolph zu Schwarzenberg was working on a biography of his famous ancestor, a project that intrigued Patton more than the deer that were abundant in the Schwarzenbergs' wild-game preserve.

on the visiting general," McCrary told Vogel, "will depend the future of this camp." Vogel carried the news to the battalion chiefs, and from them it spread quickly, until every one of the inmates knew about it. Seized by excitement and great expectations, they fell to scrubbing and sweeping and polishing. By the morning of the eighth, the camp was all *blitz und blank,* spic-and-span, exactly as Patton liked it.

Carl Vogel was the *Deutscher Lagerkommandant*—the *German* camp commander—so called to distinguish him from his opposite number, the *American* camp commander, not equals by any means, but an arrangement under the rules that somehow left the impression of an esprit de corps among colleagues in Vogel's mind. Vogel had been a successful publisher in Kufstein, Austria, a member of the SS since 1933 and an officer in the elite Mountain Chasseurs since the outbreak of the war in 1939.

Named the German camp commander, an administrative job that carried only limited authority, because he was fluent in English and knew the camp from the time it was the barracks of the mountain troops of General Eduard Dietl, the "hero of Narvik," Vogel proved to be competent, efficient, and pliable. But he was also unrepentant, unregenerate, and a hypocrite. He was a paragon of cooperation with Major McCrary—to his face. Behind his back, he kept "the eternal light" of Nazism at least "flickering in the darkness," as he put it, and showed his "inward resistance" by deprecating "the enemy" and making a mockery of his regime.

In his own right, Major McCrary was sly, but he was no hypocrite. Still quite new as the camp commander, having inherited the job from Major S. D. Perrin of Winchester, Massachusetts, who had organized this camp, he was trying to strike a delicate balance between the mollycoddlers of Bad Toelz and the taskmasters of Frankfurt. And he proved to be an excellent tightrope walker. He was considerate of his charges and went as far as he possibly could to accommodate them in their predicament. But he was firm and authoritative, and never left these Nazis in any doubt as to who was in command of Camp 8.

Vogel discovered this at the very outset. Summoned to McCrary's office the morning after the major's arrival, he found the new commander—"a typical staff officer with a West Point veneer and American informality"—sitting behind his desk with cap on head, his legs crossed on the desktop, playing with a sleek horse whip, which he thrashed about from time to time to emphasize certain of his words. "Outwardly," Vogel wrote in his diary, "he was not different from the typical German staff officer—sporting-lean, controlled, with quick reflexes and admirable empathy. He spoke slowly and to the point, and knew what he was talking about."

At this session, McCrary questioned Vogel about his former rank, his years in the service, his assignments and decorations. Vogel on his part asked permission to be "brutally frank" when the occasion warranted, then inquired pugnaciously whether the major intended to observe the provisions of the Hague and Geneva conventions, which regulated the treatment of prisoners-of-war, and asked whether habeas corpus would apply to the inmates. "No," McCrary replied. Put in his place, Vogel now asked more meekly: "But what will apply?"

"Exclusively and only the commands of the United States Army," McCrary said. That cleared the air.

MCCRARY AND VOGEL were at home in this camp. Vogel had had his basic training and then had served here in 1939. And McCrary had captured it. He was in the 10th Armored Division under Major General Fay B. Prickett during the "Tigers'" triumphal end run, and participated in the taking of the barracks of General Dietl's mountaineers by the 21st Battalion, of which he was executive officer.

The "Tigers" had been on the road a long time, and their arrival at the foot of the Zugspitze, Germany's highest peak at 9,710 feet, signaled an end to their long journey. It was a far cry from stopping Field Marshal Gerd von Rundstedt just outside of Bastogne during the Battle of the Bulge to capturing him in Bad Toelz, where the tired old man had holed up only four months later. After Toelz, the "Tigers" spearheaded the drive into the highlands of Upper Bavaria, which was crowded with the sacred shrines of Nazidom. Landsberg, where Hitler was imprisoned in 1923 and paroled promptly so he could resume his meteoric career, was taken on April 28. Across the border in Austria, Braunau, the holy city of the Führer's birth, surrendered on May 1. And Berchtesgaden, the vast Nazi playground, fell on May 5.

The campaign that netted Garmisch-Partenkirchen was interesting, if only because it stamped its mark indelibly on the character of Camp 8. On April 30, the day of Hitler's suicide, Prickett's "Tigers" rolled over this land. The 21st Battalion took Partenkirchen first and then Garmisch, the famous winter resort where the 1936 Winter Olympics were held on the slopes of the Zugspitze.

Unhampered by the mountains, unhindered by any organized resistance, the division encountered only one obstacle—a major roadblock near Fernstein attempting to close the pass. At one moment the order came to halt and await the passage of the infantry, which arrived soon in the form of the 317th Regiment of the 80th Division, commanded by Major General Horace L. McBride. During these heady days the "Tigers" had slashed through big pockets of desperate people—fugitives rather than refugees. The area had been set aside by the Nazis as a "safe haven"—as their last resort. Many of them, assuming that they were among the most wanted on the American suspect lists, sought desperately to escape to the protection of these mountains.

These hard-core Nazis, both in and out of uniform, were on their way to the National Redoubt—that dream fortress of the propagandists—into which the diehard among them were supposed to retire to prolong resistance, perhaps indefinitely.

The redoubt turned out to be but a pipe dream, and the protection it was supposed to afford these Nazis a futile hope. Abandoned to their fate by their Führer, they sat tight and waited—the AAs, the STs, the BLs, and the WCs—all the heavies in the four major categories of guilt the

"Eclipse" plan had stipulated for the treatment of these people.* Reversing the tradition of Anglo-Saxon jurisprudence, they were assumed to be guilty until they could prove their innocence.

When Major McCrary's unit captured Garmisch-Partenkirchen and took over the old compound, it found the barracks in excellent condition and ready to be used as a *Lager* (camp) to house the tens of thousands of prisoners and internees. It was enormous, covering one and a half square miles in the valley of the Loisach River, a super-scenic spot beneath the Zugspitze, embraced on all sides by the incomparable beauty of the Worsenacher Land. Originally a cavalry school, then the proving ground of Dietl's mountaineers, the compound consisted of twenty buildings, including dormitories, stables, and houses for the various services, even a theater whose auditorium was now used as a courtroom for hearings in the denazification cases. It was now fenced in by the heaviest barbed wire the OSS could find, and was surrounded by thirty-foot-high watchtowers whose machine guns and searchlights were manned day and night by the toughest troopers of the 317th Regiment, whose 1st Battalion was on guard duty there. But the place still retained its natural attractiveness, what with the magnetism of the mountains and the animation of the air.

The compound was first given over to displaced persons, deserving of a haven after their ordeal. But they made such a mess of it that they had to be transferred to other camps where such damage did not matter. Also, they had to move to make place for a special brand of Nazis—"the scum and the brutes," as it turned out—who were thus given the best accommodations and the most attractive place of any of the several *Lagers*.

---

*The AAs; most of them members of the SS, were those subject to "automatic arrest"; the STs were the so-called "security threats," members of the Gestapo and the *Sicherheitsdienst*, or of the Abwehr; the BLs were major war criminals and close collaborators on a special "black list"; and the WCs were run-of-the-mill "war criminals," so to speak. Based on accurate intelligence, the Allies knew exactly who had been what, and whom to look for, among the millions of Nazis on the loose. The big roundup was a remarkable and efficient enterprise.

By September there were 4,811 of them in residence here, all dyed-in-the-wool Nazis. The camp also housed the biggest contingent of SS troops, kept together and intact. They were organized into "regiments" of 700 men each, under a former SS general and with their own officers. The camp held 2,300 of them, vigorous, unspent, proud young men, still smart and suave, erect and blustery, full of bounce—and of bluff. They pretended not to hear when their GI guards called them "Nazi dogs" and "fucking Ass-Ass," an ingenious epithet coined by interlocking "SS" and "AA."

WHEN MAJOR MCCRARY told Hauptmann Vogel that much in the future depended on the impression the Germans would make on the visiting general, he did not inform him who the visitor would be. But Vogel suspected, of course, that it was General Patton. It was exactly ten o'clock in the morning on September 8 when the strident cortege, with foghorns blowing, drove down Zugspitze Street, turned right and right again, and entered the camp through the main gate, where an honor guard of the 317th Infantry Regiment was lined up to welcome Patton. Greeting all by his silver-topped swagger stick to his helmet, Patton was received by General Prickett and General McBride, who had come over from their division headquarters, and by major McCrary and First Lieutenant Edmond F. Waterman, the Provost Marshal, at the head of their staffs. Also present was Captain Jack Carver, a young officer who headed the CIC detachment, a newcomer at Camp 8 who had the job of trying to do the impossible—denazify these diehard Nazis.*

The inspection was humdrum. Patton seemed bored and fidgety, and he was obviously in a hurry. He did commend McCrary on the exemplary cleanliness of the premises, and congratulated General McBride on the smart showing of the men from the 54th Battalion who were on guard duty in the barracks. But he rushed through the dormitories, paid no

---

*I agreed to use a pseudonym for this officer; it is the only instance of my using any but actual names in this book.

attention to the kitchens and the laundries, did not look even at the elaborate stables, reminders of the day when the place was a cavalry school. He was about to depart without reviewing another guard of honor—the inmates whom Hauptmann Vogel had lined up in front of the supply depot opposite the camp commander's post—when the unheard-of happened. Leaving his spot at the head of his contingent, Vogel marched up to Patton in a slightly modified version of the goose step, clicked his heels, saluted stiffly, and addressed the general in his excellent English, tinged with an Austrian accent:

"Captain Carl Vogel, formerly Twentieth Mountain-Chasseur Army, respectfully reporting, sir, and begging the general's permission to address the general."

Startled, but only for a moment, Patton smiled at the interloper, and said: "Go ahead, Captain. What can I do for you?"

"Sir," Vogel said loudly, for he was addressing not only Patton but all the assembled spectators, Americans and Germans alike, "I beg the general to select at random some of the internees at Camp 8 and question them about certain conditions that trouble them." He pointed at a long row of men and women, lining up for lunch with their canteens in hand outside the kitchen. "I am sure," Vogel continued, "that they will provide the general, sir, with firsthand information about the unusual circumstances of their arrests and the contrived reasons for their continued presence here."

"Go on, Captain," Patton said, showing interest for the first time during his so-called inspection.

"Sir," Vogel said, standing rigidly at attention and pulling a sheet of paper from a pocket, "I have here a list with a representative sample of the men and women who are interned in this camp without apparently having committed any offenses to warrant their detention." He began to read the case histories of the eight men he had on his list—of minor officials during the Nazi regime, of people in their fifties and sixties, and younger men with large families, of an officer of the Wehrmacht, and a simple peasant who had been the elected foreman of his village. "Common to all these cases is, sir," Vogel said almost triumphantly, "that none was a member of the National Socialist German Workers' Party and, therefore, could not have committed the alleged political crimes of which he is accused."

Encouraged by Vogel's bold initiative and the American general's patient interest, another German stepped forward to present his petition, but Patton waved him aside. "Thank you, Captain," Patton said. "What I found so disturbing here was that most of the prisoners look so downhearted. What's the matter with them? All they do is gaze at the beautiful mountains in the distance."

He shook hands with Vogel, even as he himself looked up to the Zugspitze, now bathed in the glorious noon sun, then turned back, moved closer to the column of the Germans as if ready to address them. But he apparently changed his mind, and merely said: *"Nur Kopf hoch!"* He said it in German. Hold your heads high! Chin up! Turning on his heels, obviously moved, Patton returned to the two generals and the little group of American officers who had observed this extraordinary spectacle in stony stillness. Addressing them so loudly that the Germans could easily hear him, he said:

"It's sheer madness to intern these people."

With that, he saluted, walked with fast steps to his car, and climbed in—the foghorns turned on, the engines roaring—and Patton was gone. After the reception committee had dispersed in embarrassed silence, Vogel walked to Major McCrary and asked: "Excuse me, sir, who was this general?"

McCrary hesitated. He himself disagreed with some of the harshest provisions of the rules and regulations, and, for instance, delayed the signing of his directives as a passive protest against what he considered undue hardships in the treatment of these internees. On the other hand, he was in full agreement with the policies of the detention system and especially with the need for denazification. He was deeply disturbed by Vogel's arbitrary intervention and even more by Patton's reaction to his appeal.

But Vogel asked again, this time with a touch of irony in his voice: "What's the matter, Major McCrary? Is the name of the general a top secret?" McCrary was still trying to sort out things and figure out how to interpret Patton's remark. But then he said: "All right, Vogel. I don't like what you did, and I have under consideration relieving you as the *Lagerkommandant*. We'll see. You've heard of General Patton. Blood and Guts and all that jazz, haven't you? Well, this was General Patton." He paused, then said, his tone almost melancholy, "But I'd advise you, Vogel, not to jump to conclusions. If I were you, my man, I'd forget what you've just heard."*

That night Carl Vogel wrote in his diary: "General Patton's entourage listened to his remarks in icy silence. Evidently they do not share his views. But Patton seems to be a man of good will. And also a voice in the wilderness."

ONE OF THOSE who had heard the remarks, and refused to believe his ears, was Captain Jack Carver, formerly Schnitzler, of Washington Heights in New York City. He was fifteen years old when he and his family fled from his native Frankfurt after a horde of drunken SA men had vandalized their house. In the United States, the Schnitzlers changed their name and became Americanized, especially son Jack, who was studying at New York University to become a lawyer when the war broke out. He volunteered and wound up in the Counter-Intelligence Corps because he spoke German and knew his way around in Germany. He was now in command of the CIC detachment sent to Camp 8 to handle the denazification of those people.

Captain Carver was liked by these Nazis. They had come to realize that he was strict but fair, and even Vogel conceded that much. "Jack is a *German* Jew, after all," he said, with the accent on "German," which was meant to say that Carver was a *better* type of Jew. He and Jack were on a

---

*After the incident, McCrary was ordered to *tighten* the rules. One of the results of the inspection was that all releases were suspended, as were minor privileges the inmates enjoyed, like the publication of their own mimeographed newsletter and participation in foreign-language courses. Less than a month later, Major McCrary was replaced by Lieutenant Colonel Howard L. Selk, executive officer of the 317th Infantry Regiment. Camp 8 was eventually closed down on June 15, 1946. Carl Vogel was transferred to other camps before he was released in the summer of 1947. He was still unrepentant in 1951, when he published a little book about his experiences, first as an AA and then as a PP, political prisoner.

first-name basis by now, but when Vogel once tried to switch to the intimate *Du* in addressing the American captain, he was rebuffed.

Captain Carver was mortified. No sooner had Patton left than he went to his quarters and wept. Did General Patton know exactly who these Germans were? *The Thundering Herd*, newspaper of the 84th Division, had called them "the putrid dregs of the former Hitler regime." And *The Tiger Cub*, the paper of the 10th Armored Division, described them as some of the most dangerous Nazis, and the most despicable—among them the SS guards at Dachau and Buchenwald, including a woman, an inconspicuous little brunette, who was charged with having sent four thousand men, women, and children to their deaths. Did General Patton know that 238 of the inmates were former bloodhounds of the Gestapo with a frightful record of torture and murder? Did he know that twenty-three of them were kept here because they had clubbed and trampled to death American flyers who had had the misfortune of parachuting from their stricken planes into the Nazi's arms?

Did Patton know all these details? And if he knew, would he have still thought that it was sheer madness to intern these people? Jack Carver could not comprehend how an American general, whose duty it was to punish this scum for their gross misdeeds, could characterize as "sheer madness" their internment. Was this how Patton understood his job and interpreted his mission?

In the privacy of his quarters, Jack Carver wrote out in longhand a report of what had just taken place. He addressed it to the colonel at SHAEF who was in charge of these camps, with a copy to his major in Wiesbaden, asking him to alert the colonel to his letter.

The fat was in the fire. The days of grandeur were coming to an end.

13.

⭐ ⭐ ⭐ ⭐

The Shadow of Ike

FROM CAMP 8, without staying for lunch, Patton motored to an abandoned Luftwaffe airstrip nearby, boarded his personal C-47, and flew to Pilsen for yet another sojourn with Lieutenant General Ernst N. Harmon, who had become his favorite oracle.

"Hell on Wheels" Harmon had joined the traveling Patton circus in Morocco in 1942 and presented him with his first victory in Safi and Mazagan. He was now the commanding general of the XXII Corps, stationed in the part of Czechoslovakia that was to be handed over to the Russians. Harmon disliked that prospect even as he disagreed with the other arrangements of Yalta. In this and in everything else, he was following in the footsteps of Patton, whom he idolized. But in his own domain, he was hellbent on surpassing his idol. Everything Patton was doing, Harmon was doing better. And he did it first. His regime in Bohemia was, therefore, a sort of pilot project of insubordination, his impetuosity and intolerance providing a pattern for the elder man. And Patton liked it fine. "Harmon is the greatest," he said. "We need more of his kind around here."

In these parts, General Harmon had become a legend in his own time. No day passed without the outspoken general adding to the stuff of which knights errant were made, bred as he was to the profession of arms and their rattling.

Harmon's influence on Patton during these days of easy impressionability was considerable. He was egging on the Old Man in the two major areas in which Patton was most susceptible to dubious advice: his loathing of the Russians and his tolerance of the Nazis. Harmon thus joined the handful of counselors who contributed to Patton's self-destruction.

Within hours after the incident at the camp, Patton was carefree again, on a duck shoot with his aristocratic hosts in the Sudetenland. It lasted until three o'clock in the afternoon on this September 8. He then walked briskly through seemingly endless potato patches, bagging those ubiquitous Hungarian partridges. In the evening he went to a dinnerdance at the Grand Hotel in Pilsen that Ernie Harmon was giving in his honor, and retired late. But he was up again bright and early the next morning, stalking deer in the hilly countryside for hours and encountering none.

By this time, during his absence from his desk, his remarks at the camp had produced echoes, not only in the hearts of the Nazis, but also in the minds of some members of his entourage. As it turned out, young Carver was not the only one to send in a report. Other junior officers, whose roots were in Central Europe, were outraged. When they observed the euphoria Patton's visit had caused among their prisoners, they decided to bring the incident to the attention of Brigadier General Clarence L. Adcock, the brilliant engineer and administrator of the Sixth Army, who had succeeded General McSherry in July as Eisenhower's G-5 in Frankfurt.

Major McCrary also sent a report to General Adcock, and Lieutenant Waterman mentioned the strange events in his weekly report to his superiors in Wiesbaden. What mattered most was a personal letter one of the generals in attendance sent to Major General Walter Bedell Smith, Ike's chief of staff, whose patience with Patton was wearing thin. So by the time "Beetle" Smith was briefed by Adcock, he had an idea of what had happened, and told his senior civil affairs aide: "There is no rational explanation for what General Patton is doing. I don't doubt any longer that old George has lost his marbles."

Clarence Adcock turned out to be an outstanding custodian of the difficult task that Frank McSherry had pioneered. The fifty-one-year-old West Point graduate from Waltham, Massachusetts, had been with Eisenhower since

1942. He accompanied Ike to London in the summer of
1942 and helped him plan the North African invasion that
was to become Patton's baptism of fire. He then remained
close to Eisenhower until his transfer to the Sixth Army
Group as General Jacob Devers's supply chief.

After being named assistant chief of staff for civilian
affairs on July 4, 1945, General Adcock had no excuse for
the Germans, and was more convinced than his predecessor
of the need to tighten the treatment of the Nazis among
them. "We didn't come here," he said, "and fight this war
and give American lives and money merely to reestablish
democracy in Germany or restore a minimum economy. We
came over here to deprive Germany of her war leadership
by denazification and demilitarization and to deprive her of
her equipment and war potential."

THE REPORTS from Garmisch-Partenkirchen reached
General Adcock on September 9. He discussed them with
Bedell Smith the same day. In turn, his chief of staff in-
formed General Eisenhower that the Patton affair was coming to a head. A civilian aide in Adcock's office, Professor
Walter Dorn, on leave from Ohio State University, then
drafted a letter for Ike's signature, to remind Patton of the
policies of the occupation which he was so apt to forget.
This was no longer a relatively narrow issue, like the handling of DPs and the feeding of the Jews. This was a case
of chronic insubordination. Patton was defying Ike, his commander, and in the process he was sabotaging the will of
the government of the United States.

The letter stated in no uncertain terms: "As you know,
I have announced a firm policy of uprooting the whole Nazi
organization regardless of the fact that we may sometimes
suffer from local administrative inefficiency. Reduced to
its fundamentals, the United States entered this war as a foe
of Nazism; victory is not complete until we have eliminated
from positions of responsibility and, in appropriate cases,
properly punished, every active adherent to the Nazi party.

"I know that certain field commanders have felt that some
modifications to this policy should be made. That question
has long since been decided. We will not compromise with
Nazism in any way.

"I wish you would make sure that all your subordinate commanders realize that the discussional stage of this question is long past and any expressed opposition to the faithful execution of this order cannot be regarded leniently by me. I expect just as loyal service in execution of this and other policies applying to the German occupation as I received during the war."

It was not the first such communication laying down the ground rules and spelling out the policies of the occupation. As recently as August 23, Patton had been reminded by Eisenhower that the "obliteration" of the Nazis was a must on their agenda. "Denazification," Ike told him, "is a most delicate subject both here and at home." And during a three-day conference of all the military governors, between August 24 and 27, General Adcock had reiterated the admonitions. "You are not here to govern," he said. "Your job is to control. And denazification and demilitarization are the two items of top priority on our schedule."

Patton had been fidgety and flippant at that conference. He had told anyone willing to hear him out that "Germany was so completely blacked out that so far as military resistance was concerned they were not a menace" and that "what we had to look out for was war with Russia." He had likened what the Americans were doing in Germany to the methods of the Gestapo, sounding an ominous note of interference in domestic politics. "If any newspaper opposed to the Democrats," he said at the conference, "should get hold of the stuff that is being put out by those in charge of the military government in Germany, it could produce very bad results for the Democratic government"—the Truman Administration, specifically.

He on his part, he had blustered, would release as soon as he could some of the Nazis interned at Moosberg and Garmisch-Partenkirchen, because, he said, many of them were "either old or pregnant." He himself conceded afterward that his remarks had "caused considerable furor."

By the time the letter of warning reached him, his rebellion had become an obsession.

He and Ike had been the closest of friends for a quarter of a century. The first time they met was in 1918, at Camp Colt, Pennsylvania, where Eisenhower, a mere captain, was the camp commandant, and Patton was training what was left of the new Tank Service. Oddly, Ike, the son of a poor railroad employee from Kansas, and Patton, the frontier aristocrat from California, got along well. Theirs was, indeed, an extraordinary relationship, rare in the Army, for Patton was ten years Ike's senior in years and two grades in permanent rank. "You are my oldest friend," Patton wrote to Ike in 1941. He was by then fifty-six years old. Eisenhower was not yet forty-six.

Himself barely settled in command of a budding tank brigade at Fort Benning, Georgia, the older man urged the young officer to leave the infantry and transfer to his outfit, either as his chief of staff or to command one of his regiments. Ike thanked him for the invitation but doubted that he could qualify for either job because, as he put it, he was still three years from his colonelcy.

But then the meteor of his career took off. He was a brigadier general only eighteen months later, running the War Plans Division of the General Staff. The change was cataclysmic. It shook the Army but it did not shock Patton. If anything, he was elated, because he had come to realize that he had only a tentative foot in the war and badly needed a friend at the top to get into it with both feet. In April 1942, nearly five months after Pearl Harbor, he wrote to Ike plaintively: "Sometimes I think that your life and mine are under the protection of some supreme being of fate. . . . But remember that my fate largely depends on you, because . . . one can very easily be forgotten."

Eisenhower returned the ball deftly. He expected Patton to make it well ahead of him. "Maybe I'll finally get out of this slave seat," he wrote from Washington, "so I can let loose a little lead with you. By that time you'll be the 'Black Jack' of the damn war." Ike was rooting for Patton and Patton was rooting for Ike.

Then the job Eisenhower had predicted for Patton fell to himself. In June 1943 the virtual unknown was named U.S. commander in the European Theater with headquarters in London. Now that his friend was in the seat of power, Patton dared to dream a little brighter.

He realized, without jealousy or rancor, that without

Eisenhower's miraculous rise, he would probably have been filed and forgotten in some desert hole in the United States, doing what Ike had done in World War I, training tankers for others to command. "I will never let you down," was soon becoming the refrain of many of Patton's letters to the Supreme Commander, and he tried hard to keep the promise.

"PATTON," General Eisenhower wrote to General Marshall in March 1945, "is a particularly warm friend of mine and has been so over a period of 25 years." But Ike was no longer just an old friend. He was the Supreme Commander of the victorious Allied expeditionary forces in the heartland of Europe.

"I think," Eisenhower wrote, "I can claim almost a proprietary interest in Patton because of the stand I took in several instances." And to be sure, his friendship for Patton never really ceased. But their professional relationship cooled.

The deterioration of their relationship was not apparent to those who observed the two men in their personal contacts. Eisenhower on his part may not even have been aware of it. And Patton was shrewd enough to refrain from parading his resentment. But when he was alone with his confidants, his anger and frustration sometimes made him vituperative and virtually savage in his references to the Supreme Commander. It was Eisenhower he was spiting and defying, blaming and accusing, for it was Ike's lengthening shadow that was darkening his horizon.

His petulance and peevishness, his acrimony projected to an uncertain future, were focused on Ike. The friend became a villain in an inane plot Patton was conjuring up, whose ramifications then put their old friendship to the acid test.

If Ike had acted upon his misgivings in the fall of 1944 and taken into consideration Patton's penchant for indiscretions, he would have saved himself countless headaches in the aftermath of the war. And he would have spared Patton the anguish and despair that resulted from the pitfalls and frustrations of the only job in his life for which he was not suited. But now it was too late.

Ike's letter reached Patton on September 11—at a time, in fact, when he had "more interesting" matters to attend to. On that very day, he at last accomplished a feat he had been attempting for some time but did not dare to perform— he had won another battle, as he explained it, in his never-ceasing war against fear. Noticing that he was becoming timid, even as he had been after World War I, he was especially disturbed when he caught himself thinking up all sorts of excuses to avoid a jump of only three and a half feet on a little course "the baron," his German stable sergeant, had built for him. Was he *afraid* to jump? On this September 11 he made it, and was so proud that he talked about nothing else the rest of the day. He even bragged to Count Felix von Luckner, the famed German commander of a surface raider in the First World War, who dropped in to ask for a job "to teach," as Patton put it with tongue in cheek, "democracy to the Germans."

More important, Ike's letter was overshadowed by one from General Maxwell Taylor, commander of the 101st Airborne, who had just been made superintendent of the Military Academy. Taylor was asking Patton to assist him with changes he was proposing in the curriculum at West Point in light of the wartime experience. Patton considered the request a great compliment, responding *in extenso* with a brilliant essay. He proposed that Max Taylor shift the emphasis from academic to tactical subjects, reminding him, as "a goat but without bitterness," that though he had been held back for flunking math in his plebe year, he later managed to outrank all members of his class.

To tell the truth, Patton no longer cared about this assignment of his in Germany. If they left him in Bavaria, he would stay, but only on his own terms. If they wanted him to quit, he would go, but only at his own time. But he still thought they could not just fire him—not Georgie Patton. Think of the uproar it would provoke—just when Ike was grooming himself for Marshall's job and Truman was trying on F.D.R.'s shoes.

As for Eisenhower's blistering letter, it was not even certain whether he really had dictated it, or even knew about it. During those days in September, Ike was in and out of Frankfurt—he had to go to Brussels to receive the Grand Cordon of the Order of Leopold, then off to Rome to see the Pope. He continued on a tour of the Riviera. Even if he had the time to put his signature on the letter, he had none to devote to the problem.

Ike was in Nice when two urgent messages reached him in the pouch General Bedell Smith was sending after him each day by couriers. One was word from Washington that he had been chosen to succeed General Marshall as the Army Chief of Staff. The other was a full report signed by Clarence Adcock, updating l'affaire Patton with later information from Camp 8 and elsewhere. In case he missed the connection between the two communications, Bedell Smith obliged by clarifying it. He cautioned Ike that the latest Patton crisis was gaining momentum, and that the news of Patton's indiscretion at the Nazi camp might break at any moment. Patton's actions might yet become a stumbling block to Ike's appointment, Smith warned. Eisenhower cut short his sojourn in southern Europe and flew to Munich, determined to do something before his friend could do him in. Delayed by the weather, it was late in the evening of September 16 when his plane could land near Munich at last, forcing him to change his plans. He cancelled his appointment with Patton he had scheduled for the morning of the seventeenth in Munich and decided to motor to St. Querin to spend the night in the Amann villa as George's houseguest.

As usual when these two men met alone, their reunion was cordial and candid. Eisenhower confided to Patton news of his imminent appointment and asked his friend what he planned to do when he, Ike, would no longer be around in Europe. Patton had come to realize that it was no longer Eisenhower who needed him but he who needed Ike. He told him frankly that he would not care to serve under his successor. As a matter of fact, he said, he would be comfortable in the Army only either as the commandant of the War College or as the commanding officer of the ground forces.

But just a few weeks before General Gerow had been chosen to replace General DeWitt as the head of the Army War College. And General Devers had been named to the command of the ground forces. There was no future in those places anyway, Eisenhower told Patton, since he believed that both would become victims of the pending unification program of the armed forces.

Uneasy in Europe, uncomfortable elsewhere, with the war in the Pacific over, Patton was becoming claustrophobic in uniform. "The only thing I can do is go home and retire," he wrote in his comments on his talk with Ike. In turn, Eisenhower was not the least encouraged by what his friend was telling him about the DPs. Patton repeated his "objections" to the Jews in so thinly varnished terms that it made Eisenhower shudder with shock. Patton's solution of the problem was to return them to their ghettos. The only concession he would be willing to make, he said, would be to send them back into some "sort of improved ghettos."

ALERTED that conditions in certain DP camps were deteriorating and that discrimination was practiced increasingly against the Jews in some of them, Ike had been coming over to see for himself, especially since word about the virulence of Patton's sudden anti-Semitism had been reaching him from various sources. Patton was becoming almost recklessly indiscreet. What astounded those around him was the intensity of his feelings and the vehemence with which he was voicing them.

Ike had a personal stake in the growing scandal. By this time, he himself had come under attack on the issue of the displaced Jews. And he became directly concerned when the dismal conditions were confirmed by such an objective authority as Earl G. Harrison, a former U.S. Commissioner of Immigration and Naturalization, who was sent by President Truman to Germany to look into this highly charged problem.

Patton questioned angrily Harrison's conclusions and animadversions. "Evidently," he wrote, "the virus started by Morgenthau and Baruch of a Semitic revenge is still

working." Discussing them with Brigadier General Mick-
elsen, one of Ike's civil-affairs officers in charge of the DP
camps, he said bluntly that he could not see why "the Jews
rated any better treatment than Mohammedans and Mor-
mons."

But Ike took seriously Commissioner Harrison's censure,
especially when it was spelled out by Truman in a sharply
honed letter of reproof. As a first step to remedy the situation, he appointed a popular Jewish Army champlain,
Major Judah Nadich of New York, to serve as his special
adviser on these problems. Then, since there was nobody
in the Third Army to "advise" Patton, and nobody on his
staff, gentile or Jew, to mitigate his impatience with the
Jewish DPs, Eisenhower "handed him," as Patton put it,
a "political adviser," an obscure State Department official
named Parker W. Burhman.

Patton received him with suspicion. "Please let me
know," he wrote to Keith Merrill, who was familiar with
the Foreign Service, "what you know about him and, if you
know nothing, speak to someone who does, as it is always
a good idea to get the dope on one's assistants." Then he
added for good measure: "Particularly—does he belong to
the chosen people."

During the night in the Amann villa in St. Querin, Eisenhower changed his mind. It had been his intention to
inspect the camps without Patton. But now he decided that
it might do his friend some good if he went along—remembering how shaken and moved Patton had been on their
visits to the concentration camps.

What followed so agitated Eisenhower that he cancelled
the rest of his tour of southern France to solve the Patton
problem without any more temporization. His friend had
been rational throughout the night, a delightful partner at
their nocturnal palaver, full of ideas and a reasonably re-
alistic picture of his future. But his conduct during the
action-packed hours of the following morning convinced
Ike that Bedell Smith was right. Patton had fits of madness,
and he had better do something fast before he destroyed
himself and did irreparable damage to Ike's career.

• • •

THE CORTEGE of the generals left early in the morning with all the trimmings of viceroyalty—the motorcycle outriders sounding their sirens, Patton's personal bodyguard on the ready at the AA gun mounted on the flatbed of a weapon carrier, jeeploads of MPs—and the entourage in sedans and command cars. The convoy was heading straight west, for Feldafing, which had been chosen for the inspection by Rabbi Nadich, summoned from Frankfurt to accompany Ike on the tour.

Feldafing had been singled out by Commissioner Harrison in his report to Truman as the worst managed of the DP camps. where discrimination against the Jews was most rampant, aggravated by the coddling of former Nazis in the same enclosure. It was an unlikely setting for such a place— to keep the wretched vagrants the Nazis had left, this human flotsam of the war. Even six months before, the beautiful resort on the western shore of the Starnberg Lake was the favorite vacation spot of Nazi bigwigs who had the most exclusive private school here for their kids.

It had a bittersweet history, and harbored within its walls the memories of one of Bavaria's legendary romances. The beautiful Empress Elisabeth of Austria, a former Bavarian princess, had spent thirty-four summers on the Rose Island in Feldafing, across a narrow channel of water from the Promenade. It was there that she had carried on a quaint affair with King Ludwig II of Bavaria, her cousin, to whom she had been drawn by their common infatuation with the arts. Watched by the emperor's spies, and by agents of the Munich government, their love blossomed mostly by correspondence. The desk whose drawers served as their secret mailbox is still there in the little château on the island.

"The beauty of the land," read the tourist flier that advertised Feldafing, "the garden and park-encrusted villas, silent walks and noiseless promenades give this lake resort the countenance of pronounced elegance, distant from all urban hustle and bustle, so calm and calming."

It was in Feldafing, nevertheless, that thousands of Jews were housed after the war. If an example were needed to validate any apprehension that the Army would botch up the job of governing the Germans, the DP reservation at Feldafing supplied it. The camp was huge and it had everything—reasonably comfortable dormitories, ample recreation areas, medical facilities run by Jewish doctors whom General Patton rated as "excellent." But nothing seemed to work.

Unaware or unmindful of traditional animosities within the special world of the Diaspora—the friction between German and East European Jews, the isolationist attitudes of the Hasidim and the hostility of the Galitzianer (the Jews from Galicia) toward other Jews—the Americans had crammed these DPs indiscriminately into the camp, resulting in some king-size brawls as Jew pitted himself against Jew. And there was no leadership to resolve the tension. The voice of the United Nations refugee organization was ineffectual, and the organizations of American Jews were represented by as many factions as the inmates, each with a different axe to grind.

GENERAL EISENHOWER was appalled when he found that Germans, some of them still wearing their SS uniforms, had been assigned to guard duty at the camp. Ike stopped to speak to one of the guards. He was found dead in his blood the morning after, bludgeoned into pulp during the night. Inmates at the camp recognized him when Ike had singled him out. He had been one of the most hated SS guards at Buchenwald.

Patton called Ike's attention to the fine bearing of these German guards, especially that of the sentry at the main gate. Ike stopped to talk to the man briefly, and learned that he, too, was a former SS man, fresh from a *Lager* of his own in the AA category. He had been, as it turned out, an armed escort on the freight trains that shipped fodder for the ovens of the extermination camps.

The compound was a former German military hospital, and Patton was quick to point out to Ike how rapidly it had deteriorated under the new tenants. "These buildings," he said, "were in a good state of repair when these Jews arrived. But look at them now! I'm telling you, Ike, these Jewish

DPs, or at least the majority of them, have no sense of human decency. They give the impression they've never seen a latrine before. They're pissing and crapping all over the place on the floor!"

"Shut up, George," Eisenhower said.

"I'm afraid, General Patton, you don't seem to understand." It was the UNRRA lady from New York, "the most talkative Jewish female," as Patton described her. "These people are just recovering from the most inhuman experience a human being could have had. They have to relearn their manners, General, if that's what you have in mind."

Courteous even to talkative females, Patton told her: "As a matter of fact, young lady, I commend you for having done an excellent job."

"You can't make these people responsible for these conditions," she said. "They are still dazed—they still don't know what's happening to them. You'll find that things will get better with every passing day."

"I doubt it," Patton said. "I've never seen a group of people who seem to be more lacking in intelligence and spirit. Incidentally," he turned to Ike, "there's a German village not far from here, deserted. I'm planning to make it into a concentration camp for some of these goddamn Jews."

THIS WAS September 17, Yom Kippur, the Day of Atonement, the Jews' most sacred day. At Feldafing they were all gathered in a large wooden building they used as the synagogue of the camp. General Eisenhower suggested that he make a speech to the congregation from the pulpit, and his proposition was welcomed gratefully.

Patton described the occasion. "We entered the synagogue, which was packed with the greatest stinking bunch of humanity.... When we got about halfway up, the head rabbi, who was dressed in a fur hat similar to that worn by Henry VIII of England and in a surplice heavily embroidered and very filthy, came down and met the General. Also a copy of the Talmud [sic; he meant the Torah], I think it is called, written on a sheet and rolled around a stick, was carried by one of the attending physicians.

"However, the smell was so terrible that I almost fainted and actually, about three hours later, lost my lunch as the result of remembering it."

After that, they returned to St. Querin, and Patton went fishing on the Tegern Lake, to remove, as he put it, the nauseous odors from his nostrils and take "the aspects of the camp" off his mind. He then took as long and as hot a bath as he could stand, to cleanse himself.

"I believe," Patton mused, "this was the first time General Eisenhower had inspected or seen much of Displaced Persons. Of course, I have seen them since the beginning, and marvelled that beings alleged to be made in the form of God can look the way they do or act the way they act."

14.

★★★★

Snares and Pitfalls

A still small voice spake unto me: "Thou art so full of misery, Were it not better not to be?"

TENNYSON, *"The Two Voices"*

USING THE new airstrip at Bad Toelz from which General Eisenhower had departed on the morning of September 18, General Patton took off for Pilsen, where General Harmon was awaiting him with another set of incendiary ideas and a tight schedule of shoots at the Schwarzenbergs'. Then, back in Bad Toelz in the afternoon of September 20, he was greeted with the news that his regime, which had been tottering on the brink of exposure, had made *The New York Times* that morning.

The dispatch was written by Raymond Daniell, a correspondent they knew in Toelz only by his reputation as a pugnacious if not obnoxious Canadian. At this time, only the barest of facts about Daniell's article were available to Major Ernest C. Deane, Patton's press officer and formerly a working newspaperman. But from the wording of the headline it did not sound promising.

Eisenhower's Order for Their Ouster Is Being Flagrantly Ignored, Survey Shows

When the text arrived the next day, it turned out to be worse than expected. The report attacked Patton personally, rather than the military government in general. As proof that Nazis still monopolized banking in the American zone, Daniell quoted a remark he had allegedly overheard during a conversation between the general and Colonel Charles E. Milliken a couple of days before. "Don't you think it's silly," Patton was supposed to have said to his finance officer, "to get rid of the most intelligent people in Germany?"

Daniell's article depressed Patton. If that was what they thought of him, after what he had done in war and peace, they could shove it. His most immediate reaction was to instruct his wife not to send him any Christmas presents at Bad Toelz because he probably would be leaving for home sooner than he had expected. "If I am not relieved by that time," he mused, "I shall try to get a leave." He was so shaken by the attack that he assembled his closest aides and told them to look for other posts. And they had better grab what they found because, he said, the Third Army would be just "a corpse losing a toe one day and a finger the next." All he had left, he wrote to a friend, was the squash court. But that was a good thing because it enabled him to let off some steam.

Patton still refused to make concessions. If anything, he was becoming more obstinate in his interpretation of his mission and in the management of his duties.

IT WAS in this mood that he discussed with General Craig the sticky problem of "taking care of the Jews," and agreed to face the press on the morning of September 22. Patton had taken a liking to Louis Craig—for "the elegant way," as he put it, the XX Corps commander had conducted himself as acting commander of the Third Army in June— by doing nothing during his absence. Craig had asked for "the audience," as General Gay called these sessions, because he was anxious to discuss with Patton yet another headache the Jewish DPs were giving him. When they met in the morning of September 21, Craig told Patton: "I have to move twenty-two rich German families out of their houses and give them to these animals. It's against my instincts to do such things."

"It's against my instincts, too, Louis," Patton said, "but

that's how Ike wants us to take care of the chosen people. Just see to it that pictures are taken before and after—to show how the houses looked before the Germans were kicked out and how they looked after the Jews moved in."

"Do you have any ideas," Craig asked, "what I should do with the Germans? After all, they will become the displaced persons now."

"Move them with as much consideration as possible," Patton said. "Give them all the trucks they need so that they can take with them as much of their property as they possibly can."

General Craig told General Patton, "I inspected another Jew camp yesterday and found that men and women were using adjacent toilets in full view of one another. They have screens, and they could separate the toilets. But these goddamn Jews are too lazy to put them up. The filth," Craig went on, "is unspeakable. In one of the rooms I saw six men and four women in four double beds. These people either never had any sense of decency, or else they must have lost whatever they had during their internment by the Germans."

"No, Louis," Patton said. "My personal opinion is that no human being could possibly sink to the level of degradation of these people in the short space of time of only four years. We are dealing with animals—they're the cross we've got to bear."

This was the main line of his thinking on September 22, when he was ready to face the press, clamoring as it was to confront the general in the wake of Ray Daniell's dispatch in *The New York Times* and a couple of articles in the newspaper *PM* in New York. Press conferences had once been great fun. Patton handled them like a virtuoso, and his correspondents, accredited to the Third Army during its halcyon days, lapped up everything he said because he tended to level with them, on or off the record, and was always amusing.

Things had changed. Instead of the daily wartime sessions, Patton was now holding only one briefing each week, on Saturday morning. Now he agreed—for he, too, had a few things to get off his chest—to allow the reporters to listen to the presentation of the staff reports, then let them ask questions. At the appointed time, only eleven correspondents showed up. Some—like Pierre J. Huss of the International News Service, Nora Waln of *The Atlantic Monthly* (being a Boston magazine, it presumed to have a proprietary interest in Patton), and Kathleen McLaughlin of *The New York Times*—were from the Third Army's own press camp in nearby Bad Wiessee.

Later, Patton saw a few strange faces in the crowd— Carl Levin of the *New York Herald Tribune*, Edward P. Morgan of the *Chicago Daily News*, and Raymond F. Daniell of *The New York Times*, who came with his wife, Tania Long, also working for the *Times*. It was Miss McLaughlin whose confidential reports to Edwin L. James, her managing editor in New York, about Patton's odd regime were the first to alert the *Times* to the story and who had suggested that Daniell come over from Nuremberg.

As if he had changed his mind at the last minute, Patton got up after the staff meeting and started to leave. But he was asked to stay, and he sat down again. The issue of his treatment of the Nazis was among the first to be raised by Daniell. Then Levin inquired about relations with the Fritz Schaeffer government, whose "ultraconservatism" was supposedly "distasteful" to Ike.

Patton responded to the questions sluggishly, unmindful of the fact that he was skating on extremely thin ice. He belittled the denazification program and asserted that the military government "would get better results if it employed more former members of the Nazi Party in administrative jobs and as skilled workmen."

The reporters gasped. One of them, sensing the opportunity to coax Patton into a major story, asked casually, "After all, General, didn't most ordinary Nazis join their party in about the same way that Americans become Republicans or Democrats?"

"Yes," he said, "that's about it."

The story made headlines. "Patton Belittles Denazification" in the *Times*. "American General Says Nazis Are

Just Like Republicans and Democrats" or words to that effect appeared in newspapers in the United States and around the world.

THE VIOLENCE of the reaction was a surprise to Patton as well as to others who had attended the session, because the press conference seemed to have been rather dull. Patton was bored to begin with and listless throughout it, coming to life only when he defended his policies. In general, the give-and-take had seemed innocuous. Colonel George Fisher, who attended both the staff briefing and the press conference, gave the journalists, who impressed him as "men of distinction in their field," the benefit of the doubt. "It did seem," he wrote, "that what they wanted to know was reasonable enough." They wanted it from Patton himself rather than from one or another of his aides—from Colonel Roy L. Dalferes, for example, who had succeeded Nick Campanole as G-5 and was now in personal charge of civil affairs—and they wanted it straight, as only Patton could give it to them. "They bore credentials," Colonel Fisher pointed out, "from Washington as well as from Frankfurt. And they did evidence a degree of deference toward the Old Man that was notable."

On the other hand, Patton was just not in the mood for all the foolishness. "Something was gnawing his guts that morning," Fisher recalled. "His own people knew enough to let him alone at such moments. But of course the press could not wait."

And Patton seemed to be deliberately reckless. He "barked out," as Fisher phrased it, the first answer that happened to pop into his head. It was he, Fisher thought, who baffled and teased the correspondents and not the newspaperman who tried to irritate and entrap him.

Patton was upset, to be sure, but not with the reporters. He was angry because one of his officers had talked too long and too loud during the briefing. Patton referred to this residue of the great press corps that had followed his camp throughout the war as "the ragtag and bobtail remnants of the great U.S. press." But he did not think that their hostility was aimed at him. "I always had them on my side," he wrote that evening. "Today there was very apparent hostility, *not against me personally*, but against the Army in general."

He recorded the event in a remarkable diary entry that was far more devastating than anything the correspondents wrote, for the light it shed on Patton's ignorance of the issues. He conceded in so many words that he had no idea of what this was all about—knew only vaguely who Dr. Schaeffer was—and could not figure out why the opposition to the man Colonel Keegan had made the Minister President was so vehement. He apparently did not even know—or could not remember in the heat of the moment—what Dr. Schaeffer's exact job or proper title was. "The special gripe [of the press] seems to be," he wrote, "that we are backing the wrong horse in the choice of the Governor or President of Bavaria."

He singled out Levin's oral belligerence for censure but exposed his own ignorance in the same breath. Complaining of Levin's temerity to suggest, as Patton put it in a revealing phrase, that "he knew more about who we should have than I did, although I know nothing, made me mad which I think is what they wanted." The morning after, when the impressions were still fresh in his mind and his political naïveté as pronounced as ever, he wrote to General Hugh C. Gaffey, his former chief of staff and division commander, back at Fort Knox by then:

"All the correspondents who have nothing better to do go around and attempt to form political parties and then accuse me of being either pro-Fascist, pro-Republican, or pro-Communist, according to their desires." A few days later he thought he had weathered the storm. "The assault on me in the papers is still going on," he wrote, "but [it] is losing its steam."

Actually, nobody knows exactly just what went on and what was said. No official record or transcript of the press conference exists because no formal notes were taken. So Patton's statements cannot be either confirmed or contested, quoted verbatim or paraphrased, on or off the record—they can be reconstructed only by the recollections of those who were present—and memories dim, survivors diminish. Nobody knew the exact story—except Pierre Huss, one of the fixtures in the press camp, the mercurial correspondent whom nobody could make out. In the end, he would stamp his own indelible mark on the record of this historic session.

A NATIVE of Belgium who represented the Hearst empire in Patton's world, Pete Huss had languished in the second rank of war correspondents, overshadowed by such giants as Drew Middleton of *The New York Times* and Bob Cromie of the *Chicago Tribune,* and even by his own colleagues at Hearst, like the veteran Carl von Wiegand and the brilliant Bob Considine. Even though most of the ace reporters had left, abandoning the field to the newcomers, Huss, the old-timer, was not making it to the top.

He was not liked, partly because he impressed his fellow correspondents as one who tried too hard. There was something unsettling about Huss, as if he had a secret to hide. His continental manners were taken for cant, his courtesy for hypocrisy, his eager polish for opportunism. The consensus was that Pete was a creep, a plodding journalist who could not be trusted. There was talk that he had been less than critical of Hitler during his tour as the Berlin correspondent of Hearst before the war, and still had links to his former Nazi friends. Ernie Deane, the press officer, did not share this animosity, for he had come to know Pete as a rather capable reporter, although perhaps something of an enigma.

The agency he was working for stood at the right of center among the news associations, frankly reflecting the *Weltanschauung* of William Randolph Hearst. Huss represented it with gusto, for he himself shared Hearst's philosophy. He was, like his formidable master, vehemently anti-Communist and reckless in his habit of branding people whose politics he disliked as Reds.

At the press conference of September 22, Pete did not like what he saw and heard. A devout, militant Catholic aligned with Cardinal von Faulhaber and quite comfortable with the reactionary forces his clique had foisted on Bavaria, Huss directed his antagonism against the substance of the proceedings, to be sure. But in the same degree, he also frowned upon the visiting correspondents, especially the representative of the *New York Herald Tribune*, Carl Levin, who, Huss insisted, was but a stooge for another Jew, Victor H. Bernstein, correspondent of the newspaper *PM*, a leftist-liberal afternoon paper in New York, which Huss was convinced was a tool of the Communist apparatus.

When the conference had adjourned and Patton had left, Colonel Fisher feared that the atmosphere was portentous: "Lunch that noon was a serious affair," he said. "Everyone had a notion that the fat was in the fire."

WHILE THE STORM raged with mounting fury, General Patton remained strangely calm and composed. There was in his poise the kind of attitude the French describe in the phrase *je m'en fous*—which, in Patton's own language, translated into not giving a shovel of shit. There was something else in his behavior during these tumultuous days in Germany that was not there in Sicily and in England during his previous "incidents." His outbursts were not followed by a display of contrition and humility.

This latest scandal did not merely annoy or embarrass General Eisenhower. It filled him with acute concern. Obviously his recent admonition had proved of little avail. During their nocturnal meeting only a few days before Ike had sternly cautioned his old friend to beware. His time would soon run out, Ike had said, and no amount of compassion or forbearance could then take him off another hook.

"Ike had taken Patton's hide off," Commander Harry C. Butcher, Ike's personal aide, had written in his diary after an earlier incident. "But I think Patton must have as many hides as a cat has lives, for this is at least the fourth time General Ike had skinned his champion end runner." Yet Ike was still willing to give his stormy petrel the benefit of the doubt.

On September 24 he ordered General Bedell Smith to call Patton on the phone, trying to clear up the incident without the necessity of employing more radical measures. Smith was not calling to relieve Patton. He was merely conveying Ike's orders that he eat crow by immediately calling another press conference for the purpose of taking

back everything he had said on the twenty-second. Smith
also instructed Patton to read to the correspondents two
paragraphs from Eisenhower's letter of September 11 that
spelled out the official policy regarding the treatment of
Nazis in no uncertain terms.

It was at this turn that a stranger appeared on the stage,
an itinerant operative sent to Germany by former President
Herbert Hoover. He was part of an intricate scheme conjured
up by Pierre Huss to discredit Roosevelt and, by extension,
the Democrats. The plan was to expose the press conference
as a trap into which Patton had been lured, and turn the
general into a martyr for another triumphal return to the
States. It was a brazen plot in which Patton would be a
patsy or a pawn, if, indeed, he would be willing to participate at all. But it would cause the Truman Administration
considerable trouble and unleash resentment of the "Communists" who, in Huss's distorted view, had taken over the
United States.

The scheme had the makings of a conspiracy, and Huss,
who could think them up but could not make them work,
needed the help of someone with clout and connections. He
sent for President Hoover's man in Germany, who had arrived in Munich just when Pete Huss had hit upon the idea
of making George Patton the next President of the United
States.

He was fifty-two-year-old Frank Earl Mason of Lees-
burg, Virginia, a former top newspaper executive and a
colonel in the reserve, and, during the recent war, a special
assistant to Secretary of the Navy Frank Knox. Now, in the
fall of 1945, he was between jobs, and looking for one that
might come out of this tour. In the meantime he was free-
lancing for Hoover and for Roy W. Howard, powerful president of the Scripps-Howard newspaper chain, with whom
he shared a loathing of Franklin D. Roosevelt—even now,
five months after F.D.R.'s death.

For Mason, Huss's frantic call was the cue. He rushed
into the breach on this moment's notice. The two of them
could be seen closeted in the press lounge in Bad Wiessee
and huddled in Bad Toelz in whispered conversations. Then
Mason took over. Basing his information solely on what

Huss had told him, Mason constructed a melodrama in which those newcomers to the press camp under "Semitic influence" were the villains and Patton was their innocent victim. In Mason's hands, Huss's amorphous plan took the shape of an insidious plot. Mason charged that Jews and Communists had banded together in Patton's own back-yard—in an international conspiracy to destroy him.

Briefed by Huss, who pointed an accusing finger at several prominent liberals whom he believed to be the string-pullers of the plot, Mason asked for an audience with Patton in the role of the teacher Artemidorus in Shakespeare's *Julius Caesar*, who warned in similar circumstances, "There is but one mind in all these men, and it is bent against Caesar." Patton received Mason with suspicion and skepticism.

"A Mr. Mason," he wrote, "came in with a long story about the attempt on the part of Jewish and Communist elements to put the bug on people like myself. While his story sounded plausible, I have developed such a low opinion of all newspaper people that I think he is probably a liar."

At the session with the general, off the cuff, Mason named five high-echelon government officials—Treasury Secretary Henry Morgenthau, Assistant Secretary of State Harry Dexter White, David K. Niles of the White House staff, Alger Hiss of the State Department, and Laughlin Curry of the Justice Department—as members of the alleged conspiracy, working, he said, through journalists Bernstein, Daniell, Morgan, and Levin. Five of the nine were Jews. Two of them, White and Hiss, he described as clandestine Communists and practicing spies for the Soviet Union. He singled out Victor Bernstein as the mastermind and leader of the plot—"the most powerful man in Germany," as he called him, "because he [has] the support of Harry Dexter White and Henry Morgenthau."

FRANK MASON, a native of Wisconsin and product of Ohio University, had come to Bad Toelz with impressive credentials. As it turned out, he had been on duty at Langres in World War I, just when Patton was training his tankers there. After the war, he was the American military attaché in The Hague and Berlin, then stayed in Europe for INS, eventually becoming its president. He switched to the National Broadcasting Company in 1941, and was with NBC when he doubled during the war as Secretary of the Navy Frank Knox's assistant. Now, five months after F.D.R.'s death, he was in Europe, he told the general, paying his own passage, looking for a job while rekindling the memories of his own experience after World War I. After his audience with Patton on the morning of September 25, Major Deane, who was assembling the reporters for the second press conference in three days to correct the impressions left by the first, asked Mason to stay and see for himself.

The session had none of the heat that Huss had told Mason the earlier conference had generated. Patton was rested and in a more equable mood. He faced the reporters calmly, without any apparent grudge or rancor. But he confined himself to the reading of two paragraphs from General Eisenhower's letter of September 11, and of a long statement he had prepared to clarify his position. He allowed but seven minutes for questions from the floor, prefacing them with the remark: "As the result of our last talk together, apparently some startling headlines appeared in the home papers. I say 'apparently' because I only know them by hearsay."

"General," one of the reporters asked, "if you recall, what was the direct quote about political parties."

"I said," Patton replied, not without an impish wink, "that Nazism might well be compared to any of the political parties at home, either Republican or Democrat. I also referred to my cousin who remained a postmaster for years by judicious flip-flops, and I don't consider him a son-of-a-gun either."

As far as the controversy whirling about Minister President Schaeffer was concerned, Patton continued to plead ignorance and innocence. "So far as I know," he said, "[he] has not been proved to be a Nazi." And he disclaimed personal responsibility for the man. "Schaeffer was, as a matter of fact," he said, "picked out before I got here."

But otherwise he did not retreat from his original position. In the prepared statement, he injected the memory of his great victories at Casablanca, at El Guettar, in Sicily, and on the European continent, and equated them with what he described as his successes in Bavaria now. Then, to the point, he said:

"Unquestionably, when I made a comparison of so vile a thing as Nazism with political parties, I was unfortunate in the selection of analogies. The point I was trying to bring out was that in Germany practically all, or at least a very large percentage, of the tradespeople, small businessmen and even professional men, such as doctors and lawyers, were beholden to the party in power for patronage which permitted them to carry on their business or profession and that, therefore, many of them gave lip service only; and I would extend this to mean that when they paid party dues, it was still a form of blackmail. These are the type of people whom, while we will eventually remove them, we must put up with until we have restored sufficient organization to Bavaria to insure ourselves that women, children, and old men will not perish from hunger or cold this winter.

"I believe," Patton said with feeling, "that I am responsible for the deaths of as many Germans as almost anyone, but I killed them in battle. I should be un-American if I did not do my utmost to prevent unnecessary deaths after the war is over."

It was a friendly and even sunny session, in the style of the good old days, when press conferences were pleasant intermezzi. But Mason disregarded this follow-up conference and wrote a long account of "the incident," confining himself to the previous conference, the details of which he knew only by hearsay. As he saw it, Patton was "sound" and he was "American." But, Mason wrote, "he is getting hell for daring to block the radicals in running interference for a Red government in Germany."

His report typed neatly, he drove through the night to Wiesbaden to give his account to Colonel Fitzgerald, chief of Eisenhower's public relations. He sent copies to former President Hoover, Roy Howard, and several friends at the American Legion in Washington, scattering his version of the events as widely as he could. He then lunched with

Brigadier General R. B. Lovett, Eisenhower's adjutant general, giving him the story in the hope of getting it to Ike from another source. Each time he repeated what had become his proof that this was, indeed, a Communist conspiracy. Patton, he said, was under attack by a "small but vociferous group of newspapermen led by *PM*."

The avowed purpose of the Huss-Mason intrigue was to save Patton. But with friends like them, he needed no enemies. By the time Mason was ready to leave Bad Toelz, he had Patton fully aroused and convinced that the Reds and the Jews were ganging up on him—and not only on him. "All military governments," he wrote in one of his letters during these days, more in sorrow than anger, "are going to be targets from now on for every sort of Jewish and Communist attack from the press." In another letter he wrote: "It may well be that the Philistines have at last got me."

15.

Down to the Wire

ALTHOUGH FRANK MASON had trumpeted his jeremiad far and wide, and saw to it that at least two of General Eisenhower's top aides heard it, it never reached Ike himself. His staff still strove to insulate the Supreme Commander from General Patton's shenanigans, and, therefore, intercepted Mason's memo.

It was, nevertheless, the Mason version of this foretaste of Patton's downfall that came to be accepted as the historical account. But it was full of holes, for part of it was hearsay, and part was tainted by Mason's own bias and preconceived notions. He himself was not present at the critical first press conference and relied entirely on Pete Huss's account, badly distorted by Pete's anti-Communist slant as well as his well-known dislike of Jews in general, and of Carl Levin and Vic Bernstein in particular.

As far as the press conference and his interview with Patton were concerned, Mason assumed certain things that were not there. As he had come to see it, and as it came out in his memorandum, the Jews and the Communists had banded together against Patton because, Mason wrote, he was "daring to block the radicals in running interference for a Red government in Germany." This was the insidious scheme. Levin and Bernstein were but agents of that hideous conspiracy for which they had succeeded in subverting Daniell, Morgan, and Long.

Actually, the players were not quite up to the characters of this bizarre scenario. Daniell and his colleagues were tough reporters to begin with, and they were on the make.

Daniell was pugnacious and abrasive by nature. Morgan had puffed his pipe too vigorously, not caring that the smoke had drifted straight into Patton's face. And Levin had been too aggressive and quite a bit louder than the occasion of a press conference warranted or than a great American general would have rated. But they were, as Colonel Fisher pointed out, not harsh on the Old Man. Their offense was lack of taste and good manners, not participation in some sinister plot.

As far as Bernstein was concerned, he was conspicuous, to be sure, but only by his absence. He had already left Germany three weeks before, in preparation for switching assignments from reporting the occupation to the coverage of the Nuremberg trials. He carried with him, when he left, the respect and good wishes of Lieutenant Paul Gauthier, one of Patton's press officers. Bernstein was a meek sort of fellow in the best biblical sense of the term. He couldn't *force* a fly to go away. The press officers didn't always like what he wrote, but they never quarreled with his facts or questioned his integrity. In some sense, he could have been regarded as the American conscience in Germany after the war.

AND YET, Frank Mason's tale of a conspiracy was no mere figment of the imagination. As a matter of fact, the beleaguered general suddenly found himself in the pincers of two fast-developing plots. One was the "counterattack" Mason was hatching with Pierre Huss (who had sworn him to secrecy never to reveal the source of his information). The other was engineered by a coalition of Patton's foes in General Eisenhower's inner circle. In the end, Patton was toppled from his pedestal, not by those "itinerant" correspondents and the philistines, but by a greater design devised by his own colleagues. Bedell Smith, Gen. Harold R. (Pinky) Bull, and Clarence Adcock had concluded that Patton was unfit to govern the Germans.

Now it was September 25, three days after the fateful press conference. The crisis had moved closer to Eisenhower—too close for comfort. The front pages of the newspapers in the United States were crowding up with stories of the scandal and the radio was presenting it in angry words. The question was no longer whether Patton had done it again. The question now was whether General Eisenhower was the right man to control postwar Germany.

Earlier in September, Ike still hoped that he would gain a brief grace period for solving the problem, just enough time to arrange a more suitable berth for Patton outside of the European theater. But the scandal was spreading and the crisis was mounting. Even President Truman had inquired in a blistering personal letter just what the hell was going on. And he had sent it directly to Ike, instead of via General Marshall, although the President usually observed the channels meticulously.

The press in particular was breathing down their necks. As usual, Patton was not reading the newspapers. He refused even to glance at the headlines. He tried to dismiss the unpleasant tidings by ignoring the messengers. It was different with General Eisenhower. Like an actor in a new show, he was dependent on his notices. Now, when it mattered most, his press was bad and it was getting worse.

It was at this point that Victor Bernstein entered the stage. He had arrived back in the States on September 4, took a few days off to rest after his six months in Germany, then began briefing himself for the trial in Nuremberg, which was the next assignment on his calendar. Just before the furor erupted, the editors of *PM* had asked him to sum up his impressions in a series of four articles, and he sat down to answer such questions as whether Hitler was really dead . . . what were the Germans doing to eke out a living . . . who was getting the profit out of German industry . . . and what, if anything, was being done about the stolen Jewish property?

As originally conceived, Patton was to figure only incidentally in the articles. But then, Ray Daniell's angry piece appeared in *The New York Times*. Ed Morgan had his say in the *Chicago Daily News*. And Carl Levin had written in the *New York Herald Tribune* about the case of Fritz Schaeffer: "The whole matter leaves Patton pretty cold. He said he does not know anything about [political] parties and does not care. What is more, 'Schaeffer can run the province any way he sees fit.'"

Bernstein's first article appeared on September 21, and was still vague in tone. But the next day his second article dealt frontally with "the American failure in Germany." What was wrong, he asked, with the American policy of the occupation? Who was to blame? Patton, of course. But also Eisenhower, Bernstein wrote. In every sense, he wrote, Ike was an absolute monarch. And so was Patton, for that matter.

The fault lay, Bernstein wrote, deeper than mere personalities. "Perhaps we've made a serious mistake in expecting the military mind, which thinks primarily in terms of order, discipline, and good communications, to wrestle successfully with problems of democracy, freedom, and representative government."

As if to bear him out, *The New York Times* cited Patton as saying: "My opinion is [that] to create an anarchistic situation by not restoring normal communications and law and order is more dangerous than having some Nazis working for us." Herbert M. Clark, the ABC correspondent, charged that Eisenhower, standing in for Uncle Sam, was becoming far too soft, and the editorials asked noisily: Does Patton speak for Eisenhower? Or is he the executor of Ike's policies?

At the same time, an ominous undertone was added by John O'Donnell, the Washington columnist of the *New York Daily News*. Were the Jews at work to do Patton in to avenge his slapping of a Jewish soldier in Sicily? Neither of the soldiers Patton had hit had been Jewish, but O'Donnell insisted that they were. He had thereby aroused the ire of American Jews such as Henry Morgenthau, Bernard Baruch, and Felix Frankfurter. Was this another conspiracy of those wise men of Zion, O'Donnell asked, to make the world safe for Judaism?

Trial balloons appeared in the conservative press, testing cautiously the climate for a possible candidacy of Patton in American politics. It was then left to Victor Bernstein after all, in this cacophony of pros and cons, to orchestrate the

charges and pinpoint the attack. Winding up his series with
an editorial on September 24, he put his conclusion on the
front page in the biggest type *PM* could find:

GEN.
PATTON
SHOULD
BE FIRED

"General Patton is the issue," Bernstein wrote. "Eisenhower
is responsible. The reputation of the one is as much at stake
as of the other.

"General Patton should be fired."

The word was out.

IN THE EVENING of September 25, after supper,
Patton was handed a telegram from General Eisenhower,
who was, or so it seemed, still giving him the benefit of
the doubt. "I simply cannot believe," Ike wrote, "that these
reports are accurate." For better or for worse, he sought
comfort from Patton's insistence that he had been mis-
quoted. But the question, Ike wrote, was a very serious one
and he asked Patton to fly to Frankfurt "at the first opportunity" and see him for an hour.

This was Tuesday. Ike was expecting him on Wednesday
or Thursday. But the weather was bad. Instead of flying to
Frankfurt, he accepted the invitation of General Bethouard,
the gallant French officer imprisoned by the Vichy government in Morocco three years before, whom Patton had had
to leave there at the behest of General Noguèz but who now
was one of his colleagues as a proconsul in these parts.
They were going to hunt for Austrian gazelles in the rocky
Alps. It turned out to be a portentous outing, for storm
followed him wherever he went. Amidst thunder and light-
ning, in pouring rain, Patton was bagging one chamois after
another—out of touch with the world and apparently oblivious to its realities.

On September 26, in answer to his critics, Eisenhower
promulgated Military Law No. 8, reiterating that no member
of the Nazi Party or any of its formations could be employed

in jobs higher than laborers. At eleven o'clock in the morning of the same day, General Bedell Smith was meeting behind closed doors with a bevy of reporters, Levin, Daniell, and Morgan among them. "Tell us, General," Carl Levin asked, "whether you think that the program can be carried out by people who are temperamentally and emotionally in disagreement with it."

They were concentrating on Patton, attacking his ignorance as much as his policies and practices. They said Patton had admitted to them that he did not know exactly who the Minister President of Bavaria was and what he was doing. He had no idea, Patton had said, what the word "reactionary" meant. When asked about the *Fragebogen*, the controversial questionnaire the Germans had to fill out to sum up their life under the Nazis as a first step in their denazification process, Patton asked back: "What the hell is a *Fragebogen*?"

PATTON'S STAFF consisted of a major general, seven brigadier generals, and thirty-five colonels. But just at this time, the handful of people he needed and trusted most—the friends he regarded as his best firemen to put out the flames he set from time to time—were all gone. Secretary of War Henry L. Stimson had left office on the very day Patton's troubles had peaked, and was no longer there to protect and support him. General Bradley—"the best thing," as General Haslip had put it, "that ever happened to George Patton"—had gone home to take over the Veterans Administration. The men closest to him on his own staff—General Muller, Colonel Koch, and Colonel Codman—were in the United States, as was, unfortunately for him, Hobart R. Gay.

Wiry, erect, and properly a little shorter than his boss, Hobart Richard Gay, a devout cavalryman and irrepressible polo player, was a little like Faust's Homunculus—it seemed that Patton had cloned him in his own image. They had met seven years before, in 1938. Patton was then a colonel, stationed at Fort Myer, Virginia, when Gay was ordered up from Fort Riley to serve on his staff. Alarmed by Patton's reputation as a taskmaster and martinet, Gay moved heaven and earth to get another assignment. His first encounter with his blustering new boss then made him regret doubly that he had failed to get it.

Standing at the stable of an apparently recalcitrant horse just after Gay had checked in, Patton pointed to the wild one and ordered Gay to take it out and bust it—for nobody, he said, not even he himself, had succeeded thus far in breaking the beast. Gay said a prayer, mounted the horse, and promptly fell, bruising himself and breaking the horse's leg. The horse had to be destroyed.

Mrs. Gay was at their new quarters when Gay called from the nearest telephone to warn her: "Stop unpacking, Betty. We'll be moving on." But Patton, who had been bluff and surly with him before, but had obviously been impressed with his handling of the order, now told him with a twinkle in his eyes: "It's all right, Gay. Thank God, I won't have to ride that goddamn nag ever again." From this Pattonesque beginning to the tragic end, the two men had remained inseparable.

By this time in 1945, as he had been for some time, Hap Gay was, indeed, an indispensable man in Patton's eyes. But others did not think so—not General Bradley, for instance. He regarded Gay as "a lightweight" who lacked the sophistication his job at Patton's side needed. Gay's idol-worship of Patton, Bradley thought, and his uncritical acceptance of his boss actually pushed Patton even deeper into the quicksand of his bravado and the morass of his indiscretions. Others went along with Bradley's assessment, and Bedell Smith in particular carried his animosity to extreme. He merely disliked Patton. But he loathed Gay, and succeeded in turning even Ike against the beleaguered chief of staff.

General Gay was not easy to size up. It was difficult to get close to him, almost impossible to know him well. He was single-minded where people thought he was narrow-minded. He was tongue-tied where he gave the impression of having nothing to say. They called him "Hap" by the nickname he had acquired early in the Army, short for "Happy," and Hobart Gay was unquestionably happy in his fashion—but not happy-go-lucky, no backslapper, no politician.

He had only some of the traits and attributes an officer

needed in the caste-conscious Army, but lacked many of the others. A farm boy from southern Illinois, where he was born in 1894, and a graduate of the University of Illinois but not of West Point, Hap went into the cavalry because he loved horses and knew how to handle them. He then made up for what he lacked in pedigree with his dash as a cavalryman and wizardry in polo. He was a dedicated outdoorsman, far more at home at game preserves than in drawing rooms. Nobody ever described him as suave, soigné, or debonair. His face handsome but commonplace, his eyes small and trusting, of medium height and build, Hap Gay was average in every respect—except in Patton's eyes.

For Hobart Gay, behind that humdrum facade, was a wonderful human being and a superbly competent chief of staff, on his own as well as in Patton's shadow. And though to many he seemed remote and stand-offish, he was warm and loyal. Gay had charm, and it came through, but he had to like the people and the people had to know him to recognize that awkward charisma behind his diffidence and nervous smile. Most important, he was totally wrapped up in his devotion and service to General Patton, and his antennae were always out to pick up even the weakest signal. And, it seemed, distance made no difference.

Now in the United States, he suddenly felt in his bones that the General needed him at Bad Toelz. He cut short his leave, flew back to the Flint Kaserne, and walked into Patton's office, unexpected and unannounced. Patton was overjoyed to see him. "Oh, Happy," he said, "am I glad that you're back. . . . I don't think we would be in this mess if you had been here."

Gay shrugged off what he thought was just a compliment, but Patton insisted. "No, Happy, I mean it. Nobody knows exactly what I said to those goddamn shysters of the press, and I can't prove that I didn't say any of the things they're now putting in my mouth. Harkins and Maddox didn't think of it, and neither did Deane. But if you had been here, Happy, you would have seen to it that a goddamn stenographer was present and took down every word."

• • •

WHEN IKE could no longer avoid staying out of the fracas, he asked Robert D. Murphy, his longtime diplomatic adviser, now serving with General Lucius Clay at the Control Council in Berlin, to look into the matter, as a last resort. Actually Murphy's presence in the controversy was regarded suspiciously as a sign that he had been sent into the breach to lay the groundwork for a whitewash. "There is one indication," a dispatch of the United Press conjectured, "that [Patton] may escape with a reprimand and a promise to obey orders." Robert D. Murphy, the correspondents warned, had a record of expediency not unlike Patton's own. "Murphy has been Ike's political right arm since Africa," one of them wrote, "where he backed such French politicos as Giraud, Noguèz, and Peyrouton against de Gaulle."

Ambassador Murphy called from Munich and was invited to lunch with the general in St. Querin on September 27. Murphy arrived a little early and had to wait while Patton, as nonchalant and flamboyant as ever, was sitting for a Polish artist for what turned out to be a stunning portrait. He was serene in his Sunday best, dressed for his portrait, with seven rows of ribbons on his chest, a pearl-handled pistol hanging from a broad leather belt, one gloved hand holding the other glove. The rays of the afternoon sun played with the ruby of his West Point ring, which he wore on the middle finger of his right hand. Patton looked formidable. But he was tired. His fair hair had turned gray and become sparse. The rings under his eyes had become permanent. Wrinkles danced around his lips, which seemed thinner and paler than before.

After lunch, while Patton was conferring with Murphy, his new WAC secretary came in with word that General Bedell Smith was on the telephone. Patton took the call. Pointing to the extension telephone on another table, he said to Murphy: "Listen to what the lying s.o.b. will say." Then, as Murphy described it, he vigorously pantomimed for his visitor's benefit his scornful reaction to Smith's "placatory spiel."

Murphy's visit solved nothing. He was later said to have tried to straighten out Patton, so to speak, suggesting that he fire Dr. Schaeffer and shift the setup in Bavaria from

the right to the left of center. But Ambassador Murphy
himself later denied indignantly that he had ever done any
such thing. As a matter of fact, just before he had left for
the meeting in St. Querin, he had dined with a friend in
Munich who had brought Dr. Schaeffer along to show that
the controversial Catholic politician had no horns. "The
three of us had an agreeable discussion," Murphy recalled,
"and I was favorably impressed with Schaeffer."

Behind what Murphy described as "the embarrassing
mix-up" was a man whom Patton described as "a very slick
individual." He was Walter Louis Dorn, a fifty-one-year-
old historian on leave from Ohio State University, the son
of a distinguished German-American pastor-teacher, scion
of a family whose roots went back to Martin Luther in
sixteenth-century Germany. The Dorns represented a different brand of Germans and Christians. They were steeped
in the spirit of reform and rebellion, in the tradition of uphill
liberalism that had its halcyon days in 1848, only to be
crushed under Bismarck's jackboots.

Now Professor Dorn was to bring to bear the ingrained
liberalism of his forefathers on conditions in Bavaria; it soon
became evident, however, that the American Zone of Occupation in Germany was not big enough to accommodate
both General Patton and Professor Dorn.

IF WALTER DORN did not surface before as a decisive factor in the general's downfall, it was not because
he was shy or wary, or lacked the courage of his convictions,
or because he had a passion for anonymity. A jovial man
of some bulk, with a smiling, round, jowly face and a
weakness for wisecracks, Dorn was gregarious. He had
many friends in Germany, both Americans and Germans,
and was making more every day. But nobody knew exactly
what he was doing. The nature of his job and the protocol
of the Army demanded that he remain faceless.

His chain of command descended from General Eisenhower to General Walter Bedell Smith, then to General Bull
and General Adcock. There, as far as Dorn was involved,
the buck stopped. He dealt with and was directly accountable
only to General Adcock. His consuming passion was to aid

in the establishment of democracy in Germany on the American pattern. And he had succeeded in convincing General Adcock that it would be possible to accomplish this goal—and without the Nazis.

Dorn's anonymity was so pervasive that Robert D. Murphy, who was one of Dorn's nominal bosses, never referred to him by name. The pliant diplomatic adviser, who had pioneered the business of civil affairs in North Africa, dismissed Dorn as a wild-eyed intellectual. "A subordinate civil-affairs officer," he described him, "who had been recruited from the history department of an American college," as if an academic background had been a disqualifying blemish.

And Patton? Dorn was indubitably one of the key men in the apparatus of military government. But Patton did not know him. When they met at last, Dorn impressed him as one of those smooth, smart-ass academic types, and Patton distrusted him at first sight. "He is I think pure German," he wrote after their one and only meeting, "and very probably a Communist in disguise."

WALTER DORN had been snooping and sniffing in Patton country since August, on orders from General Adcock, assembling the data needed for the recommendations Adcock was preparing for General Eisenhower about the future of Bavaria. The trouble apparently stemmed, not merely from Patton's views, but from the fact that he was imbuing his subordinates with his own dangerous ideas.

Patton's regime was a festering scandal on which the lid was tenuously kept. Something had to be done, if only because the Army was hanging on to the military government of Germany by the skin of its teeth. A scandal would be certain to hasten the termination of the monopoly.

The preferential treatment of the Germans—even the Nazis for whom the directives prescribed thirty-three different categories of automatic arrests—amounted to crass discrimination against all others. Professor Dorn's quiet investigation then brought the picture into sharp focus. It was not merely a matter of using Nazis in jobs for which apparently they were regarded as indispensable by Bad Toelz, but the deliberate pampering of the Germans in general that was so scandalous. They were permitted to live far better than the millions of victims of Nazism who were still in Germany. The Germans were better housed, better fed, and better clothed than anybody else in Germany—much better than the liberated foreigners, the former slaves, and especially the salvaged Jews, better even than some of Patton's own GIs.

Improvements in the feeding of the Germans—including the Nazis in the internment camps—began as a legitimate humanitarian gesture on Patton's part, when he discovered that certain camp commanders in their punitive zeal had been keeping them on a starvation diet of 800 calories or less. But when Patton was through remedying a bad situation, the pendulum had swung to the other extreme. The Germans were given rations of up to 4,000 calories each day, even in Camps 6 and 8, where the hard-core Nazis were detained.

The misfeasance of the Patton regime that Dorn decried as the most outrageous was in housing—particularly in the consideration shown even high-ranking Nazis, who should have been put into internment camps but were permitted to occupy their own residences now as before. Although Frankfurt stipulated firmly that the Nazis must "not be allowed to retain wealth, power, and influence," Patton objected to their removal from their sumptuous homes on legalistic rather than humanitarian grounds. For one thing, he argued, the removal of an individual from his home would have been "the punishment of an *individual*," although his understanding of the principle of such retribution was to "punish the *race*." Moreover, he said, it was against his "Anglo-Saxon consciousness"—contrary, that is, to the ancient tenet that a man's home was his castle—to evict persons from their homes in this peremptory manner. Counseled by Colonel Charles E. Cheever, his judge advocate, Patton objected to what he regarded as "intolerable punishment without due process of law."

While many of the Nazis were left at large or but lightly guarded in their places of deluxe internment, entire units of the U.S. Army were living in tents and the GIs had to sleep in the rain. The reason for this was a directive Patton had issued on July 12, shortly after his return from the United States, listing five priorities for the housing of the troops of the Third Army: (1) barracks, (2) public buildings and schools, (3) warehouses, factories, and office buildings, and (4) hotels in that order of commandeering, with a fifth category given the lowest priority.

Privately owned residences and apartments were to be requisitioned only as a last resort. No distinction in this last category was made between the homes of ordinary Germans and of "ardent" Nazis. Under this directive, the home of a Gauleiter or the commandant of a concentration camp was as well protected against American confiscation as that of a former inmate of a concentration camp.

A castle that a unit of the Seventh Army had occupied in the immediate wake of the hostilities was given back on Patton's personal orders to its former aristocratic owners rather than transferred to an antiaircraft unit of the Third Army whose men needed it to have a roof over their heads. A quartermaster outfit was ordered to vacate another Schloss, because supposedly it was too far from the materiel dump it was servicing. Actually the distance was less than a mile. But when they moved out, in moved its former owner—a dowager countess with four servants. Around Regensburg, Dr. Dorn had found that German soldiers, now prisoners-of-war, were still occupying their old barracks, while the American soldiers were quartered under tents in the nearby fields.

THERE WAS an even more explosive issue festering in the Patton scandal. It was the retention of the Nazis' armed elite—both from the General-SS, that had supplied the guards for the slave labor camps and the extermination chambers, and the Waffen-SS, which was Heinrich Himmler's private army fighting as the Wehrmacht's rival. Also "sequestered"—or "hidden," as Walter Dorn put it—were caches of their arms.

Dorn was first tipped off to this "army" by Major Ordway

in Munich; Ordway was chief of a special unit of investigators working for General Adcock, even as Dorn was, but with the paraphernalia of regular sleuths. Ordway cautioned that it was but a phantom army—a mishmash of rumor and wishful thinking, somewhat like the heavenbound force of Andreas Hofer, the legendary Tyrolean leader of the peasant rebellion against Napoleon in these parts 135 years before. But Dorn tracked them down in the cages Ordway had mentioned as the staging points of a budding conspiracy. And he was shocked when he found them there in fact.

Were the Russians right when they insisted that Patton was scheming to provoke a clash with them, using these Nazi troops in a showdown? Dorn could not deny the justification for their apprehension. No explicit orders—nothing in writing, that is—could be traced to document the scheme. Nobody came forward to testify that orders had been issued orally by Patton or in Patton's name to assemble such a secret army. But the design was unmistakable. And the evidence that Dr. Dorn was piecing together was overwhelming. By simply tracking on the map the disposition of these SS-units, Dorn became convinced that there was a pattern in their "deployment." Their intended use appeared to be implicit in Patton's policies.

When the war had ended, prisoners were taken wholesale, in greater number than ever in history. Patton had his orders to disarm and disband them as quickly as they were pouring in, process them, and send them home. The wheat and the rye were tall in the fields, ready to be harvested. These hands were needed, or else famine would be added to the Germans' woes.

The system of releasing these prisoners daily by the tens of thousands was a masterpiece of efficiency. The Third Army's record was the best. But there were exceptions— the SS in particular. The "Eclipse" plan provided special treatment for them—it made SS men AA men—subject to "automatic arrest." They were to be segregated in special camps and dealt with more harshly. That was the theory. In practice, it was different.

Actually it was no big secret in the Flint Kaserne that

certain units of the German army had been left intact. And apparently it had made no difference whether they had been Wehrmacht or Waffen-SS. Entire quartermaster, engineer, and signal corps battalions were kept up in their own uniforms, with their arms cached nearby. There seemed to be a pragmatic purpose in their sustenance—these were disciplined and trained men with skills indispensable for the rapid rehabilitation of Germany. Some of them were sent into the forests, singing their old songs, in tight formations, to gather firewood and forestall one of the crises Patton anticipated—the cold. Nobody would be freezing through this winter in his district if he could help it! Others restored communications ahead of any other segment in occupied Germany. The roads were maintained, and the railroads were made to run virtually on time by these men. What if a soldier had been SS? The criterion was his immediate usefulness to the running of Bavaria!

Dorn found that other units, too, were maintained uniformed and armed, and no justification could be produced for their retention. Their very appearance was alarming. It belied the fact that these men were prisoners-of-war from a vanquished army. The German units vied with the Third Army in the polish of their showing. Their exemplary neatness and martial poise had little to do with the Germans' much-vaunted discipline and love of orderliness. It was these men's response to what they assumed was General Patton's call to arms.

It may have been but a ringing in their ears or the echo of their shattered hopes. But Patton, it seemed, did nothing to discourage their expectations of rebirth.

The great German army was a shambles. On one of his first inspection tours of the P/W cages, at a gigantic former compound of the Luftwaffe in Fuerstenfeldbruck near Munich, Patton had refrocked part of this unfrocked army. It was an SS cage, its inmates already segregated—presumably from the evils of their past. "On both sides of the broad road that ran through the camp," recorded the German Regiments-Adjutant, a Standartenführer only four weeks ago, arrested in the first wave of the roundup of SS officers, interned *sine die,* elected by his own comrades, and accredited to the Amis, "are housed two regiments of four battalions each, and a number of independent units. Every one of the batallions occupies its own cage, under joint command. The German command has its headquarters in one of the buildings on the airfield. Next door are the Americans."

The prisoners, lined up to greet the American general, all had the typical earmarks of defeat—they were listless and empty-eyed, clad in the tattered remnants of their uniforms. They were unshaven, unbathed, unkempt. Patton was appalled. He sent for the German camp commandant, who turned out to be a former Wehrmacht colonel with the old snap. "Aren't you ashamed?" Patton yelled at him. "These men belonged to a great army only a few weeks ago. Look at them now! They are a bunch of vagrants at a convention of goddamn tramps. Get yourself together, Colonel. Show me that you know how a German soldier is supposed to look."

Within twenty-four hours, the men were scrubbed and cleaned. When Lieutenant Colonel William J. Horne, Jr., exec of Patton's G-1, returned a few days later to see how the orders were carried out, he found nothing but spit and polish—SS men almost resplendent in their black uniforms—delighted that they were allowed to come out of their doldrums of defeat.

In several of the P/W camps—at Woergl, Kufstein, Oberaudorf—Walter Dorn discovered American officers serving stealthily as legates to these German units, practically performing the functions of liaison officers. With the help of a lieutenant colonel who was an assistant judge advocate, Third Army—an officer in Patton's own backyard who was as scandalized by these excesses as was Dorn—four such liaison officers could be pinpointed. One of them was a captain of the 301st Military Intelligence Company, another was a first lieutenant serving with the CIC, a third was a captain in G-5, the fourth was another captain, with USFET G-2. Each was an American of German or Austrian descent, one naturalized in 1939, the others made citizens when drafted into the Army. They had distinguished themselves in the Third Army during the fighting, and their loyalty to the United States was never disputed. But their lingering allegiance to their Germanic past and their common hatred of the Soviets singled them out as the perfect liaison officers to what Walter Dorn suspected was Patton's secret army in the making.

ON SEPTEMBER 25, Professor Dorn was back in Frankfurt with his report, and General Adcock recognized at once that the eleventh hour was upon them. The two men were in complete accord on these issues, and not because they were inherently dedicated to the same principles. No two men could have been more different by background, upbringing, and outlook on life. Dorn, whose philosophy harked back to Aristotle, Luther, and Jefferson, and who was the ideologue in G-5, had been a member of a brilliant group of scholars in Washington who had originally devised the basic design for the postwar weaning of the Germans away from Nazism. He was especially qualified because he knew how to strike an ingenious compromise between the different constituents of American and German political philosophies. His doctoral thesis at the University of Chicago in 1925 was a paper on "The Conflict of Humanitarianism and Reasons of State under Frederick the Great."

Dorn's ideas struck a gratifying response in the mind of his superior. Clarence Lionel Adcock was an engineer, not a historian, and a professional soldier, not a scholar. At West Point he was a classmate of Lucius D. Clay, who then pulled ahead of him and became the deputy military governor of Germany.

But while Dorn was impatient and righteous in his indignation, Adcock, the perfect West Pointer and ideal staff officer, preferred to go about the difficult case subtly and tactfully. Persuaded by Dorn that Patton was mad, for he could offer no rational explanation for what the general was doing and saying, Adcock borrowed a psychiatrist from the Medical Corps and sent him to Bad Toelz in the disguise of a supply officer, to observe Patton as closely as possible.

Then, knowing how indiscreet Patton could be and how reckless in the free expression of his innermost thoughts, he asked the Signal Corps in great secrecy to place a tap on General Patton's telephones and sneak a few microphones into his house in St. Querin. The latter arrangement appeared to be necessary because it was assumed, from certain passages in the Russian communications to General Eisenhower, that the Russians were also tapping and bugging Patton.

It might seem that Patton, never a paragon of mental stability, had become temporarily imbalanced. He was not mad by any means. But he appeared to be unsettled by the conflict between the spirit of his convictions and the letter of the directives to him. And in turn, that conflict produced, it seemed, a confusion, making him lose sight of prudence and common sense, and of control over his deeds and words.

There was no need for taps and bugs to record clandestinely Patton's incriminating pronunciamentos. He was scattering them far and wide at the slightest provocation, even to Adcock and Bull. When he was accused of having voiced his belief that Germany should be strengthened because, as he put it, "we were going to fight Russia in five years," he noted ruefully: "I never made the statement to anyone [except to Adcock and Bull], and only made it to them under the erroneous assumption that they were my friends."

At this critical time his exasperation erupted in a strange telephone conversation on the tapped wire with General Joseph T. McNarney, another old friend who had come to Germany to take over when Ike would go to Washington. Patton's outburst was precipitated by McNarney's admonition to speed up the release of SS troops, relaying the Soviet complaint that he was too slow in disbanding them.

"Hell," Patton exploded, "why do you care what those goddamn Russians think? We are going to have to fight them sooner or later, within the next generation. Why not do it now while our Army is intact and the damn Russians can have their hind end kicked back into Russia in three months? We can do it easily with the help of the German troops we have, if we just arm them and take them with us. They hate the bastards."

"Shut up, Georgie, you fool," McNarney told Patton. It was not only that he was shocked. He was fearful that the

Russians might be eavesdropping. "This line may be tapped and you will be starting a war with your talking."

But Patton refused to shut up. "I would like to get it started some way," he said, "that is the best thing we can do now. You don't have to get mixed up in it at all if you are so damn soft about it and scared of your rank—just let me handle it down here. In ten days I can have enough incidents happen to have us at war with those sons of bitches and make it look like their fault."

McNarney hung up. Patton turned to Colonel Harkins, who was in his office during the telephone conversation, and said to him: "We will need these Germans and I don't think we ought to mistreat people whom we'll need badly."

This conversation with its fantastic indiscretion and political naïveté, marked the beginning of the end. It was eventually the irrepressible sharing of his misgivings and hopes with colleagues in the Army, whom he regarded as like-minded friends, that buried him. Walter Dorn had formidable witnesses to bear him out.

16.

★★★★

The Professor versus the General

How slow the Shadow creeps, how when 'tis past
How fast the Shadows fall. How fast! How fast!

—*HILAIRE BELLOC, "For a Sundial"*

IT WAS SEPTEMBER 28, 1945. The weather was still too bad
to fly. Patton had to spend almost eight hours on the rain-
soaked road to meet General Eisenhower. En route he was
grandstanding to Major Merle Smith, his new aide, who
was the only member of his staff to accompany him. He
whiled away the boredom of the trip by plotting imaginary
attacks on enemy positions in the changing terrain, em-
placing his own forces here and there for rearguard action,
until he caught himself at daydreaming. "Hell," Patton said
with a bashful little smile, "I have fought my last war,
fellow. Other people will have to pick positions for the next
one."

Outwardly he did not seem to be worried. Somehow this
journey in the rain reminded him of the day less than a year
before when Ike had summoned him to Bastogne under
similar circumstances and he had thought that he might be
fired. But it turned out that the Supreme Commander was
merely "desirous," as it seemed to Patton, of the pleasure
of his company.

Now he thought the odds were in his favor—that he was

better off this time than on similar trips in the past. When called to London in the spring of 1944, after the ludicrous Knutsford incident, he was apprehensive that he might be relieved *and* court-martialed. Now he was certain that no court martial loomed in his future. And his feelings about being relieved were mixed. "Every time," he said, "I've been in serious trouble or thought I was, it has turned to my advantage."

He was confident, too, that he knew how to handle Ike—he had done it often before. His was a tricky and perhaps a little unseemly method, mixed in equal portions of contrition and opportunism. Sometimes it would be almost indecent, the lengths to which he would go with flattery and feigned humility. But usually it worked, even though Ike saw through some of his tricks and laughed them off.

WHEN HE ARRIVED in Hoechst, where Ike had his huge command post in the former I. G. Farben building, Patton was late, delayed by the downpour that plagued him all the way from St. Querin to Frankfurt.* He followed the special etiquette he had devised for such confrontations. His boyish grin wiped off his face, his expression was serious and serene. Even more than the solemnity of his look, the uniform he chose for the occasion was meant to show that he was cognizant of the gravity of the situation. He was wearing plain trousers instead of his fancy riding breeches, and had on the simple Eisenhower jacket. He had left his swagger stick and pistols in the car.

---

*What follows is the first complete account of the confrontation that cost General Patton the great army he had commanded in some of the greatest victories in history. The four men who participated in the showdown are dead. By the reluctance of three of them to publish their recollection of the proceedings, we only had Patton's version for all these years—dramatic and touching, and not entirely inaccurate. But it suffered from his habit of giving the benefit of the doubt mostly to himself. It was possible, nevertheless, to round out Patton's narrative with notes General Adcock had left behind, and especially with the rich lode of Professor Dorn's papers. Dorn's record was the more detailed and dramatic, but Adcock's jottings supplied a pungency that showed the mood of the meeting. From a synthesis of the three descriptions of the same session there emerges at last a more balanced version of the showdown.

It was already half past four in the afternoon when Patton was ushered into Eisenhower's enormous office, and whatever misgivings he may have had were dispelled by the old grin with which Ike was receiving him. The Supreme Commander tried to be friendly even as he was giving him a long harangue about his inability to keep his mouth shut. That may be so, Patton replied. But he also had his virtues, he said, the greatest being his honesty and his lack of any ulterior motives.

"No, George," Eisenhower said, almost solemnly. "Your greatest virtue is also your greatest fault. It's your audacity."

When they came to the topic of this emergency meeting, Patton still appeared incapable of facing the realities of his predicament. He was either unwilling or perhaps unable to comprehend the meaning of what Ike was telling him. The two friends were speaking on different wavelengths. On his part, Patton agreed that something had to be done and volunteered the opinion that it might be best if Ike simply relieved him. But Eisenhower said no, he did not intend to do that. As a matter of fact, Ike assured him, there was no pressure from the Pentagon to do anything so drastic at this time.

What then? In what seemed to be a sudden brainstorm, Eisenhower asked how would it be if Patton gave up command of the Third Army and transferred to the Fifteenth Army? Patton thought it was an idea off the top of Ike's head. "Apparently," he concluded, "Ike has to a high degree got the Messiah complex for which he can't be blamed, as everybody bootlicks him except myself."

Suddenly, Eisenhower stiffened as he pushed a button and barked to an aide: "Ask General Adcock to come in."

Patton was jolted. He considered Adcock a friend—but friendships had an elusive quality in Patton's circle. Some of his best friends wielded the finest stiletto at times, stabbing him in the back. (Even Bedell Smith! Only a few days before he had called to say: "You're my best friend, George. Probably that is the reason why you always give me my worst headaches." But Patton had no illusions. "He's a goddamn snake," he told Colonel Harkins when they hung up.)

But Adcock? General Adcock came in with a tall, well-fed, smugly smiling civilian whose properly deferential poise was obviously tempered by some cocky self-assurance. Adcock turned to Patton and asked, apparently in lieu of an introduction: "You know Professor Dorn, don't you, George?"

"No," Patton said. "I don't think we've ever met."

"Sir," Dorn said cheerily. "We didn't actually meet. But I believe Colonel Dalferes had spoken to you about me."

"Oh, yes," Patton said, still uncertainly. "Yes, yes. You're right, Professor. He did speak to me about you. Pleased to meet you at last."

Patton's confidence in the outcome suddenly sagged. He was not quite sure how to conduct himself in front of the civilian whose unexpected presence made him uneasy. But his nervousness was dissipated when it appeared that Eisenhower was more irritated with Dorn than with him. Moreover, it was obvious that Ike himself was also meeting Dorn for the first time.

"Who are you, Mr. Dorn," Ike asked, "and what do you do for a living?" His voice was edgy, his tone was testy.

"I am a professor of history, sir, on leave from Ohio State University," Dorn replied. "I am serving in your theater, General Eisenhower, as a special assistant to General Adcock for civil affairs, on account of my long interest in German history. It goes back to my study of Frederick the Great and the conflict between his humanitarian concepts, as reflected in his relations with Voltaire, for instance, and the demands of statecraft."

It was heady talk, heavy going, and it made Ike even more uneasy. Eisenhower was eager to come to the point. He was thinking beyond the confrontation—of the aftermath—and that agitated him. He thought it unbecoming to discuss Patton's fate with a civilian. But he was prepared to review with Dorn the crisis in Bavaria and the future of Minister President Fritz Schaeffer, whom he had always distrusted. It was, therefore, on this topic that the session began, with General Adcock telling Ike bluntly that Dr. Schaeffer had outlived his usefulness. "When the scandal erupted in the headlines," he said, "I asked Dr. Dorn to go to Munich and conduct a personal investigation. He's here, sir, to give you a firsthand report."

"Go ahead, Professor," Eisenhower said, his irritation still coloring his voice.

"Sir," Dorn said, "upon my arrival in Munich, I immediately notified Colonel Dalferes, General Patton's G-5, of the purpose of my visit. I then called on Major Ordway, chief of the special investigation unit concerned with the apparent collapse of the denazification program. I was amazed to find out from him that General Patton had ordered him to discontinue all further investigation of the Schaeffer government."

By then, Dorn said, it had been proven that Schaeffer had deliberately sabotaged the program. "He had instructed a number of his officials," Dorn continued, "to conceal their Nazi past in the questionnaires, and was employing sixteen prominent Nazis in his Department of Agriculture alone. I promptly revived the Ordway investigation, then sought an interview with Dr. Schaeffer himself." As Dorn related it, Schaeffer had admitted to him that he had disregarded his instructions. He had kept a former Nazi in his own Ministry of Finance, for instance, in spite of explicit orders to dismiss the man.

Dorn went on to relate how he had briefed Colonel Dalferes on his findings. "While I was with him in Munich," he now said, "a call came in from General Patton, who was in Bad Toelz. Apparently General Patton then told Colonel Dalferes that you, sir, had just asked him to come to Frankfurt to report on the denazification program directly to you. While I sat there, I heard Colonel Dalferes giving General Patton the substance of my findings."

Patton, who was listening intently, suddenly said: "That's true. Dalferes did tell me what the professor had told him. That's quite correct."

"I returned to Frankfurt," Dorn said, "and submitted my report to General Adcock, who at once turned it over to General Bedell Smith. It is my understanding, sir, that it has been communicated to you. I was also made to understand that this is why General Adcock has been ordered to be here and bring me with him."

This was a firm issue and a safe topic. Not only Dorn and Ordway, but several other investigating agencies also recommended that the Minister President and at least three members of his cabinet be dismissed on specific counts. They added up to the charge that Schaeffer and his cohorts represented "reactionary and generally undesirable elements in German life."

The matter of Schaeffer in Bavaria was a legitimate reason—indeed, a categorical imperative—to question General Patton's stewardship, especially when General Adcock now said that he concurred with Dorn's findings and recommendations. He urged that Schaeffer be relieved, not with just three members of his cabinet, but with scores of officials in his administration.

Ike turned back to Professor Dorn and asked him, still in an irritated tone and with subtle sneer: "You say you are a university professor. Well, tell me, Mr. Dorn, what would happen to your university if suddenly the president and that many faculty members turned out not to be acceptable, and had to be dismissed so peremptorily?"

"Nothing would happen," Dorn said. "Actually it may even be to the advantage of the school."

"Nothing would happen?" Ike asked incredulously, but with a slightly different emphasis in his voice.

"No, sir," Dorn replied, "nobody is irreplaceable."

"Well, Professor," Ike asked, "do you have any substitutes for Dr. Schaeffer and the people you tell us to fire?"

Adcock now felt it was his turn to answer that question. "Yes, sir," he said emphatically, "we have."

Suddenly, General Eisenhower was seized by what Dorn later described as "a holy rage of anger." Using his most colorful language, he exclaimed: "What in hell is the American Army doing in Germany if not to rid the German administration of notorious and conspicuous Nazis? The Russians are killing them off and we are keeping them in office." He launched into a long lecture about the thousands of GIs he had sent to certain death "in order to destroy this foul and inhuman thing called National Socialism." Then he stopped pacing in his enormous office, went to Dorn, and asked him brusquely: "Who the hell has the full responsibility for this goddamn mess?"

"Colonel Reese, sir, our executive officer at the Bavarian government," Dr. Dorn said bluntly, "and certainly the G-5 of the Third Army, Colonel Dalferes."

"As far as this Schaeffer is concerned," Eisenhower said, "I want him removed from office right away. As a matter of fact, I think he should really be thrown into prison for having so flagrantly evaded the real purpose of denazification and for his attempt to circumvent the military government." His fury still raging, he asked Dorn: "Could you name a person who'd be reliable enough to replace him?"

"Yes, sir," Dorn replied eagerly. "For Minister President we propose Dr. Wilhelm Hoegner, a moderate Social Democrat. He would, we submit, represent more properly and faithfully the American policies than Dr. Schaeffer."

"We've screened Herr Hoegner," General Adcock said. "He's a distinguished man in Bavaria's public life, highly respected as a politician even by his opponents. Although we haven't been directly in touch with him, we understand he would be available to take over on a moment's notice."

"Will it be safe?" Eisenhower barked. Adcock replied, "Yes, sir. We don't expect any untoward repercussions."

PATTON now felt completely left out. He hardly knew who Schaeffer was. He had never heard of Dr. Hoegner. Actually he did not think he had done anything to warrant this uproar. He was satisfied that his progress in denazification was second to none in the American zone. But Ike's apparent acquiescence in the proposed changes made him realize that he had just lost. A little stiff and distant when they were first introduced, he now went out of his way to be courteous to Dorn. In a tone dripping with honey, he asked: "Would you mind, Professor, spelling the name of the gentleman you've just recommended as a successor for Herr Schaeffer?"

"Not at all, General Patton. The name is Hoegner, sir, Wilhelm Hoegner—H-O-E-G-N-E-R," Dorn said. "General

Adcock has a copy of his curriculum vitae for you, General Patton. Moreover, General, we have all our recommendations down on paper, and if General Eisenhower so directs us, General Adcock will give you a copy of our memorandum as well."

"Could you tell me the names of the cabinet members," Patton now asked, "we ought to remove right away?"

"The three men in the cabinet are Langer, Rattenhuber, and Otto Hipp, General Patton," Dorn said, then went on to spell their names, too.

It was 6:30 P.M. The session had lasted an hour already. Patton now asked Ike whether he could use the telephone to call Colonel Harkins in Bad Toelz. He told Harkins to fire Schaeffer and the others, and to remove "all members of their ministries in any way tainted with Nazism"—adding in his notes afterward that he had done it "regardless of the setback it would give to the administration of Bavaria, and the cold and hunger it would produce."

Sitting in Ike's office like a student in a classroom, alert and eager in what had turned into a seminar, Patton was taking notes, nodding his head, polite and cooperative, and seemingly in full agreement even with Dorn's critical remarks about his management in Bavaria.

THE MEETING broke up shortly before seven o'clock in the evening. It was raining outside, harder than before, and it was pitch dark, one of those nights when one curls up in front of a fireplace with a drink, for a cozy time to be had indoors. The great outdoors was not fit for a dog. It had become a sort of ritual in every one of their showdowns for Ike to dish it out and George to take it on the chin—but when it was over, to revert to their old routine. Usually Ike had canceled everything for those evenings, in the wake of the reprimands, and entertained Patton with greater than his usual geniality and with a better meal than his usual bill of fare.

Patton now waited for Ike to drop the iron mask, and ask him whether he had any plans for the evening. But no— their long friendship was on the rocks. "I guess," Eisenhower said, "you're anxious to return to Bavaria as quickly as possible. You can have my special train, George." He looked at his watch and said gruffly: "It's leaving in half an hour."

Ike had wielded the ax this time. He had taken the Third Army away from Patton.*

---

*Like a bee after expending its sting, Dorn did not survive his victory in his job. Eisenhower somehow made him responsible for the distasteful "hatchet job" he had to perform, and told General Adcock to "get rid of that goddamn professor." Transferred to Berlin, where he worked for General Lucius Clay, he was fired again—"booted out" was the actual phrase—in the summer of 1947. He was the victim of "the conflict between humanitarianism and reason," which was the very title of his magnum opus about Frederick the Great—between ideals and realities, as it were, whose clash, as Sir Halford Mackinder recognized in *Geopolitics,* was the basic compromise democracy had to make in politics and geopolitics. It was an accommodation Walter Dorn was incapable of making.

17.

★ ★ ★ ★

Out of the Fog

"Duty, Honor, Country"

—*Motto of the United States Military Academy*

AT FIVE O'CLOCK in the afternoon of October 2, 1945, when General Patton was already at the door in his office to go home to St. Querin, the telephone rang. It was General Eisenhower calling from Frankfurt, in a tone that Patton recognized at once as Ike's special voice of discomfort. He said, "Yes, General, what can we do for you?"—and signaled Colonel Harkins, who was with him in the room, to pick up the extension telephone and listen to what Ike had to say.

"George," Eisenhower said, "word of the pending change has leaked in Berlin, and I have no choice. The pressure is mounting on me to announce your transfer, and I might have to do it earlier than we planned."

"How much earlier?" Patton asked.

"Well," Eisenhower said, "tomorrow at noon." It was that cut and dried.

The exact date of the transfer had been left up in the air—as a matter of fact, it was Eisenhower who had suggested that Patton keep the Third Army for another ten days to two weeks, until about the middle of October. The decision to relieve him virtually overnight was sudden and demeaning. But Patton understood. "I can't see that it makes any difference, General," he told the Supreme Commander, leaving the informality to Ike. "I'm all packed and ready to go, sir."

"Thank you, George," Ike said. "I knew I could count on you."

Alone with Harkins in the car, they started a little game of guessing at the source of the leak. It could have been only Robert Murphy, Harkins thought, and he was right, because it was Ambassador Murphy, back in Berlin, who had tried to be helpful by telling Edward Ball of the Associated Press about the disgrace of Patton's dismissal. But Patton did not blame Murphy. "Him I trust," he said. "It's that sonuvabitch Bedell Smith I suspect."

Then, however, he zeroed in on Eisenhower. "It must have been Ike, Paul," he told Harkins. "He scares easily, the bastard. He must have suddenly thought of the possible effects of giving me the sack, and decided to get this thing over with as quickly as possible, before it hurts him." He actually grinned. "The so-called leak," he said, "was a figment of his imagination, a euphemism for a damned lie."

He blamed the Jews as well as Ike and Bedell Smith— "the non-Aryan press" in the United States, prominent Jews like Henry Morgenthau and Felix Frankfurter in Washington, D.C., and, of course, the DPs in Germany. "I know the expression 'lost tribes of Israel' applied to the tribes which *disappeared,*" he told General Horace L. McBride when he called to commiserate, "and *not* to the tribe of Judah from which the current sons of bitches are descended. However, it is my personal opinion that this too is a lost tribe—lost to all decency."

Then another bombshell hit, more unexpected and bizarre than Ike's call. John O'Donnell of the *New York Daily News,* victimized by the Mason-Huss clique, "exposed" in a startling column on October 3 why Patton had been fired and who the string pullers had been behind the scenes. As O'Donnell put it, the soldier Patton had slapped in Sicily in 1943 was a Jewish boy—in fact, the columnist wrote, Patton had called him "a yellow-streaked Jew." Behind Patton's disgrace now, O'Donnell professed to know, had been "this republic's foreign-born political leaders;" waiting in ambush to avenge the insult to "their race."

Patton seemed to be too numbed to become excited about O'Donnell's scoop—although he knew, of course, that neither of the soldiers he had slapped was Jewish. The one, in fact, whom O'Donnell had singled out was a member of the Nazarene Church. Right or wrong, true or false, O'Donnell echoed his feelings. It was the Jews who had done him in.

But it mattered no longer. He was performing, as he put it, with his usual efficiency, playing the part of the undertaker at his own funeral. He cleaned out Rommel's desk in the Kaserne and emptied the drawers in Herr Amann's villa—days ahead of the original schedule of his departure.

IN THE EVENING of October 3, lounging in a plush hotel in Bad Nauheim, a group of middle-aged to elderly Germans sat in some puzzlement—as usual, they could not make out these Amis. Judging by their modest appearance— their ill-fitting suits and battered shoes, their close-cropped haircuts and bland cast of countenance—they seemed to be members of that nondescript class that supplied the town notaries, provincial bank managers, and station masters. But only four months before, these men had been resplendent in their uniforms with their lavish gold braid and the crimson stripe of their exalted rank on the pants. They were, in fact, some of the German generals whose name used to be featured breathlessly in the *Sondermeldungen*—the florid victory bulletins issued by Dr. Goebbels.

They were in Bad Nauheim on parole—prisoners-of-war in minimum-security custody—to help the American Army in the compilation of the history of the war by supplying the German side, in an unprecedented venture of this kind. It was unique for an army so fresh on its laurels to pause and take stock, in a project that was one of General Eisenhower's most significant but least known contributions as Supreme Commander. Not only did he conceive this monumental enterprise of scholarship to write the history of the war while the facts were still fresh in the minds, but he insisted absolutely that it be devoid of partisanship, chauvinism, or considerations for any personal sensitivities, including his own.

"Gentlemen," he told the staff, "I want you to come up with the warts and all—no cover-ups, no whitewash, no consolation prizes. Let the chips fall where they may! But let us learn from our mistakes."

The Fifteenth Army was the product of this concept, and it was living up to Ike's expectations. Even as the American staff had been handpicked, a search was undertaken for *German* senior officers who could supplement them—who knew the inside stories of their side of the war and were capable of recording them for posterity without fear or favor. By this time, even if only a few weeks after the end of the fighting, these former war lords of the Führer were settled comfortably and adjusted to their new roles—and on easy terms with their captors, pouring forth the innermost secrets of Hitler's general staff without any qualms or inhibitions.

They had experienced many surprises since their arrival in Bad Nauheim—the proof, for example, of the American Army's professional competence, infused as it was with a true spirit of democracy, the principle of civilian control that worked, the historic consistency of the Army's traditionally inferior place in the American government. But none of the surprises that these strange postwar days had in store for them had a greater impact on them than the banner headline in the afternoon's *Stars and Stripes*, which read:

PATTON FIRED

Written by Ed Ball with a Berlin dateline and by Wes Gallagher, chief of the AP Bureau in Frankfurt, the story, picked up from the AP wire by *Stars and Stripes* placed the blame squarely on the media. "Patton had come under the direct fire of the press," they wrote, "when correspondents quoted him as stating that he saw no difference in politics between the Nazi problems and Democratic-Republican squabbles back in the United States."

As for the Siberia for which he was heading, Ball wrote: "In his new post Patton, who commanded the Third Army in the drives across France and Germany, will head only the headquarters and special troops engaged in research work. The Fifteenth Army, newest of the forces in the ETO, no longer controls any occupation area or any divisions. At present it is a paper army."

The German generals had some difficulty in believing what they were seeing. Was it possible that this could happen to the great General Patton? Was this how his nation showed its gratitude to its most successful warrior? Was this the American way of making and breaking heroes? Yet in the light of their own recent history—when their Führer had rewarded Field Marshals Kluge and Rommel by forcing them to commit suicide and had sent the venerable Field Marshal von Witzleben to die on a meathook in the death chamber of the Moabit Prison—General Patton's fate was relatively humane.

In the column next to the big story was a smaller headline, closely related: "Jewish Camp Improves," it read. The story attributed the change for the better to Ike's intervention and Patton's dismissal. Both stories seemed to be overshadowed, however, by news whose headline topped them all, printed *over* the familiar logo of *Stars and Stripes* across the whole width of its front page. It read:

BOROWY, NEWHOUSER
TO START WORLD SERIES

On this October 3 in 1945, Americans were doing their best to forget the war. It was no longer the GI against the Kraut. It was Detroit against Chicago—and to hell with the rest.

THE SEND-OFF Patton was getting in Frankfurt was a mix of some regrets and plenty of relief. The United Press reflected the mood at SHAEF by quoting Lieutenant General Walter Bedell Smith. "George's mouth," he had quipped, "doesn't always carry out the instructions of his brain."

This time Patton planned his farewell himself, because he wanted it to be quick and painless. He was getting ample help from the elements for that. October 7, the day of his departure, was dismal for so early in the fall—with a driving rain, high winds, and a biting chill in the air. Held in the

cavernous gymnasium of the Kaserne, the transfer ceremony
of command of the Third Army from Patton to Lieutenant
General Lucian K. Truscott, his old cavalry chum, took less
than an hour, with another hour for lunch afterward. His
four corps commanders had assembled on the stage—the
Stars and Stripes on the right, the colors of the Third Army
on the left, his and Truscott's flags in the middle. They
were fluttering bravely in the breeze of the fans and gleamed
in the beam of the floodlights.

At noon on the dot, General Patton came in with General
Truscott, followed by Colonel Harkins and Colonel Car-
leton, the new chief of staff. Four ruffles and flourishes
greeted Patton, the four-star general. The ceremony ended
with the playing of three ruffles and flourishes for Truscott,
who was only a lieutenant general. The lunch reminded
Colonel Fisher of George Washington's farewell at Fraunces
Tavern. Chaplain James H. O'Neill thought of the Last
Supper. Patton himself quoted William Ernest Henley: "My
head is bloody, but unbowed." But he turned to Harkins
and told him in a whisper: "Let's get the hell out of here.
I've had enough."

At 2:30 P.M., General Patton boarded the Third Army
train for the last time. Gone by 3:00 P.M., he stood at the
window and looked out at the dripping skies. "I'm terribly
hurt, Paul," he said to Harkins. "Actually, though, it may
all work out for the best."

FOR ALL practical purposes, this was the end of an
era—General Patton's distinguished career was over. How
fast it had come to pass! Exactly four months before he had
been standing erect and proud by the Charles River in Boston, looking out on a multitude that had come to cheer him
and pay him homage. The passage of history, so slow when
in the making, so fast in retrospect, was not lost on Patton—
history never was. "The best thing that had ever come to
me thus far," he had told his people in the gymnasium of
the Flint Kaserne but a few hours before, "is the honor and
privilege of having commanded the Third Army." And the
best thing that had come to the Third Army, he thought,
was that he had commanded it.

His confidence in himself, in his greatness as a soldier, was unshakable in the face of the storm—it never needed any outside affirmation either. He was so imbued with that faith that he had no doubt in his mind about his firm place in history. He almost agreed with General Giraud that he was second to none—not even to Napoleon, with whom Giraud was equating him—agreed *almost,* that is. He was actually convinced that he had in fact surpassed the Little Corporal. "He and I fought the same battle," he told his son, "but my means of progress were better than his." And to a friend in Boston he wrote: "My private opinion is that practically everybody but myself is a pusillanimous son of a bitch."

Would the Allies have won the war without Patton? Of course. Could they have won it in 1945 without Patton? Perhaps. It may be an axiom that no man is indispensable, although that truism is a little limp in the case of generals. Lee was as indispensable to the Confederate cause as was Grant to the fortunes of the Union. And before them, George Washington was the indispensable man of the Revolutionary War. General Marshall had been proclaimed "indispensable at home" in so many words when he was denied his wish to get the Supreme Command in "Overlord." Admiral King proved indispensable, as did General Eisenhower, on opposite grounds—King for his tactless ways, Ike for his superb diplomacy.

Patton, too, was indispensable, certainly according to the standards of the poet—by being faithful to that which existed nowhere but in himself. Patton did not know very well how to make himself wanted. But he understood how to make himself *needed.* He thus proved indispensable to Ike's crusade in at least three great operations: the breakout of Avranches and the pursuit down the Cotentin Peninsula, the relief of Bastogne that smashed the Germans' desperate last offensive in the Ardennes, and in the Palatinate where he ushered in Germany's doom.

Yet Patton was kicked about after the war. He was subjected to certain failure by an impossible assignment, for which he was obviously unqualified. And now he was set adrift in waters he could not possibly negotiate.

It was a shabby payoff. Patton hobbled a little but remained of his feet. He even managed to produce a little smile on his pale, thin lips—probably by forgetting the humiliation on these days and thinking of the not too distant future. He could not see any yield in being a martyr too soon. "I will resign when I have finished this job," he said en route. "I hate to do it but I have been gagged all my life, and whether they are appreciated or not, America needs some honest men who dare to say what they think, not what they think people want them to think." He was getting his case in order for that day, by assembling the *evidence*—collecting his papers in numerous big boxes, and keeping them close by for future reference. Broken and hurt though he was, George S. Patton, Jr., remained a formidable foe to reckon with.

IT WAS ALREADY October 8, in the pitch darkness of the autumn dawn, when General Patton's special train reached Bad Nauheim. Only three months before, on his return from his triumphal American tour as the conquering hero, he was given that spectacular reception in Bad Toelz as the new master of Bavaria. Now he was sneaked to his new command like a thief in the night. Greeted by a single officer to show him the way, and by his new chauffeur, a fresh-faced, eager lad from Kentucky, he was driven in an old Cadillac through the deserted streets to a villa on the Hohen Weg, a home from which its owner, the manager of a coal mine, had been evicted.

The Fifteenth army had been created in January 1945, in the panic caused by the Battle of the Bulge, especially for Lieutenant General Leonard T. Gerow, till then a corps commander. But it never had a chance to fire a shot in anger. So swiftly had the Germans crumbled west of the Rhine, that no need was left for the employment of Gerow's army as a combat unit. It was ordered to hold the west bank of the Rhine as a quasi-occupation force.

Then another mission was found for this stillborn army. It was left in the care of Gerow, a veteran infantry leader with a well-known intellectual bent, to prepare a broad-based history of the war in Europe. For Patton, though, the

Army's fightingest general, this seemed to be another incongruous assignment. The Fifteenth Army had no troop units except the handful it needed for keeping house. It operated through committees of officers who wrote so-called General Board Reports—actually analytical studies on the tactics, techniques, organization, and administration in both camps of the late war.

It had worked with smooth precision under Gerow, but in a casual atmosphere at a leisurely pace. Now that Gerow had moved to a job Patton was coveting, to command the Army War College in the States, and Patton took over the paper army, the work picked up speed. He had set a deadline for the completion of the Board Reports: December 26, 1945. It was a reasonable date. His people were straining on the leash. Like Patton himself, everybody was eager to go home. His policy was sound and scientific. "I am convinced," he told his new staff on his introduction, "we should avoid the error we made at the end of the last war of taking this war as an approved solution for future unpleasantness. We must use this factual account simply as a datum plane from which to annually build a new set of jigs and dies."

Patton did not dislike his new job. Somehow the paper army appealed to him. It was in keeping with what he called his natural academic tendencies. And it was so much better than governing Bavaria. Like the Army's old historical section in Washington, he told his wife, it was a place for "writing a lot of stuff which no one will ever read."

Imperceptibly in his tranquil assignment, with the momentum of the change growing but slowly, Patton was reverting to his former self, becoming, in fact, a little wiser, and much more patient and tolerant. It seemed he was being calmed by the salty fresh air and steady climate of Bad Nauheim after the mystic haze and rampant ghosts of St. Querin. Closest to him now as before, and most sensitive like a seismograph to the tremors of his mood, Colonel Harkins was the first to notice the change for the better.

Here in his custody and care were assembled the great captains of the defunct German army—officers and gentlemen, it seemed, whom Patton always professed to respect

even across the barriers of war, and had come to regard
with something akin to admiration and affection as his sym-
pathies for the Germans grew. Here working for him now
was the erudite Hasso von Manteuffel, ace among the Panzer
generals, as was Kurt Student, the brilliant and adventurous
commanding general of the parachute troops. Here in this
institute for advanced military studies, picking the best
brains the Wehrmacht had, were stars like former Panzer
generals Erich Brandenberger, Gerhard Count von Schwerin,
and Fritz Kraemer; such proven greats among the infantry
leaders as Franz Beyer (who had a doctorate of philosophy
aside from his rank of full general)—also Hans Schmidt,
Siegfried P. Macholtz, Guenther Blumentritt (the former
chief of staff of Marshal von Rundstedt), Wolfgang Lange,
and a host of other crackerjack German commanders.

Yet Patton, for all his new-found respect for their skill
and prowess, ignored them. He regarded this elite of German
military leadership exactly as what they were—prisoners-
of-war, just performing a chore—and apparently it did not
make any difference to him whether they did sentry duty
in Feldafing or wrote military history in Bad Nauheim. He
had withdrawn into his shell on the Hohen Weg, coming
out only to accumulate more honors from those foreigners
who evidently appreciated him more than did his own countrymen. He collected citations, the freedoms of cities like
Metz, Toul, Reims, Château Thierry, Saarguemines, Thion-
ville, and Verdun, more and more decorations (including
a big one from the French general he called "Du Gall")—
and tremendous cases of indigestion after festive banquets
honoring him in Copenhagen, Paris, Stockholm, Brussels,
and Liège.

The Russians still bothered him. "Anyone," he told an
AP correspondent in the only interview he granted after the
fall, "who says there won't be a future war is a Goddamned
fool." He devoured anti-Russian literature his brother-in-
law was sending him from Boston, avidly read correspondence describing the horrors of life in the Soviet Union, and
studied tracts about the global conspiracy of the Communists. But even in this respect, his flamboyance evaporated
and his ardor cooled. He refused to discuss, as he phrased

it, "American-Russian relations." And, for that matter, he kept mum about his own relations with General Ike.

Apparently the trance was over. There were distinct signs that the nightmare was gradually lifting from his mind.

IN THE MEANTIME, the O'Donnell column of a few weeks back was having reverberations. It was so wrong in its details and so preposterous in its inference that the roof was caving in and the columnist had to scurry for cover. On October 19 he had to print an abject retraction, conceding that the soldier Patton had slapped was not Jewish, and the "foreign-born political leaders" had no part in Patton's downfall. O'Donnell then closed the case by apologizing.

But his column had done some good—it had brought the Jewish issue into Patton's sharpest focus. All of a sudden, he was not so sure. Jews and gentiles were writing him, some applauding his anti-Jewish views, but in such uncouth terms that he recoiled from their praise. Most of the letters protested the very insinuation that he was ever really motivated by anti-Semitism.

A telegram that moved him to tears came from Joseph Wilner in Washington, D.C., who had lost two sons in the war, one of them a captain in the Third Army. He knew, Wilner wrote, from his dead son's letters that Patton would have been congenitally incapable of making such a scurrilous remark about a Jewish soldier fighting under him. Would Patton himself set the record straight?

From Little Rock, Arkansas, Adolph Goldsmith mailed him approvingly an editorial from the *Arkansas Democrat* that called Patton "the soldier's general." "We former soldiers of the Third Army," Goldsmith wrote, "are practically unanimous in [our] belief that '[our] boss' got a d--ed rotten deal."

This was Middle America, and it did not make any difference that it was speaking with the voice of Jews.

Then came missives from people he knew and whose views he trusted. Daisy Harriman—Mrs. J. Borden Harriman, American Minister in Denmark, and a woman of considerable attainments—was advising him that "certain ultra-nationalistic groups are seeking to exploit your high prestige for their own selfish purposes." She implored him to "disavow the implications" read into his reported remarks.

What really settled the issue in his mind was a letter from Bernard Baruch, the financier, writing with exquisite tact, but forcefully, in language Patton could not misunderstand. Back at "Lucky Forward" in April he had played host to Baruch, so old and frail, it seemed, that he had to travel with a doctor and a nurse. But Baruch proved affable and ebullient, with so many interesting stories to tell and so close in his views to Patton's opinions, that he thoroughly delighted his host, who insisted that he stay for lunch. It had been the beginning of an important friendship. It was Baruch, back in Washington, who had lobbied most vigorously for Patton's transfer to China or the Far East, intervening personally with their friend, General Marshall. Although he failed, they kept in touch, and their correspondence reflected the sincere admiration they had developed for each other. "We are all proud," Baruch had written, "of our soldier-general, George Patton, and a glow of pride goes over us for your many accomplishments." Not even Patton himself could have said it any better. And Patton was prompt in returning the compliment. "Meeting you was a very great pleasure," he wrote to Baruch, "because, when one meets famous men, one is sometimes let down. In other words, they do not live up to their reputations. In meeting you, this was certainly not the case. You were just as great as I had always pictured you."

"I feel very strongly," Baruch wrote on November 8, "that when an Army or Navy man has made a good record in service, he should not be taken and placed in a position where an entirely different kind of ability has to be shown or developed." He went on to say in retrospect, "I wanted to see you when you were here as I wanted to warn you of some of the things I thought you would have to meet in Germany. However, that is all past."

It was becoming rapidly so. Now, in the heat of Patton's weirdest battle, Baruch found the right theme and the wise words to set Patton straight. He sent him a clipping in which another former officer of his, one Kurt E. Wallach, protested vigorously the charge of anti-Semitism raised against Patton. Interviewed at a hospital in Galesburg, Illinois, where he was recuperating from his wounds, Lieutenant Wallach said: "The attacks on General Patton as an anti-Semite sound strange to a Third Army soldier. Our general was on the record as knowing only good soldiers or bad soldiers and not soldiers of different religious preference." The young lieutenant closed with a flourish by saying, "It will be the pride of my life that I had the honor to serve under a man like General Patton."

In his covering letter, Baruch reassured him that Patton was "a great soldier" no matter what his detractors said, and that he resented the criticism leveled at him. The Wallach letter, and Baruch's note, then set the tone for Patton's replies. To Wilner in Washington he wrote, still rather subdued: "I am glad to have the opportunity of categorically denying that I have ever made any statement contrary to the Jewish or any other religious faith." To Goldsmith in Little Rock he was more personal and friendly. "I am deeply moved," he wrote, "by the fact that one of my soldiers who, so far as I know, I did not have the pleasure of meeting personally should take this much interest in my career."

"I cannot understand," Patton wrote to Bernard Baruch, "who had the presumption to attribute to me anti-Semitic ideas which I certainly do not possess." To Daisy Harriman he denied indignantly that he had ever made the statement attributed to him, and added with new emphasis that he never had the temerity of as much as examining the religious or racial antecedents of the men he "had the honor to command." Discussing the malodorous aftermath of O'Donnell's column, he told Colonel Harkins, closing the case: "I feel like Leonato—done to death by slanderous tongues."

HE WAS FORTUNATE to have the colonel so close to him, when General Gay happened to be at home on leave, because Harkins, a proper Bostonian, the son of a noted music critic, and a man of good taste and delicate sentiments, fathomed better than Gay the depth of his anguish, and knew best what Patton needed in this period of his delayed change of life. It was November—and Harkins was arranging a surprise party for him that was designed as more than just a celebration of his birthday.

It was held on November 11, in the ballroom of the Grand Hotel in the famous spa of Bad Nauheim, reputed to be the best hotel in Europe, where during happier days William Randolph Hearst regularly summered with Miss Marion Davies. It became a grand show. The waiters wore their tails for the first time in years. The sommelier reopened the hotel's celebrated wine cellar. The chef was a distinguished Hungarian, found in one of the DP camps, who had been for three decades master chef of the National Casino in Budapest, the exclusive old club of Magyar aristocracy, whose cuisine before the war was reputed to be the most exquisite in the world.

Patton had a great time among his friends, who had come for the occasion from far and near. He had stopped smoking a few weeks before, as he did from time to time. But now he was handing out big cigars, and lit one himself from a box which his friend Harry Whitfield had sent him from Virginia as a birthday gift. At his best again, Patton was a synthesis, as the historian Emil Ludwig described him, of a high-strung, gallant horse, a poet in Lord Byron's mold and an artist of war—the perfect grand seigneur.

Patton was sixty years old on this birthday, and he had forty days to live.

BOOK THREE

★ ★ ★ ★

Whiplash

I am forgotten as a dead man out of mind: I am like a broken vessel . . .

—Psalm 31:12

18.

$$\star \ \star \ \star \ \star$$

Into the Valley
of the Bug

"THE THEATER COMMANDER directs as necessary in the military service," the orders read, "that General George S. Patton, Jr., 0-2605, USA, Hq, Fifteenth U.S. Army, proceed on or about 14 December 1945 from his present station to Paris, France, for movement by first available air transportation to the United States."

Signed by Brigadier General R. B. Lovett, Adjutant General of the ETO, the orders allowed Patton only 165 pounds of baggage while traveling by air. That would be all the spoils of war the conquering hero could take home. But Patton did not care. He was eager to leave. In fact, he had already arranged to be with his wife and children in plenty of time before Christmas. And though officially he was going on a thirty-day leave, he was planning the trip as his last junket in the Army. He was getting out.

Patton was all packed, whiling away his last Sunday in Germany. He was in one of his *Que será, será* moods, resigned at last to the idea that he might be better off "outside the tent pissing in, than inside the tent pissing out." As usual, he viewed his prospects with the touch of opportunism that eased his pride through many a crisis, rather than the fatalism he now feigned.

He was planning to make the homeward journey in the grandest style. Although the Adjutant General had arranged for him to go by the first available air transportation, Patton secured berths for himself and Meeks on one of the battle-

ships that had escorted him to Casablanca almost exactly
three years before—only three years! Making the crossing
in five days, he could not be sure where he would land.
But then he would take a month to decide what to do. "If
I get a really good job," he wrote, "I will stay. Otherwise
I will retire." The only sure thing in his plans was that he
was through with this job. "I don't intend to go back to
Europe," he vowed.

General Geoffrey Keyes, his protégé and devoted friend,
who now commanded the Seventh U.S. Army in Heidelberg, hated to see him leave. Yet he was relieved at the
same time, if only because, he mused, Patton might get out
of all the controversy once he was back in the States. Keyes
had driven up to Bad Nauheim the night before, to have a
sort of last supper in the villa on the Hohen Weg, and was
Patton's house guest overnight, planning also to spend the
Sunday. But early in the morning, before breakfast, a call
from his headquarters summoned him back to attend a conference at 11:00 A.M. By the time Patton was up and dressed,
Keyes was up and gone.

Patton was peeved when told that Keyes had left, because
now he did not know what to do with himself in the stifling
boredom of this miserable place where it was getting so
dark so early. He then decided to do what he usually did
on Sundays—go hunting birds in the fields below Mannheim, a little over a hundred miles away, beyond the urban
conglomerate that blighted the region south of Frankfurt.
He still had Major General Hobart Gay, his perennial chief
of staff and friend, to keep him company. Gay was always
ready and willing to go wherever Patton went.

WHAT HAPPENED on this December 9, 1945, had
its beginning just a little over six months before. On May
20, in the process of dissolving his household staff, Patton
sat down to write a farewell note and commendation for
Master Sergeant John L. Mims, the young soldier who had
served as his driver throughout the war. It was a most
unusual document in the Army and extraordinary even for
Patton for the extravagance of its praise.

"You have been the driver of my official car since 1940,"

it read in part. "During that time, you have safely driven me in many parts of the world under all conditions of dust and snow and ice and mud, of enemy fire and attack by enemy aircraft."

Preserved for posterity by special order of the Adjutant General, the document looms large as a memento in the light of what happened to General Patton in the end. "At no time," he had written for Sergeant Mims, "during these years of danger and difficulty have you so much as bumped a fender."

Since Mims's departure, however, Patton was living dangerously on the road, racing from one mishap to another. He almost perished in a crash when the pole of an ox cart hit him on the head. As recently as October, he had again been in an accident, and had been slightly hurt. Patton was accident prone all his life. But his close shaves had become ominous after Mims's replacement by a succession of drivers picked at random from the Third Army's motor pool.

Then Patton was given a regular driver again as one of the changes wrought by his transfer to the Fifteenth Army in Bad Nauheim. He inherited the man from General Leonard T. ("Gee") Gerow, whom he himself was replacing; the new man came with glowing recommendations. His new chauffeur was a handsome GI—a mere kid from Sturgis, in western Kentucky, near the confluence of the Treadwater and the Ohio northeast of Paducah, a coal, grain, and livestock area.

Nineteen-year-old Horace L. Woodring—called Woody by all—raised Cain and raced fast cars with his brother Hickman in whatever little blue grass there was in Union County. His whole life seemed to have been wrapped up in automobiles. His passion for the road drove him from home at the age of fifteen to become a truck driver. In the Army three years later, he attended chauffeur's school in Fort McClellan, Alabama, and was assigned to the infantry, of course. But when frostbite disqualified him for other jobs as an infantryman, he was placed in the motor pool at last.

He had become General Gerow's driver by a fluke after he was demoted from sergeant to private for being caught in several acts of fraternization. When every man in the motor pool seemed eager to become Gerow's chauffeur in the newly formed Fifteenth Army, it was decided to end the contest by giving the job to the lowest-ranking and youngest man in the °outfit. Woody qualified on both counts. He was not yet nineteen. And he had just hit rock bottom after his third demotion.

Neither his addiction to speed nor his youth appeared to be special assets in the responsible assignment, but Woody Woodring had other advantages going for him. He was a dashing young fellow, a smart dresser, an eager beaver at everything he did, and was not unduly awed by the biggest of brass. Gerow had grown to like him, and Patton took to him instantaneously. After Mims's cautious driving, Woody's ways at the wheel were like a fresh breeze. Patton ran at an accelerated rate everywhere he went. Mims was wont to defy him, but Woodring drove to suit his desire for speed, ignoring bystanders and military police alike, rushing through checkpoints and railroad crossings at seventy miles per hour. "Woodring is the fastest and the mostest," Patton quipped, and related proudly how Woody had driven him from a meeting in Belgium, where he had lunched with King George VI at Liège, to a ceremony back in Bad Nauheim in under two hours—covering the distance of one hundred fifty miles at a clip of more than seventy miles per hour. "He's better than the best Piper Cub," Patton said, "to get you there *ahead* of time."

On this morning of December 9, Horace Woodring, who had been upped a notch to Private First Class by General Patton in the meantime, although he was fraternizing more briskly than ever, was called out of bed. He had his quarters across the street in a handsome villa he shared with the rest of the household staff. "Get the *limousine* ready," Meeks ordered him on the intercom. "The General and General Gay are going hunting."

There were no garages in the houses on Hohen Weg, so Woodring kept the general's cars on the street—the jeep, the command car, the sedan, and the limousine. The limo, which Meeks had ordered for this outing, was a sturdy

Cadillac, vintage 1938, Model 75—one of the last of the hybrids designed especially for European roads—assembled in France from parts made in Detroit. It was a roomy automobile built for seven passengers; the distance between the partition behind the front seat and the rear of the back seat was at least six feet. It was spic-and-span as usual— Woody was spending hours at a time to give it the high polish Patton insisted on, whether it was the liner of his helmet or his limousine.

It had a clock on the partition, and Woody remembers that it stood at three minutes to seven o'clock in the morning after Sergeant Meeks had called and he went out to the street to make ready the Caddy. Then a call was put in to Joseph Spruce, a sort of sergeant-at-arms, to join the caravan on the Hohen Weg with his quarter-ton truck.

The party left some time between seven and eight, with Patton and Hap Gay in the old limousine, and Joe Spruce in the truck with the guns and the dog. It was cold to begin with, and it was getting colder as they moved out of the balmy hollow in which Bad Nauheim was situated. With plenty of time on his hands, Patton decided to do something he had always had in mind—to inspect some ruins on the way down. He told Woodring how to get there on a side road that wound up a hill. It was cold below, but it was freezing on the hill. The ruins were covered with fresh snow. As was his custom on such excursions, Patton climbed out of his warm limousine to subject the ruins to close examination. His stomping around had thoroughly soaked his boots and socks. Returning to the car, he climbed in up front next to Woodring, to dry his feet in the warmth of the heater and the motor.

This was the first in a series of coincidences that made Patton's passage totally unpredictable and impossible to monitor. Back in the valley after leaving the ruins, the general's limousine was about to pass a checkpoint on Route 38, one of those Woodring was wont to ignore or race by. As if someone were shuffling his fate this time, the mighty conveyance was flagged down by a young MP, himself shivering in the cold. The rookie compounded the insult by demanding that they identify themselves, despite the four stars on the car and the unmistakable presence of General Patton in it.

"The guy must be crazy," Woody exclaimed as he got out to berate the obviously inexperienced sentry. Then Patton, too, climbed out of the front seat and walked around to the boy. As unpredictable as ever, he patted him on the back and told him in a pleased paternal voice: "You are a good soldier, son. I'll see to it that your C.O. is told what a fine MP you make."

Then occurred another unexpected turn. Patton yelled back to Sergeant Spruce to bring over the dog and place him next to Woodring in the limousine. "The poor thing," he said, "is going to freeze to death in your goddamn truck." Instead of climbing back in front, he took his seat in the rear again, and that was where he was, sitting in his favorite half-assed way for the rest of the trip—squatting at the edge of the seat, as if ready to jump out, instead of leaning back and enjoying the comfort of the limousine.

They were riding through the Kaeferthal, on the outskirts of Mannheim, half built up and half a shambles, with rows of depots and modest factories all along the road, and the drab houses of the people who worked in them. It was the dismal landscape of suburban slums, bad to begin with and left in worse shape by the war. No landmarks distinguished this stretch, only the litter of that war, still piled high everywhere.

It was now about half past eleven. They had been on the road for more than three hours—having lost time inspecting the ruins, and more time coming upon General Keyes's car, in which he had left Nauheim ahead of them. Keyes's driver was with the stalled car. But Keyes was nowhere in sight. Apprehensive, Patton insisted that they investigate. They discovered that not even the commanding general of a conquering army could prevent a car freshly serviced in the motor pool from breaking down. Keyes's car had died, and his driver had not been able to make it start again. The general had then thumbed a ride back to Bad Nauheim to get a mechanic or another car. On the way up, he passed Patton in the limousine but did not stop him. When Keyes's driver told them that his general had gone for help, Patton continued. By his mishap, Keyes only missed his eleven o'clock appointment. But Patton never made it to the pheasants.

THIS TEN-MILE STRETCH of the Autobahn just outside Mannheim running through the Kaeferthal was lightly traveled on this crisp late fall morning in 1945. Nobody professed to know why it was called the "Valley of the Bug." The neighborhood had no more insects than the other suburbs in this marshy land between the Neckar and the Rhine. But perhaps the bugs had been there in force before the asphalt came, and cement and brick covered every square inch of the countryside. Now it was the birds to the south— Hungarian pheasants by the thousands—bringing in hunters from near and far.

On the romantic Rhine, Mannheim was celebrated mainly for its cultural heritage—Mozart lived there briefly, and Schiller saw his early plays performed in the city. For a passing touch of melodrama, the playwright August von Kotzebue was murdered in Mannheim by a wild-eyed student who objected to the reactionary propaganda von Kotzebue was spreading as the paid secret agent of Czar Alexander I.

The Kaeferthal itself had but a vague claim to fame. Until this morning, it was marked only by a Castle Eichholzheim on one of the hills over the river, where the notorious Baldassare Cossa, the antipope who called himself John XXIII, had been confined by order of the Council of Constance in 1418. But this morning, more than five hundred years later, the spot was fated to enter the history books of Americans.

Traffic was sporadic. Few Germans were permitted to drive, and there were not many American installations in these parts. Strategic though it was, the area had been taken at a somewhat leisurely pace by the Third Army and Sixth Army Group. But resistance, offered by remnants of the army Hitler managed to scrape together, flared up now and then, as middle-aged men with ulcers pitted themselves against the American juggernaut. Boys of the Hitler Youth

caused most of the trouble. Because of the decision to prolong the war, the region had been badly damaged by bomb-
ings and artillery barrages. And now, seven months after
V-E Day, the people were just climbing out of the ruins,
tidying up the landscape by piling up the rubble of the battle
on both banks of the Autobahn.

At this time of the morning, three vehicles in particular
were moving on this stretch of the two-lane highway, all
of them American. One was a big GMC Army truck, the
second a windswept jeep with a couple of young officers
of the military police. The third car was General Patton's
Cadillac. They were going their separate ways—until suddenly they converged in an event that would link their passengers for the rest of their lives.

SHORTLY AFTER it left the checkpoint and passed
a Polish DP camp on the left, the Cadillac was brought to
a halt at a railroad crossing, as its red lights flashed and its
gates came down to let a train pass. It turned out to be an
enormously long freight train, but Patton did not seem to
mind—he did not stop chatting with General Gay and never
changed his precarious way of sitting on the left rear seat.

He was carefree and genial, his curious little eyes darting
from left to right as he surveyed the countryside. The litter
of the recent war was still there, everywhere, forming an
endless canyon of junk. Pointing to the right bank of the
road, Patton said: "How awful war is! Look at all those
derelict vehicles, Hap!" Then he turned in the other direction
and said: "And look at that heap of goddamn rubbish!"

On the far side to the south, waiting also for the lights
to stop flashing and the gates to go up, the GMC truck stood
in a row of waiting vehicles. It was a Signal Corps truck,
not one of the Quartermaster Corps as it has been identified
previously. And it was not heading for a depot on the southern side of the road, which did happen to be in the neighborhood. Its driver was T/5 Robert L. Thompson, supposedly from Chicago, Illinois—he was never pinpointed with
any exactitude. On the contrary, he was allowed to vanish
before long to become the mystery man of the incident.
Thompson was on the road, it seemed, in violation of the

rules and of his own routine. He had no orders to go anywhere this Sunday morning; he had taken out the truck as a lark for a joyride, with a couple of his buddies, after a night of drinking, mostly beer. The three of them were in the cabin, in another infraction of the rules. Only two persons were allowed, and there were no exceptions for hitchhikers.

Lieutenant Peter K. Babalas, a twenty-year-old Bostonian, one of the MP officers in the jeep, was on his way to his office in town to check on any overnight reports. He was mildly hung over from too much celebration the night before, but that Saturday night was not different from all the recent Saturday nights in the officers' mess, now that the war was over and the beer from a nearby brewery and the wines of the Rhine were plentiful. With him was his second in command, Lieutenant John Mertz, a young lawyer from New York. When they had seen the Cadillac bearing its four-star insignia, Mertz asked, "Who do you think he is, Peter?"

"There's only one four-star brass left in the European Theater," Babalas said. "Patton. He must be Old Blood and Guts, Johnny."

It was now 11:45 A.M., and the train was gone at last. The gates were up and the traffic began to move. Hardly was the limousine over the tracks and rolling when Lieutenant Babalas heard the muffled sound of a crash to his rear. He looked over his shoulder and saw "the dust of a collision rise from the pavement," as he put it—the big car entangled with the truck. From what little he could find out, by questioning Woodring and Thompson only perfunctorily at this time. Lieutenant Babalas concluded that the truck had made a sudden sharp turn to the left just as the Cadillac was moving up, and the famous crash on Route 38 had become unavoidable.

"The driver made no hand signal," Woodring told the lieutenant. "He just turned into my car. I saw him in time to hit my brakes, but not in time to do anything else. I was not more than twenty feet from him when he began to turn. The GMC was barely scratched, but it hit us solid with its front fender."

The morning after, the South Germany edition of *Stars and Stripes* described the accident in a one-column headline: "Sedan Runs Head-on Into Army Truck." But it was nothing so violent as that. Just starting up after the idle wait at the railroad crossing, neither the truck nor the limousine was moving at even twenty miles per hour. Judged solely by the velocity of the crash, the accident appeared to be trivial. The radiator of the Cadillac was smashed, but not a single window of the big car was broken. The right front fender of the sedan and the motor were pushed back, but no other part of the body had so much as a scratch. And though three persons were riding in the car, only one appeared to be hurt.

"My neck hurts, Lieutenant," the four-star general complained to Babalas, who leaned over to him, ready to help. He *was* Patton. "I'm having trouble breathing, Hap," he told Major General Hobart R. Gay. "Work my fingers for me."

Gay tried it several times, until Patton said: "Go ahead, Hap. Work my fingers."

Babalas's attention was distracted by the more spectacular injury Patton had suffered when he bumped his head into the steel frame of the Cadillac's partition. He was bleeding profusely, his entire face smeared with blood.

The lieutenant took charge, radioing for an MP detail. By then an ambulance was on its way. In a nearby doughnut dugout, a pretty Red Cross girl had looked up from her cup of coffee at the instant of the crash. She jumped to her feet and ran five blocks to the 290th Combat Engineering Battalion, where she summoned help. Moments later, Major Charles Tucker, an upstate New Yorker commanding the engineer outfit, was at the scene with Captain Ned Snyder, his medical officer, and the ambulance.

Doc Snyder found Patton motionless, reclining in the back seat. As he bent down, the young Texan heard the general say in a voice that was barely audible: "I think I'm paralyzed."

"How serious is it?" Babalas asked the doctor, trying to decide where to take Patton. The nearest hospital was in Mannheim. The better and bigger one was in Heidelberg, twenty miles away. "He broke his neck," Captain Snyder whispered. "He needs the very best we've got."

In a maneuver of quiet efficiency that was remarkable if not unique, General Patton was properly bundled up in minutes and eased into the ambulance. At 12:20 P.M. the little convoy left the Kaeferthal, rushing Patton to the outskirts of Heidelberg, to the new station hospital of the Seventh Army.

Patton was conscious throughout the trip and composed, but he did not utter a word on the twenty-five minute ride.

19.

★ ★ ★ ★

Ward A-1, Room 101

AT SEVENTEEN MINUTES before one o'clock in the afternoon the ambulance turned left, passed through the guarded gate unchallenged, and stopped outside the second entrance to a three-story whitewashed building. The big sign on the narrow turf in front of a long row of attached houses was new—only recently had this compound, formerly the barracks of a German cavalry unit, been taken over by the Seventh U.S. Army. As the sign proclaimed, the former *Kaserne* was now the HEIDELBERG HOSPITAL—OPERATED BY THE 130TH STATION HOSPITAL—COMMAND-OFFICER COLONEL LAWRENCE C. BALL.

General George S. Patton, Jr., arrived at his destination to take up residence in the last home he would ever occupy.

Word of Patton's coming had been flashed ahead in a roundabout way, from the radio of one of the MP jeeps at the scene of the accident. But apparently the signal failed to arrive or was pigeonholed on this lazy Sunday. Nobody was at the gate when the ambulance turned in, and the hospital was unprepared for the coming of its most illustrious patient. Colonel Lawrence Ball, the commanding officer, was around but hard to find. But Lieutenant Colonel Paul S. Hill, Jr., the thirty-nine-year-old chief of the surgical service, was quickly found by a young medic who stopped him outside the mess hall, just coming from lunch.

"Colonel Hill," the young man told him breathlessly. "General Patton has just come in, sir."

Hill was skeptical. "Oh yeah?" he said. "Who else?"

"He was in an accident, sir. He is badly hurt. He was brought from Mannheim..."

Before the sentence was finished Dr. Hill was at the ambulance outside the emergency department, which he himself had just set up, and which was about to be put to its first big test. Scion of a family of distinguished surgeons from Maine, Paul Hill was the chief surgeon—a first-rank operator with three years of experience in the war and a big peacetime practice back in Saco, a bustling factory town in the southern part of the Pine Tree State.

Even before he took the time to fill out the usual forms, Hill busied himself with more urgent matters. He interviewed Captain Snyder, the ambulance driver, who called his attention to Patton's ghastly head wound on which dressing and adhesive tape had been applied in the ambulance, to hold down the scalp, which was hanging in a loop. Hill also received the sketchy details of the accident from Lieutenant Babalas.

GENERAL PATTON was formally admitted to the 130th Station Hospital of the Seventh Army at 12:45 P.M. on December 9, 1945, only an hour after the accident and less than three minutes after his arrival. Dr. Hill had found him lying on the litter fully clothed. His neck was flexed forward, causing him some pain on the left side. He was fully conscious, oriented, and alert. But he was very pale. His lips, congenitally albino-pink, were now cyanotic with a light bluish hue. His feet were cold. Evidently he was in considerable shock.

They had to move him up only a few steps and barely fifteen feet inside the pavilion to the outpatient room in what now became Ward A-1, where the litter was placed on the operating table so that Patton would not be unduly disturbed. For the same reason, his clothing was cut away but not removed from under him, and a portable machine was brought in to take the preliminary X rays. Hill immediately sent for plasma and whole blood.

During his first ten hours in the hospital, Patton received a total of 1,500 cc. of plasma and 300 cc. of whole blood, type "A" Kahn:N, from four GI donors—Salvatore Di-

Bernardo, Serial No. 4201611; Jack DiMesa, 42044833;
John Mazzarella, 420171166; and Nick Lorro, 4207267—
carefully crossmatched in the laboratory by Captain
J. B. Cherry. The donors did not know, of course, whom
their donation was helping over the first hurdle.

Color quickly returned to his face. And his blood pressure, which registered 86-over-80 on arrival, began to rise
slowly, going to 110-over-76 in the afternoon. His pulse,
45 and soft at the time of admission, became a regular 60.

The first thing Dr. Hill did in the outpatient room was
to attend to the head wound, which was still bleeding a
little. The temporary dressing had come off, and when he
peeled off the adhesive tape, he got a good view of the
forward part of the skull down to the bone, through the
flaplike laceration. There was no fracture, it seemed, but
a long, deep Y-shaped ragged gash that extended from the
bridge of the nose up and over the scalp from which the
skin was hanging like a noose.

Patton had been thrown forward and upward when the
truck hit his limousine, and had either struck the railing
above the driver's seat or hit the glass partition between the
front and the back of the car. Patton himself told Colonel
Hill that he thought he had fallen against a clock in the
partition and was scalped by its sharp edges. "The goddamn
thing," he joked feebly, "must have been an Indian time-
piece." Pending more elaborate surgery, Dr. Hill cleaned
out the wound and gave Patton a tetanus shot.

Shortly after 1:00 P.M. Colonel Hill was ready to make
his first examination, a task he approached with some trepi-
dation. He found no evidence of any long-bone injuries.
But he was dismayed to find flaccid paralysis of all mus-
culature of the thorax, the abdomen, and the extremities.
There was loss of sensation beginning about an inch below
the collarbones, the slender bones joining the breastbone
and shoulder blade. There was no sensation to the tip of the
shoulders, none in the arms, and the legs and flanks were
similarly anesthetic. The ankle reflexes were absent. Several
times when Patton coughed, his right leg was drawn up.
But when Dr. Hill asked him specifically to move his limbs,
his sole response was a feeble outward rolling of his right
leg.

Although he was paralyzed from the neck down and was in a mild shock, and although he was punctured by an assortment of needles and was lying on his back with plasma dripping into his veins, Patton was rather amused by the attention he was getting. Actually, he had some of his zest, and was genial. While Hill was working on him, the general was repeating to himself in a low whisper: "This is a damned ironical thing to happen to me." Seeing his lips move, Captain Frank S. Yordy, an attending physician who had rushed over to help, asked Patton what he wanted, and Patton replied with a genuine smile: "I don't want a damned thing, Captain. I was just saying, 'Jesus Christ, what a nice way to start a vacation.'"

Then seeing how solemn and cramped everybody around him was, apparently intimidated by his rank and awed by his reputation, Patton told them in a clear, bantering voice: "Relax, gentlemen. I am obviously in no condition to be a terror." He chuckled and the others chuckled right back.

An officer looked in tentatively; Patton spotted him, and called out: "Come in. One more or less can't hurt." He turned out to be Father Andrew J. White, a Catholic chaplain. When he finished reading the ritual for the sick at the operating table, the padre said: "Incidentally, General, your own chaplain has just arrived and will soon be here to see you." He was speaking of the Reverend William P. Price, an Episcopalian, who was the hospital's regular chaplain. "Well," Patton said, "send him in right away and let him go to work. Obviously I need it."

He was composed, completely cooperative, complaining only of the pain in his neck. He responded to all the tedious questions doctors ask on admission. No, he could not move his arms or legs. Yes, he had bled only moderately from his head wound. No, he did not know whether he had become unconscious at any time. But General Gay chimed in to say that he had passed out once, for about a minute. The last time he urinated, Patton recalled on request, had been up on the hill amid the Roman ruins, at around 10:00 A.M. And the reason, he thought, for his breathing with all that difficulty was that he had had a severe cold recently and his nose was still stuffed up.

As Colonel Hill was stumbling on scar after scar of quondam injuries, Patton delved keenly into highlights of his medical history, his rich prose becoming slightly blue in retelling some of his more outré mishaps. He had broken his nose, his ankles, both legs, several ribs—too numerous to list them all. He had wounds galore—a head wound, injury to his left eyebrow, a gash over his right eye, lacerated lips again and again. He had fallen on his head twice, and had been kicked in the head by horses. "Do you think it shows?" he asked.

Most of his injuries were brought on by horseback riding and in football, except the one extra-special wound, remnant of World War I, whose prominent scar was enshrined, so to speak, in a crease in his right buttock. Patton made the most of this. "It may be symbolic for something or another," he said, "that the only permanent memento of my historic service in the First World War is this goddamn scar on my ass."

WHEN CAPTAIN SNYDER recommended that Patton be taken to Heidelberg although there were hospitals closer by, he made a fortunate choice. New as it was—it had opened only in October—and though its equipment was not quite complete yet (in fact, they had to send away for an iron lung when it was thought Patton might need one), it had other advantages. Its excellence was guaranteed by Colonel Ball's ability as a medical administrator.

The colonel had been found in the meantime, and he did his best to make General Patton comfortable. A true Southerner from the corn-and-tobacco belt in Tennessee, he was an outgoing, jovial man in his late forties, and though a regular officer in the Medical Corps, he oozed the geniality and informality of a country doctor. An administrator of skill and tact, Ball left the treatment of Patton to his professional staff, primarily to Dr. Hill, who, as chief surgeon, was the most competent to take the case.

With Hill, Ball's relations had blossomed into friendship during their service together in the 116th Evacuation Hospital, which Ball had commanded until it was broken up at the end of the war. When Ball was then given this hospital in Heidelberg, he immediately sent for Hill, and for other members of his old staff: for Captain J. B. Cherry, for instance, in charge of the laboratory, and Gerald P. Kent, a young captain in the office of the chief of the Medical Service.

The three nurses Ball assigned to the case were Lieutenants Ann Maertz of St. Paul, Minnesota; C. Bertha Hohle, who also hailed from Minnesota, from a tiny place called Grygla; and the chief nurse, Lieutenant Margery Rondell of Indiana. A number of German orderlies were also assigned to Patton—Horst Limbeck, Carl Yunck, and Heinz Goslar.

Ball's team was a devoted, dedicated, and competent group of first-rate medics. But it was still not good enough, or classy enough, for a patient of Patton's importance. The super-hero of the war deserved the super-doctors the Medical Corps could supply. As soon as he had talked things over with Paul Hill, Colonel Ball called Major General Albert W. Kenner, the chief surgeon of the theater and one of Patton's old buddies, who had been his chief medical officer in "Torch," the landings in Morocco in 1942, to discuss with him the care Patton needed.

Colonel Hill then phoned Colonel Earl E. Lowry, a thirty-eight-year-old native of Robeson County in North Carolina, a graduate of Vanderbilt University Medical School, who had moved up quickly from a residency at the St. Thomas Hospital in Nashville, Tennessee, to chief surgeon at the Army's Lawson General Hospital in Atlanta. Since the end of the war, Lowry had served as the chief consulting surgeon of USFET (U.S. Forces European Theater), and was Colonel Hill's immediate superior in Frankfurt. Hill asked Lowry to assign the best neurosurgeon he had in the huge general hospital in Frankfurt, and Lowry told him he would send Captain William R. Duane, Jr., a handsome, elegant young Philadelphian. He did more than that. He and Kenner boarded a plane right away, bringing Duane with them.

By two o'clock in the afternoon, the calm of the 130th was shattered. Within a couple of hours, a dozen generals, led by Geoffrey Keyes, came to call, and then it seemed that every correspondent, reporter, stringer, free-lance rubberneck, and press photographer in the ETO was descending on the hospital. It was getting so bad that special guards had to be posted at the gate to curb the traffic. Inside, white-helmeted, white-gloved MPs were stationed as sentries, a couple standing stiffly at the door of the outpatient room to keep out the flock of uninvited callers.

DOCTORS KENNER, Lowry, and Duane flew down from Frankfurt together and checked in at 2:30 P.M. Their examination confirmed Colonel Hill's diagnosis, which, in turn, was supported by the grim evidence of the X-rays. The spinal column behind the neck had been fractured or dislocated at the third or fourth vertebra, and that injury had apparently caused the spinal cord to be transected. It was a classic case of whiplash—the cervical injury caused by a violent thrust of the head forward and back. In simple layman's terms, Patton had suffered a broken neck. Because of the damage to his spinal column, which had damaged the nerves of the spinal cord, he was paralyzed from the neck down. And there was that awful laceration of his head.

The doctors decided to combat the apparent dislocation of the vertebrae with Crutchfield tongs, which are placed on the head to hold pounds of traction, five pounds initially in Patton's case. The urinary bladder had to be kept empty by what is termed an indwelling catheter. And, last but not least, the laceration had to be repaired.

At 5:00 P.M. the head wound was cleansed and sutured. The catheter was inserted. The tongs were put in place under local anesthesia. Patton was keenly interested in what the doctors were doing to him. When the first stitch was taken, he exclaimed: "Seventy-two." Colonel Hill asked what he meant, and Patton said: "That was the seventy-second stitch I've taken in my life."

The operation was over in forty minutes. At 6:45 P.M. Patton was moved to a small room on the floor that had been prepared for him across the corridor, next to the commandant's office, and was put to bed, off the operating table and the litter at last. The hectic day had five hours left to midnight, and Patton was kept busy most of the time. He was given penicillin several times. Then more X-rays were taken, this time of the painful neck, confirming the worst. Patton's spinal column had been fractured, not merely dislocated.

There was a momentary excitement when the tongs slipped off, apparently because of the shape of Patton's head—it was too flat and square, not the best for holding up Dr. Crutchfield's weird contraption. Then came another fleeting commotion at the bedside when a flicker of movement was noticed in the shoulder region of the left arm. It proved a false alarm.

His temperature rose to 102 degrees, but otherwise his general condition was becoming stabilized. The most hopeful sign was that his old heart held up well and strong. And his mood was steady and good—Patton took everything in his stride, and he was proving a model patient. With the help of a little morphine, he slept a few hours—oblivious at last to all that was happening to him. Otherwise, too, the discomforts of the traction apparatus, the repeated blood transfusions, and the frequent punctures of the hypodermic needles did not disturb him. His paralysis was too far gone for him to feel anything and to be bothered by these routine inconveniences of the sickroom.

His condition was critical. The prognosis was guarded.

HE AWAKENED at 9:00 P.M. and saw Colonel Hill sitting on his bed with a piece of paper in hand, obviously waiting for him. "Sir," Hill said, "I have here something for you that I am sure will please you." He began to read a telegram from Washington, D.C., which he had taken down in his own handwriting.

"I am distressed," the message read, "at the painful accident which you have suffered and want you to know that I am thinking of you at this time. You have won many a tough fight and I know that faith and courage will not fail you in this one. I am thankful that Mrs. Patton will be at your side to strengthen and sustain you."

It was from the Commander in Chief, former Captain Harry S. Truman.

It really pleased Patton. He was fond of the new President, an old comrade-in-arms from World War I. And this was the first word he had that Mrs. Beatrice Patton was coming.

Then things calmed down, the lights were dimmed, the last wayward intruder was evicted, and the hush of the night enveloped Ward A-1. Colonel Hill dropped in once more to supervise the last transfusion of the day. Then he called on Colonel Ball, who was holding his own vigil in the office next door. His commanding officer asked the surgeon what he thought of the case.

Dr. Hill pulled a sheet from his pocket, the typewritten first summary he had prepared from notes he took during the day and night.

"What do you think of General Patton's chances to recover, Paul?" Colonel Ball asked.

"None," Hill said.

"What chances does he have to live?"

"From very slight to none."

They stopped at the door to Room 101 and looked in. General Patton was asleep. It was time to turn in.

20.

★ ★ ★ ★

"Hooray for Colonel Spurling"

INJURIES to the spinal cord had accounted for about twelve percent of all neurosurgical casualties in World War II, a number considerably greater than had been anticipated. Damage to the spinal cord resulted mostly from gunshot wounds, but also from fractures or fracture-dislocations of the vertebrae, some of which were caused by traffic accidents like the collision that had just felled General Patton. There had been, to begin with, no inclination to subject these injuries to surgical exploration. There was, in fact, a dominant school in the Medical Corps that questioned the value of such explorations of spinal injuries.

The opposing school conceded that, by and large, an operation might improve the lot of only a relatively small proportion of patients. But it was argued that in certain cases, especially those in which the bone injury was limited to the vertebral arches, debridement of the spinal canal— the excision, that is, of tissues and dead matter from the interior of the injured part, designed principally to prevent infection—occasionally did result in dramatic improvement. After a battle royal between the two schools, those in favor of surgical intervention eventually carried the day. During World War II, the Medical Corps adopted the policy of giving neurosurgical casualties the benefit of prompt surgical exploration, certainly in cases when there was reasonable doubt concerning the true extent of the damage to the spinal cord or the brain.

The author of this dictum and the victorious champion of the policy was a towering genius in American neurosurgery, Dr. R. Glen Spurling, a fifty-one-year-old Kentuckian, who had given up his practice in Louisville shortly after Pearl Harbor to serve as one of two chief neurosurgical consultants in Europe throughout the war. Spurling was a rare man for all seasons in his chosen profession. He excelled as a teacher of neurosurgery to general surgeons in the Army, and was given credit for holding "mortality and morbidity from battle wounds of the nervous system to an unprecedented low" in his theater. He had been awarded the Legion of Merit earlier in the year, given him as a parting gift. Colonel Spurling and his distinguished colleague, Dr. Barnes Woodhall, were by this time on their way out of the Army. In December 1945, seven months after V-E Day, there was no American neurosurgical consultant of their caliber in the European Theater.

As soon as General Patton's condition was diagnosed definitely, and his doctors concluded that his spinal cord had been transected, General Kenner sent out an SOS for Colonel Spurling, calling the Surgeon General in Washington and pleading that Spurling be sent immediately to Heidelberg to take over the case. But the Colonel was not at his station. Inquiries revealed that on December 7 he had gone home to Louisville to reopen his practice in preparation for his imminent separation from the Army. He was expected back in Washington on the twelfth, but it seemed nothing could be done about him in the meantime.

Nobody questioned the surgical skill of Doctors Lowry and Hill. But they were not neurosurgeons, and Dr. Duane, though recognized as one of the outstanding specialists in a younger generation of neurosurgical consultants, lacked the stature and the experience the celebrity of the patient and the complexity of the case demanded. The Surgeon General in Washington instructed General Kenner to get in touch with the War Office in London and ask for the loan of Brigadier Hugh Cairns, professor of neurosurgery at the Oxford University School of Medicine and chief neurosurgical consultant to the British Army. An Army plane was sent to London to fetch him, and on the morning of December 10, in heavy weather, Brigadier Cairns flew to Heidelberg.

Accompanied by Lieutenant Colonel Gilbert Phillips of the British Army, Cairns arrived at the hospital at 11:00 A.M., took the history from Lowry and Hill, then saw Patton at noon. His examination confirmed the earlier diagnosis of flaccid paralysis of all four limbs. Even as Cairns was going over him, there was indistinct movement at each of the shoulder joints, but even this was but a sign of involuntary motion at best. No tendon reflexes could be produced. There was complete loss of all sensation below the fourth vertebral body in the neck. The impression that Professor Cairns gained was that the spinal cord had been transected as it was feared, albeit only partially, with an incomplete lesion apparent at the fifth neck vertebra.

The new stereo X-rays were brought in, and they showed more distinctly that the body of the third neck vertebra had been fractured and was slightly compressed. But Brigadier Cairns believed nevertheless that Patton's chances of improvement were not entirely hopeless. He did find some encouraging signs—a questionable motion, for instance, in the right hand. Patton himself professed to have felt the tapping of the patellar tendon (his right knee), also the pinching of the skin of the chest on the right thoracic wall, which he localized accurately.

The prognosis was uncertain. The only change Brigadier Cairns recommended was in answer to a recurring trouble with the Crutchfield tongs that refused to stay in place. He was all in favor of the traction, of course, to correct the dislocation of the vertebrae, but he suggested that they dispense with the tongs and use zygomatic hooks instead. These are like ordinary fish hooks, and are affixed to the cheekbones on the side of the skull. The hooks were inserted into Patton's cheekbones under the eyes at considerable discomfort to him, especially since they were now holding ten pounds, twice the weight of the earlier traction.

In spite of the ordeal, and despite the guarded prognosis, Patton remained the perfect patient. Although he was lying on his back most of the time, had pain in his neck, and was uncomfortable with the hooks, he was conversing easily with Brigadier Cairns about mutual acquaintances, joking with Colonel Phillips, and had a reasonably good time in general. His color was good and his breathing was fine except for the blocked nose. His temperature was still high—102.6 oral—but it was coming down (it registered 100 the next morning). His pulse, respiration, and blood pressure were all stable, even if each was slightly off.

There was really not much even Brigadier Cairns could do. After he had seen Patton again later in the afternoon and on the morning of the eleventh, he recommended that they force more fluids, and keep him and his room cool. If sedatives should become needed, he proposed Luminal. But no change in traction.

This turned out to be his last consultation. Word had reached Colonel Ball that Spurling had been found, was flying to Germany by special plane General Eisenhower had assigned to him, and would be arriving in Heidelberg by the twelfth. It was good news—not because Colonel Spurling could be expected to do anything drastic to improve Patton's lot, but because he was bringing with him Mrs. Beatrice Patton. Much was expected from her presence at her husband's bedside.

IT MAY BE A CLICHÉ to say that Patton was like a drowning man who saw his whole life pass before his eyes, but he was in a sense drowning, and was in fact thinking back on incidents and episodes in his past. There were so many, and they were so interesting. He had lived an exciting, compulsive life, never standing still for a moment, always searching, seeking, probing.

The hurdles were high and so were the stakes. He had his ventures and his adventures, his ups and downs, his summers of fulfillment and his winters of discontent. Even after the recent chain of disappointments, nothing rankled him any more. He was looking back on the bygone years without misgiving or remorse, satisfied that he had lived a useful life and that God had been good to him. "It is rather sad to me to think," was the way he put it, "that my last opportunity for earning my pay has passed. At least, I have done my best as God gave me the chance."

This willful and resolute man, flamboyant and egotistical, had flirted with destiny and frequently seduced fate. But looking back on it all, he concluded that it had been worth the effort. The long pursuit was yielding its supreme reward. He was passing into history.

Would he want to live? Or would he prefer to die? Colonel Hill was seeing him all the time, dropping in at regular intervals, and then in between, to check up, to take his pulse, to comfort, but mostly to listen. For Patton, paralyzed as he was, turned out to be great company. He was, it seemed, too new to this unexpected dénouement and did not know yet how to adjust to it. After all, he was no longer giving orders but was taking and obeying them. There he was in bed, on his back looking at the fresh white paint of the ceiling all the time, nowhere to go, nothing to do, nobody to cuss out.

He had been in hospitals before, with all kinds of mishaps like broken legs, acute indigestion, mysterious headaches, tonsillitis, conjunctivitis, influenza, and chicken pox. But he was never really *sick*, he now told Colonel Hill—there never was anything *really* wrong with him.

Thinking back on his hospitalizations for the benefit of Hill, he recalled one particular instance most vividly, and not only because it spoiled his Christmas in 1919. G. S. Patton, Jr., yes sir, a full colonel in the Tank Corps at thirty-four, commanding the 304th Brigade at Fort Meade in Maryland, even though his permanent grade in the Regular Army was still merely captain. His job at Meade was a big joke amid the doldrums of the postwar Army—he served as the recorder of the board deciding whom to retain and whom to release among the temporary officers. It was a sinecure, enabling him to do as he pleased, especially to go on riding to his heart's desire all over the lovely Maryland horse country.

He was extraordinary as usual, corresponding with General Pershing almost on equal terms, inviting the Chief of Staff repeatedly to come down to Meade for a cavalry outing. Pershing could not make it, he was too busy with his own boards. But Patton kept on riding, rain or shine, summer or winter—until December 22. On that day, he was exercising a horse on the target range when the animal bucked. He was thrown forward on the pommel of the saddle, sustaining an obscure injury that Major Herbert C. Mallory, surgeon of the Tank Corps, diagnosed as bilateral orchitis.

Patton went out of his way to secure the proper treatment for his orchitis, whatever it was. He took to bed for a whole month, then hired a famous specialist, Professor Hugh Young from nearby Johns Hopkins in Baltimore, to help Major Mallory keep his promise and cure him "entirely."

"And do you know, Hill, why I was so determined to get well?" he asked with a chuckle. "The reason was simply because the injured part of my anatomy happened to be my testicles, and no man worth his salt should regard a disability like that as trivial."

Colonel Ball and Brigadier Cairns also caught him in anecdotal moods. Composed and lucid, and astoundingly cheerful and talkative, he was making life very easy for his doctors and nurses, and for the obsequious German orderlies doing the menial chores. It did not take long for everybody at Ward A-1 simply to adore him.

Patton's body may have been moribund. But there was nothing macabre in his spirit. "Everybody," Dr. Hill recalled, "who was privileged to observe his last battle from close up was awed and fascinated by the incredible contrast between his *joie de vivre* and his inward reconciliation that his end was near. The same afternoon that he entertained me with the tale of the inflammation of his testicles, he told one of his nurses that all the fuss about him was a waste of the taxpayers' money, because he was 'fated to die' within the fortnight. He didn't guess, he didn't contemplate. He knew."

It was only a few weeks before, on October 22, that he had confronted the prospect of death in a letter to Major General James G. Harbord, one of his oldest confidants, whose friendship harked back to their Mexican days under Pershing. "It had always been my plan to be killed in this war," he wrote, "and I damned near accomplished it, but one cannot resort to suicide."

The mysteries of death did occupy his thoughts. They intrigued him. He often talked about death and wrote an ode to it. People die naturally, soldiers die professionally. His favorite anecdote about Frederick the Great was the tale of Old Fritz in one of his battles, egging on a timid platoon of young soldiers. Standing up while the youngsters cowered to escape the enemy's fire, the Prussian king poked them with his cane, shouting at the top of his creaky voice: "Attack! Attack, you cowardly rascals! What do you want, you miserable poltroons? *You can't live forever!*"

WHEN HE WAS TOLD that his wife was coming, he had been flat on his back for thirty-six hours, awake most of the time, doing a lot of thinking and thinking a lot of her. He never brought up the question of his clinical chances in his conversations with his doctors, and skirted the issue of life or death even with Ball and Hill.

He never liked to worry Beatrice. He always apologized when he did something that upset her. He never wanted her to be around during any of his crises. But now he could hardly wait for her arrival. They understood each other. She was the only person in the world whom he could tell that he expected to die, without getting back the usual happy talk. Beatrice Patton was a real soldier.

ON DECEMBER 10 Colonel Spurling's three-day leave was up, and he was returning to Washington, because he had an appointment scheduled for the twelfth that he could not miss or postpone. He was going by train. He did not want to take a chance on flying in the unpredictable winter weather.

Midway between Louisville and Cincinnati, the conductor brought him the message that an emergency had come up and he was to get off in Cincinnati, where he would find out what it was. At first Spurling was apprehensive that something might be wrong at home. But in Cincinnati, the station master, who greeted him on the platform, handed him a telegram signed by James Ulio, the Adjutant General. It read as follows: YOU WILL ABANDON THE TRAIN IN CIN-

CINNATI, PROCEED TO THE AIRPORT IN CINCINNATI, WHERE
AN ARMY PLANE WILL FLY YOU TO WASHINGTON, HENCE TO
GERMANY.

"What's this?" Spurling asked the station master.

"Haven't you been listening to the radio, Colonel Spurling?"

"I haven't. I have been on the B&O since noon," he said.
"There's no radio on the train."

"Well," the station master said, "General Patton has been
seriously injured in Germany and I have a suspicion, Colonel, that this has something to do with your orders."

An Army car was waiting for him at the station, and he
was driven to the airport. It was late in the day—seven
o'clock and dark. The weather was very cold and sloppy.
Yet a C-47 was waiting for him with its motors warmed up
to start on a moment's notice. When Dr. Spurling was
hustled onto the plane, he chanced to tell the pilot that he
had had nothing to eat since noon and was getting hungry.

"Okay," the pilot said, "so am I. This isn't much of an
airport, sir, but they have a snack room and we may be able
to get a couple of hamburgers if we hurry. They close at
eight."

"Do we have time?" the doctor asked.

"You ought to know," the pilot said.

"As a matter of fact, I don't. What happened to Patton?"

"Don't you know?"

"Nobody's told me anything."

"From what I heard on the radio," the pilot said, "he was
in an automobile accident and broke his neck."

Colonel Spurling understood instantly why they needed
him in Germany. But he also sensed instinctively that there
was not much he would be able to do. He forced a smile.

"Well," he said, "in that case we do have time for the
hamburgers."

IN WASHINGTON at that late hour, he found a little
woman waiting for his arrival in a small room of the terminal
of the Military Air Transport Command. She was Mrs.
Beatrice Patton, all set to fly to her husband's bedside in
the company of Lieutenant Colonel Kirwin, an aide General

Marshall had assigned to her. At 10:00 P.M., they boarded a C-54 and were off. Except for a small curtained cabin improvised for Mrs. Patton, the plane was the usual bucket-seat job, the type from which paratroopers were dropped. Now there was seven thousand pounds of mail tied down in the center. Aside from a few aluminum seats, the interior was otherwise bare. And it was cold in the cabin. Even as Colonel Spurling was freezing under a couple of blankets, Mrs. Patton materialized.

Coming from the mild weather of Louisville, Dr. Spurling was clad in a light woolen uniform, wearing shorts, a cotton pullover, and summer socks, and his trenchcoat without the lining. "Here," Mrs. Patton said, "put this under your battle jacket." She handed him a heavy sweater and ski pajamas.

The flight to Newfoundland took five and a half hours. Dr. Spurling spent most of the time spread out on the floor, trying to sleep under a layer of five blankets. At Stephensville, they were received by the commanding officer of the base with his staff. "Twice before," Spurling recalled, "I had landed here. But then I was just another officer, herded through the crowd with the usual sharp, curt commands." Now they were given a royal welcome. Whisked in the C.O.'s limousine to the officer's club, they were escorted to comfortable rooms to rest up for the second leg of their odyssey. It was five o'clock in the morning. December 11. From frozen Stephensville, under three feet of snow, they took off for the Azores. When they were perhaps an hour or so out, the pilot picked up an SOS with orders to look for a wrecked plane in the waters below. Diving out of an overcast at ten thousand feet to a thousand feet, they circled in a thirty-mile radius and spotted an orange raft with people on it but no sign of life. The pilot radioed the position of the craft to the control tower, then flew on. It was later found that the survivors of the wreck had frozen to death on the craft.

They were behind schedule. It was already 5:00 P.M. when they were allowed to leave the Azores, and even then only at the resolute insistence of Mrs. Patton. The weather was too foul ahead, but she insisted that they take a chance.

It was then between the Azores and France, on the next to last leg of the journey, that Spurling received the first detailed word about Patton's condition. "According to the signal," Spurling wrote, "he had sustained a fracture of his cervical spine, with paralysis—a bad outlook under any circumstances." And there he was on what struck him as a hopeless, even a senseless, mission. "I had doubts," he wrote, "over the wisdom of risking the lives of ten perfectly healthy people, three passengers and a crew of seven, in order to get to the bedside of a man who probably had no chance at all to survive."

21.

★ ★ ★ ★

The Countdown

ON DECEMBER 12, when *Stars and Stripes* arrived in the hospital, the day's Patton story on the front page was delivered in a two-line banner headline over three columns:

FLAT ON HIS BACK, SKULL CLAMPED,
PATTON CALLS FOR SHOT OF WHISKY

It was set in type considerably larger than that with which the paper had broken the news of the accident. Giving Lieutenant Bertha Hohle, Patton's night nurse, as the source, the piece described how the general, hovering between euphoria and depression, required the constant attention of nurses because he refused to take any nourishment. "I have to be there," the article quoted Nurse Hohle, "because he never wants to eat or drink. He says he won't drink unless he gets a shot of whisky."

Ward A-1 was scandalized. Lieutenant Hohle was close to a nervous breakdown. Frantically she asked Ken Morgan, the hospital's public information officer, to issue a denial, insisting that she had not told "anything like that" to any of the reporters. "He is a patient patient," she added tearfully, "ideal, does not complain. If I were in his position with that uncomfortable traction apparatus, I'd probably be doing a lot more griping than he has done."

On the tenth, the slight signs of improvement appeared to be more pronounced. The temperature was down at last. And though Nurse Hohle thought during the night that Patton was slightly disoriented as to the time, he woke up quiet

and lucid, rested and refreshed. As if bearing out Professor
Cairns's initial impression that he had suffered an incomplete lesion of the spinal cord, he produced a twitch of the
right and a lesser movement of the left hand.

"General condition very satisfactory," Captain Duane
wrote on his chart. "There has been a definite slight improvement." Even Colonel Hill, for all his skepticism, noted
that his condition was "good."

Actually, Lieutenant Hohle noted during the night that
her patient had to be given Luminal before he dozed off,
and then slept only intermittently. While he lay awake, he
seemed to be in a deeply contemplative mood, taking out
his misgivings on the I.V. bottle whose exasperatingly slow
drops he was counting like sheep. "Nasal congestion bothers
patient a great deal," Bertha noted at two o'clock, and added
at five: "Raising mucus from throat—*mucus appears to be
blood tinged.*"

But when Lieutenant Ann Maertz took over in the morning, Patton greeted her in a clear voice: "Good morning,
Lieutenant. I feel much better today. Look," he said, "I can
move the index finger on my right hand." Ann had to strain
a little, but she decided in the end that a slight movement
was probably there. Since his condition remained good, the
general was served a Lucullan lunch, consisting of soup
with noodles, a little coffee, and half a pear.

But then at 1:00 P.M., Patton startled the nurse by asking
for a sip of water, apparently trying to push something down
in the esophagus. "I have a queer sensation in my hands,"
he told her a few minutes later, "as if my skin and flesh are
trying to fall off my bones."

He was so depressed, in fact, that the nurse sent for
Colonel Hill to come and cheer him up. Hill came promptly,
sat down at his bedside and, as was his wont by now, began
to quiz Patton about certain of his operations in the war
that, Hill said, never ceased to intrigue him.

It was a game, part of a special therapy that Hill had
designed to take Patton's mind off the present. But the
general this time did not respond well and appeared to have
sunk deep in his depression. Then, however, he suddenly
said: "You know, Colonel, exactly a year ago, I was ap-

proaching the most glorious moment of my service to my country. Unlike the anointed geniuses at General Bradley's headquarters, we at the Third Army had more than just an inkling of the imminence of the Ardennes offensive, what's now called the Battle of the Bulge. On this very day just a year ago, I issued orders to my staff to get ready for it, five days before it came."

He paused, brought up some more mucus that was bothering him, then told a story that enthralled Hill. "I never told this to anybody before," Patton said, "so you better listen carefully, Hill, and make notes, because I don't want this story to go with me to the grave." He chuckled, but only a little. He then related in detail how he had gone to Luxembourg to warn Bradley and to plead with him not to give the Ninth U.S. Army to Field Marshal Montgomery. "Monty," he said, "was dead set against everything I was doing. He wanted all available forces, British, Canadian, American, up in the north under him, for the big crossing of the Rhine that was the brightest goddamn gleam in his bloodshot eyes. Actually, I came to think, he was playing into the hands of the Germans. They could never have launched the offensive without Monty."

Patton was becoming depressed again, and Colonel Hill, who was a true believer in the medicinal efficacy of a shot of good whisky, remembered that he had a bottle of Johnny Walker Red Label in his office. He now volunteered to bring it over for a little celebration. Patton smiled and nodded. When the bottle arrived, it turned out that not much of the whisky was left in it, just enough for a single modest round. Colonel Hill brought a couple of little medicine glasses with him, filled one for Patton, the other for himself, then held his glass to Patton's lips, said cheers, and watched the general take a couple of sips.

If it was not the Scotch, for it was hardly enough to cheer him up, then probably it was Colonel Hill's ministration as a bartender that amused him. So much so, in fact, that when Captain Duane dropped in at 5:00 P.M., Colonel Hill recommended that he prescribe whisky officially as part of Patton's medication, and Duane ordered a bottle, with instructions to give the patient a teaspoonful whenever his condition seemed to call for it. It was on the chart, squeezed in between an order for Seconal and the instruction that urine specimens obtained from the indwelling catheter be sent to Captain Cherry in the laboratory every morning.

This, then, was the story of the big whisky rebellion. When Patton found out about the commotion it caused, he was hugely amused and went on one of his joke binges with it. Each time he did not feel like taking a sip of water or eggnog, he told the nurse he would take only a shot of Scotch. Sometimes he did get a little, at other times he got none, but at no time was he given more than a fourth of a jigger.

His nurses thought Patton was "cute." Now they thought his whisky routine made him even "cuter." It was to demonstrate what a pleasant patient he was that Lieutenant Hohle talked about the incident to the other patients in Ward A-1, one of whom happened to be a young reporter of the Associated Press, Richard H. O'Regan by name. Hard pressed for anything newsworthy, he had sneaked into the hospital in search of an "exclusive" by posing as a patient.

General Patton's accident provided a welcome news break in an otherwise bleak situation and ended the Yuletide doldrums on the German beat with a bang. What followed was a big scramble for bits and scraps of "items" until the plight of the stricken general became a journalistic freak show—a media event.

Out of thin air, more and more reporters showed up at the hospital, straining Ken Morgan's meager facilities beyond the breaking point. First there were five of them, then ten, then twenty. By Monday morning on December 10, a nose count showed there were thirty. Some were famous war correspondents, like Carl Levin of the *New York Herald Tribune*. Others were stringers like Dan Howell, a starry-eyed free-lancer and Patton buff from Winston-Salem, North Carolina. Some were regulars like Kathleen McLaughlin of *The New York Times* and Pierre J. Huss of International News Service. Others rushed in from all over, a whole contingent deserting the trials at Nuremberg for Patton's tribulations in Heidelberg.

They were loud, and demanding, and since the news was

scarce and they had little else to do, they stepped on each other's toes, swiped each other's little stories, all of them out apparently to cap their assignment to Europe with one big exclusive scoop. As more and more reporters flocked in, Ken Morgan assigned additional MPs to the ward. Every exit and entrance was given its special guard. Doors were locked. New press passes and I.D. cards were issued. But no precautionary measures could keep all of them out all of the time.

To organize things and calm them down, General Keyes authorized Colonel Ball to issue daily bulletins, detailing professionally and frankly Patton's progress. When elaboration was needed, a press conference was held in which Spurling, Hill, and Duane faced the mob, outlining the case and answering questions. It was a major concession, essentially violating the sanctity of physician-patient relations. Colonel Hill, whose respect for the Fourth Estate was diminishing rapidly, was shocked by the inanity of the questions asked. Was it orange juice or grapefruit juice Patton had for breakfast? What was the color of his pajamas, and were they his own or government issue? Was Patton swearing as profusely as he used to and if yes, could they give a few juicy samples of his expletives? Which of his three nurses was his favorite? Was his penis also paralyzed?

Even the press conference failed to satisfy the demand, and the correspondents seized the initiative from the doctors and harassed Ken Morgan. Several of them donned hospital gowns and ran up and down the corridors until they were spotted and evicted. One of them accosted Heinz Goslar, the German cook who prepared a special eggnog for the general and was given the honor of serving it personally, with a deal the man was not expected to refuse. For a carton of Lucky Strikes, a couple of pairs of nylon hose, and a pack of ten Hershey bars, the German was supposed to yield the tray to the reporter and let him go to Patton's room posing as the dietician.

AT LAST Mrs. Patton arrived at the snowbound airport at Mannheim, after a bumpy transatlantic flight in a mail plane that took twenty-nine hours and twenty-five minutes from the United States to France, with stops at Newfoundland and the Azores. Unable to land at Orly Field in Paris after four attempts in the fog and rain, the C-54 took her to Istres Field in Marseilles. There she was met by Lieutenant General John C. H. Lee, the grand seigneur of supplies, and made the final leg of her long journey in style, in General Lee's luxurious personal plane.

Waiting for her in Mannheim was General Keyes, who had seen her stricken husband several times since the accident and was, in a mood of determined wishful thinking, optimistic about Patton's chances to survive and recover. Keyes, who really loved Patton and could not bear the thought of losing him, was buoyed by his friend's cheer and confidence. He dismissed the doctors' guarded advisories as unduly pessimistic and concocted his own diagnoses.

Now he conveyed his optimism to Colonel Spurling (who regarded it as an order for some time) and especially to Mrs. Patton who, Keyes thought, could use the reassurance. It was, therefore, in an encouraged frame of mind, smiling, with her head held high, that she entered her husband's room at 3:30 P.M. on December 11. The reunion had been arranged at Patton's request as a strictly private affair, with nobody else to be present at the outset.

When she was escorted to Room 101 by General Kenner and his entourage of doctors, she found at first blush some of Geoffrey Keyes's optimism visibly confirmed. Her husband was resting quietly, in spite of the forbidding traction in which he was kept. His condition was slightly improved—temperature was down to 100, his pulse was 70 and regular, respiration was down from an occasional 30 and difficult to 22 and unlabored. But before the door closed on the couple, Patton, who had waited anxiously for this moment and was eager to tell her what he really had on his mind, could be heard saying in a firm voice: "Good to see you, Bea. I'm afraid this may be the last time we see each other."

Apparently he needed only half an hour to bring her up to date, take stock, and settle things. What passed between them during those thirty minutes nobody knows. But when the door opened again, it was obvious that they had an understanding. These two people were so attuned to each other in their devoted closeness after a marriage of thirty-three years that they needed few words to read each other. Mrs. Patton emerged well briefed, for she made firm arrangements immediately for a number of things. She had a list of books the general wanted, for instance, which she would read to him.

Turning to Colonel Hill, she said: "General Patton asked me to curtain his visitors somewhat, for the strain is getting too much for him." She then hardened her voice slightly as she continued: "Under no circumstances does he want to be visited by General Bedell Smith. Please understand, under no circumstances."

She hoped for the best it seemed, but was prepared for the worst, with dry eyes and an ethereal little smile playing on her lips that could be interpreted in various ways. Although she was neither pretty nor really charming, she won over the doctors and nurses right from the outset, taking her cue from General Keyes, as she told them: "You can level with me. I've seen Georgie in these scrapes before. He always comes out all right."

"HE SPARED neither pain, care, nor trouble to arrive at his end, and this applied as much to little things as to great. He was, one might say, totally given over to his object. He always applied all his means, all his faculties, all his attention to the action or discussion of the moment."

Beatrice Patton was reading to her husband. Captain Duane happened to be in the room, listening avidly to the passage about Napoleon Bonaparte, of course, which Patton had picked as the day's sutra from the 1925 English translation of General Armand de Caulaincourt's memoirs.

He turned to the young doctor with a little lecture that had a familiar touch. "Napoleon was," he said, "a man completely wrapped in his destiny. He was the supreme egoist, an isolated and self-centered man who relied on himself alone. Do you know what Napoleon himself said in 1812, just before he set out on the road to Moscow? 'I feel myself driven towards the end,' he said, 'that I do not know. As soon as I shall have reached it, as soon as I shall

become unnecessary, an atom will suffice to shatter me.'
There was a man for you who knew what destiny meant!"

Caulaincourt's two-volume memoirs had been brought
over from Bad Nauheim from Patton's personal library,
which traveled with him wherever he went throughout the
war. The most illuminating of Napoleon's memorialists, the
French general (whom the Emperor had made the Duke of
Vicenza) was his special pet, probably because Patton found
so much of himself in that remarkable portrait of his idol.
"Into everything," Caulaincourt wrote, "he put passion.
Hence the enormous advantage he had over his adversaries,
for few people are entirely absorbed by one thought or one
action at one moment."

Napoleon burned high and fast, and was burned out completely at the age of forty-five—the few years that remained
did not matter. Patton was visibly moved as Beatrice read
on and Captain Duane listened. Suddenly the affinity of
their fates became pronounced in Patton's mind, as he added
his thoughts between the lines. "Ah," he said with the elegance that came to him whenever he spoke of history, "he
was such a prophet. Look what's happening to what was
the greatest army in all history even six months ago. Look
how the American army is going to pieces. But do you
know that Napoleon said that there would be neither independence nor liberty without great armies? Oh well, the
world may not have needed him. But Jesus Christ, history
sure did!"

"Okay, Georgie," Mrs. Patton said. She put down the
book. She knew when it was time to stop. Captain Duane
stepped over to the bed to look at him. He was in the room
because Colonel Hill had told him: "I don't think he's maintaining the progress we noted yesterday. I think the reason
is the increasing edema of the spinal cord at the site of the
injury. I don't think he'll pull through."

IT WAS at 4:00 P.M. on December 12 that Colonel
Spurling was taken to Patton's room by General Kenner and
Captain Duane for his first neurological examination of the
patient, and he was pleasantly surprised by Patton's excellent mood and high spirits. It was the last thing he expected

in a general reputed to be a curmudgeon even when he was not paralyzed. "Colonel Spurling," Patton greeted him, "I apologize for getting you out on this wild goose chase, and I am particularly sorry since it probably means that you won't be home with your family for Christmas."

He submitted readily to still another examination by yet another doctor, remarking only once, lightly, on the irony of the accident, the observation he had made when he had been brought in on Sunday. "To think," he said, "that after the best of the Germans have shot at me, to get hurt in an automobile going pheasant hunting."

"Are you comfortable?" Dr. Spurling asked.

"I'm in no pain," Patton said, "other than the rather persistent drag at the site of the traction in my skull."

Spurling was pleased. The care, he found, that the surgeons at the hospital had given Patton could not have been better. By this time, General Patton was attended by three regular surgeons, four neurosurgeons, an orthopedic surgeon, and five or six doctors in other specialties—a medical staff of fourteen physicians. "The treatment was adequate from the beginning," Colonel Spurling wrote.

The findings of his first examination were recorded one by one, and they did not appear to indicate that Patton's condition was hopeless or catastrophic. He was paralyzed, no doubt about that—but there was some slight voluntary motion of the right biceps brachialis. A deep sensation was feebly present in both arms and questionably in both legs. The tendon reflexes were back and were actually hyperactive in both lower extremities. A definite sweating was demonstrated at the C-5 dermatome. The new X-rays of the cervical spine showed a complete realignment of the vertebral bodies. And Patton's general condition was stabilized, with temperature, pulse, and respiration essentially normal.

This was a full catalogue of Dr. Spurling's findings, all of them on the positive side. In layman's language this meant that the patient was in very bad shape, to be sure, but not yet at the point of no return.

The picture changed drastically, however, during the next fourteen hours. Patton did have a fair night. But he was not getting any better. On the contrary, when Colonel Spurling returned at ten o'clock the next morning for his second neurosurgical examination, he found that his patient had lost whatever little gains he had made, and that the prognosis for recovery had suddenly grown "increasingly grave." Patton's breathing was much more labored, with greater dependence on the accessory muscles of his neck. Suddenly, too, the possibility that the right diaphragm might also be paralyzed stared them in the face. This time Colonel Spurling left Patton's bedside a little less buoyant.

Perhaps because his disappointment showed or probably because Patton had planned it all the time, Spurling was paged a short time after he had left him to return to the room—alone. When he entered, he found Patton by himself. Mrs. Patton had gone to her room in the hospital. The nurse had vanished.

"Sit down, Colonel," Patton said. Then, after some casual pleasantries, he told the great neurosurgeon: "Now, Spurling, we've known each other during the fighting and I want you to talk with me as man to man. What chance have I to recover?"

"You're doing so much better than the usual patient with a cervical cord injury," Dr. Spurling replied in a mildly roundabout way, "that it is impossible to give you a forthright answer. After all, if the cord has been severed or severely damaged at the moment of impact, your chance of recovering would be very slight. On the other hand, if the cord was only shaken up, we might see some rather dramatic improvements in the next forty-eight to seventy-two hours."

"Okay," Patton said, apparently not displeased at all. "But what chance have I to ride a horse again?"

"None," Spurling said without a moment's hesitation.

"In other words," Patton shot back, showing a little greater interest in his future, "the best I could hope for would be semi-invalidism."

"Yes," the doctor said. There was a pause, then Patton spoke again:

"Thank you, Colonel, for being honest."

In a flash, he was back in his former jovial mood. "Colonel," he said, "you are surrounded by an awful lot of brass around here—there are more generals than privates cooling their heels, so far as I can gather from the nurses and the doctors. I just want you to know that you're the boss—whatever you say goes."

Spurling told him that, yes, indeed, every general in the theater seemed to be either at the hospital in Heidelberg or on his way. "Your old Army comrades are naturally anxious to see you, sir," he said. "They are clamoring for admittance to your room."

"It's your decision, Spurling," Patton said with his familiar chuckle. "Whatever you say, buddy, goes. One exception. Did Mrs. Patton tell you that I don't care to see General Bedell Smith should he ever show up? He never was a special friend of mine. It's too late to patch things up, Colonel," he said, this time with a twinkle in his eyes, "it's up to you to keep him out."

"All right," Spurling said. "No one is to see you except Mrs. Patton, General Keyes, the doctors and the nurses on duty. How does that strike you, General?"

"I think that is a good decision," Patton said, "irrespective of the medical point of view. After all, it's kind of hard for me to see my old friends, when I am lying here paralyzed all over. It may be fatal, if I have to see that old sonuvabitch."

"You need not worry, General," Spurling said. "And save your strength, sir."

In a few words the doctor explained to Patton the medical problems that made it imperative for him to save his strength, and Patton told him: "I will try to be a good patient."

THE NEXT seventy-two hours...The countdown was on....

December 13 ... Resting but not sleeping, except in short intervals...Awake, evidently somewhat apprehensive about his condition...Catheter draining...Penicillin draining...Ephedrine...Seconal...

December 14 ... Seems much more alert and talkative today...Ate a good dinner, asparagus, coffee, gelatin and chicken broth...Has a little pain at the site of the hooks...

December 15...Breakfast, coffee and orange juice, a small amount of egg...Penicillin...Coughs continuously...

Captain Duane was the neurosurgical bookkeeper of the case. On December 16, he wrote in his chart: "General condition remains satisfactory. Planning to apply friction cast tomorrow and to remove traction."

The day broke dark and gloomy. But it was not darker and gloomier than the days had been since the Sunday of the accident exactly a week before. "I've been here since the twelfth," Colonel Spurling remarked, "and I haven't seen the sun once."

Patton awoke shortly after midnight and complained of pain in his cheekbones. He kept his nurse busy. The nose had to be sprayed. He asked to be turned on his left side and then, forty-five minutes later, to be turned on his right side. His teeth had to be brushed at half past four to relieve the extreme dryness of his mouth and nose. At 5:45 A.M. Captain Duane had to be summoned. The traction had to be adjusted again.

"Patient quite restless," Lieutenant Hohle noted. A little later she wrote: "Extremely restless...."

He was sipping coffee through the glass tube shortly after 2:00 P.M. when Colonel Hill dropped in. Just then, there was that twitching again of both legs. "God," Patton said, "will this never end?"

"How do you feel?" Hill asked and Patton said eagerly, with what sounded like a non sequitur: "Look at the weather, Hill. It's exactly the kind of weather we had a year ago today. The Germans counted on it, the bastards. It kept all our planes grounded."

Of course, Paul Hill suddenly remembered. The day was the first anniversary of the Battle of the Bulge. Colonel Hill suddenly thought that, perhaps, a little anniversary celebration would dispel his blues. When Mrs. Patton had heard about their first little bout with the bottle, and how he had given up his precious last drops of Johnny Walker to cheer up the general, she replaced it with a quart of the Red Label she found in the PX. Now Hill went for the bottle, brought it over, and opened it, and they drank. "To the Distinguished Service Medal I never got," Patton toasted.

THAT EVENING, as Patton was eating again—a little grapefruit juice and some beef broth—his doctors were dining in style at Geoffrey Keyes's residence in the ornate dining room of the German tycoon who had been evicted to accommodate for the new master of Heidelberg, the commanding general of the Seventh U.S. Army. The menu included mock turtle soup, succulent roast turkey, and the famed *Torte* named for the Black Forest.

General Keyes had arranged the dinner because he was deeply concerned. "Things have gone along with satisfactory progress as to [Patton's] general condition," he wrote to his wife on December 14, "but the final outcome is still in doubt." It was "the final outcome" that worried him. He sent for the doctors to find out the score.

When they were gone after the dinner, Keyes wrote jubilantly to his wife: "The doctors are very optimistic now and say, barring unforeseen complications, Gen. Patton is out of danger as far as saving his life is concerned."

Actually, the prognosis of the doctors was not that unequivocal. And the dinner party brought out a dormant conflict—the discrepancy created by Colonel Hill's pessimism and Colonel Spurling's optimism. Since Hill was the surgeon on the case in Keyes's own command, the general had turned to him first and asked, "Well, Colonel Hill, how are we doing?"

Hill's report reflected his conviction that Patton was doomed, living merely on borrowed time. The edema was spreading and increasing. But the real complications were yet to come. It was, he said, a matter of days. But Colonel Spurling, whose authority counted more heavily than Hill's realism, told Keyes exactly what the general wanted to hear. "Twenty-four hours after my arrival there was a distinct improvement in General Patton's condition," he said, dredging up some hope. "His general condition is holding up remarkably well." He did not say it in so many words, but he hinted at the "outcome" that General Keyes was so desperately seeking.

In the end, Keyes seemed confused and bewildered. When the meeting broke up, he opted for Spurling's prognosis, dismissing Hill with something akin to rebuke. "I don't care what you do, gentlemen," he said in parting, "but do your best to keep him alive. He *must* live!" he added, and it sounded like an order. "It's absolutely imperative that he survive so that he can write his memoirs."

22.

★ ★ ★ ★

Zero Hour Zero

A WEEK is a long time to be supine in a hospital bed. After a week, even the hospitalization of a celebrity as sparkling and controversial as George S. Patton, Jr., becomes essentially a housekeeping job. Every day Dr. Spurling dispatched a confidential medical report to General George C. Marshall, the Chief of Staff, and to the Surgeon General, his immediate superior, in Washington, and a copy of his message was sent daily to President Truman. Colonel Spurling always told them "the stark truth," as he himself put it. He never left any question that "General Patton was done for." Yet the bulletins issued each day at 6:00 P.M. in Heidelberg tended to stress what was encouraging and stable in Patton's condition and played down the serious and discouraging aspects of his plight. The offshoot of such a one-sided presentation of the case were headlines like "Chances Called Good for Patton to Walk" and "Patton Able to Sit Up," for which there was no basis in fact. One of the headlines was far too sanguine, the other was simply untrue, yet both had been culled by reading between the lines of the bulletins.

THE INCONGRUITY of the situation was demonstrated by the place George S. Patton now inhabited. Generals live in grand style in the path of their conquests, and Patton the aristocrat knew especially well how to live it up. It was always the grandest and the best—the palatial Hotel Miramar, and the Sultan's Moorish castle in Morocco, the gold and brocade renaissance palace of the kings in Palermo, the ivy-covered Peover Hall, one of England's stately manor houses, in the fertile flatlands of Cheshire. But now he was confined to a former utility room that had been hastily converted for him, the only "private" room in the ward. Sixteen feet by fourteen, it was his world now, his whole world. And over it hovered Beatrice Patton.

She was a small, wiry woman, with enormous vitality. Her personality made her radiant—her smile was captivating, and her quizzical eyes eloquent. She spoke slowly, softly, correctly, and made friends easily and quickly here as elsewhere. But though she seemed unassuming and quiet to Colonel Spurling, she was, in fact, determined and domineering, making the most of the covenant she had made with George in 1910, when they decided to get married. Under it, she put up with his idiosyncrasies, eccentricities, and impetuosities, in exchange for which she was given the general management of their lives. Mrs. Patton had spent her years with Georgie in constant agony, trembling for her husband, not only when he went to war, but even when he was driving a car, riding a horse, sailing his boat, or exercising his prerogative of getting into trouble. Patton knew how worried she was, whether she showed it or not, and tried to calm her fears, soothe her apprehensions. "You always know what's best for me," he wrote to her, not once but often, in letters and notes that were humble and respectful.

After they first met in 1905 on Catalina Island in California, and had their "understanding," Patton never courted another girl, and Bea never had another beau. In thirty-three years of marriage, they were completely wrapped up in one another—the covenant worked. Her appearance was deceptive. Tiny, dainty, and white-gloved, Bea was a hard-fisted, tough woman who could ride as hard and sail as fast as her husband. And she was at her best when the chips were down.

Now, too—with the efficiency and arrogance of her caste—she took over the moment she arrived, and had been in charge ever since. Colonel Ball may have been the commanding officer at the 130th Station Hospital. But Beatrice Patton was in command so far as her husband was concerned.

She was staying with General Keyes, but had a room in the hospital, where she spent most of her days, and sometimes her nights. She was always on her toes. With the seismograph within her, she registered the smallest tremor, and responded promptly, energetically, decisively. She was more than just the wife of a stricken officer. She was the plenipotentiary of her husband, the executor of the will he had confided to her.

Having managed his life for so long, she was now arranging his death. It was an act of superb courage that required an extraordinary character, and Beatrice Patton had both in abundance. She was playing the part casually, without pathos or maudlin ostentation, for she was an Ayer and a Patton, and a woman who lived by the rule of noblesse oblige.

NOW THERE WERE only eight days to Christmas, and it seemed the spreading cheer of the holiday season was having a definite salutary effect on General Patton. December 17 was a kind of red-letter day. Because of the nearly perfect alignment of the fracture-dislocation, the bothersome fishhook traction was taken off and Major Kelleher, the hospital's orthopedic surgeon, fitted a plaster collar around Patton's neck. There were other encouraging symptoms as well. He was positioned up at a 45-degree angle, and though he was still taking nourishment churlishly, he did swallow some juices or soup several times during the day.

At 7:00 P.M. there was more good news. He was moved from the air mattress to a hospital bed, and he felt better immediately. On the whole, Captain Duane found that his condition was "excellent." There were some movements — a definite voluntary motion of the quadriceps femoris of the left thigh, a similar motion in the right abductor group, and a very slight voluntary motion in the right biceps brachialis.

Something was in the air, something mysterious like the enchanting miracle of change, reminiscent of the time a year before when Patton ordered his chaplain to pray for a break in the weather so that his planes could fly again, after which the sun came out. Whether or not Patton really expected to die, he was alive, clinging to life, and seemed to be even working at it. As if taking his cue from Spurling's optimism, he lived on, startling all, even Colonel Hill, with his stamina, resilience, and apparent will to fight it out.

Suddenly it seemed that Colonel Spurling would be vindicated and Colonel Hill proven wrong. When Spurling and Captain Duane saw him on the morning of December 19, they found him very alert, cheerful and talkative. "General Patton was a good patient this morning," Lieutenant Ann Maertz told them with real elation. "He had a whole egg and a cup of coffee for breakfast, and he wasn't making any fuss."

"Had the best night so far," Captain Duane wrote in his progress notes. And Patton himself told Lieutenant Maertz: "I am feeling really well, Ann. For the first time."

Whatever it was, Patton was not getting any worse and it seemed he was getting a little better. And nobody was fooling him. "He's undoubtedly aware of the extent of the paralysis," Captain Duane told Colonel Spurling that evening over dinner, "but he's obviously determined to grin and bear it. He's checking up on us stealthily, testing out everything we tell him. Occasionally he may be a little confused or perhaps distracted, but only for a moment or so. On the whole I'd say he is normally alert."

THE PROGRESS became even more pronounced on December 18. Captain Kent, chief of the hospital's medical service, had Patton to himself that day, for a thorough checkup that covered everything from the broken skin at the top of his skull to the superficial varicose veins on both lower legs—his head, eyes, chest, lungs, heart, and abdomen.

Patton amazed his doctors with his basic health. Even under the enormous burden of his condition, his vital organs continued to function almost perfectly. "There was, in fact, normal systolic impulse in the heart," Captain Kent said. "The heart tones were good. And no murmurs were audible. His blood pressure was 108 over 70."

Colonel Spurling was considering transferring Patton to a hospital in the United States, close to his home in Massachusetts. On the nineteenth he was encouraged enough to cable Michael De Bakey, then a thirty-seven-year-old assistant professor of surgery at Tulane University serving as a lieutenant colonel in the office of the Surgeon General, who handled the Patton case in Washington: "Arrangements being made air evacuation General Patton, 30 December."

Was it the Fowler bed after the discomfort of the air mattress or the plaster collar that replaced those painful fishhooks? Or was it just one of those typical Patton miracles? Whatever it was, General Patton appeared to be making it. As of the evening of December 19, he was to be "going home" in ten days.

IN HEIDELBERG, with back-up in Washington, elaborate arrangements were being made for the trip to the Beverly General Hospital in Massachusetts, which Dr. Spurling had chosen on Mrs. Patton's suggestion. Sergeant Meeks had to take a crash course, for he was to function as the general's nurse during the trip. General Kenner himself came over from Frankfurt to supervise the preparations, and Colonel Harkins, whom Patton had asked to accompany him, was summoned from Bad Nauheim, where he was keeping the Fifteenth Army on an even keel.

Making the trip through sleet and rain and an opaque fog, Paul Harkins arrived with his gear on the nineteenth and was received by Dr. Kenner, who was in an ambivalent frame of mind, his new optimism somewhat tempered by the pessimism of the old prognosis. As a matter of fact, the feeling that Patton was in a shape fair enough to make the trip was not unanimous by any means. The decision had been made reluctantly, mainly in deference to Mrs. Patton's pleas. She was adamant for the move, not because she really thought that her husband would survive, but because she wanted him buried in American soil.

That the patient was still touch and go was evident when Harkins arrived and asked Kenner: "Could I see the Old Man?"

"Well," Kenner replied, "I don't think it will do any harm. Go in. But stay only a minute or two. And don't show that you're upset by what you see."

What Harkins saw inside was a cheerful Patton actually propped up in bed, with an enormous collar around his neck.

He was obviously elated by the prospect of going home.

"Good afternoon, General," Harkins said, and Patton asked: "How do I look?"

"You look fine, General." Among the many assets that made Harkins invaluable to Patton was his absolute honesty. He simply could not tell a lie. He was not very convincing in fibbing now either, for Patton broke into broad laughter, and said: "Paul, goddamnit. You're a lying sonuvabitch." These were the last words Harkins heard Patton utter. He had a tough time holding back his tears, and exited quickly. He never saw the Old Man again.

SHORTLY AFTER ten o'clock that night General Patton was jolted awake by a violent coughing spell. For minutes afterward, which seemed an eternity, he remained in desperate straits, as he tried to raise mucus and catch his breath. No crisis was expected and the tension had eased in Room 101. Lieutenant Margery Rondell, whose shift was ending, was standing at the door, talking with another nurse. When she heard the patient's sudden discomfort, she rushed to his bed and sent for Captain Duane. The doctor was also taking it a little easier. He had taken the evening off and had had his dinner downtown, but was now back at his station; he was at Patton's bedside within seconds.

The general was given phenobarbital, the mild sedative that had worked well in calming him before. But the coughing persisted even after a generous dose of codeine. In this instance, though, it had its function. Patton was desperate to bring up the mucus that was accumulating in his bronchial tubes and increasing the pressure on the spinal cord.

It took Captain Duane but a glance to realize that the hour, which Colonel Hill expected would strike sooner or later, had come. Patton was dyspnoic, as Duane recorded it in his notes—his breathing difficult and labored. And he had an acute attack of cyanosis, usually present in terminal cases, when the inadequate airing of the blood gives the skin a bluish-gray hue.

Duane found Patton's spinal condition to be stable. But everything else had changed or was changing. His respiration had become rapid and erratic. His heart was faltering under the strain. The first heart sound was muffled and was followed by a loud systolic murmur. The bowels were filled with gas.

But if proof was needed that this was the beginning of the end, it was definitely there. The cough had produced frothy sputum twice and it had a slight tinge of blood—evidence, as Colonel Spurling put it, of an infarction of the lung—indicating the pulmonary embolism so dreaded at this stage—the killer complication in a case like this. An embolus is a piece of clotted blood that becomes detached from the lining of the heart or a vein or an artery, and then has an arbitrary career of its own. It travels through the bloodstream and lodges in some other part of the body—blocking a major vessel or making it to the brain, the lungs, the aorta, or an artery in the thigh or leg, obstructing the normal flow of blood. With a pulmonary embolism, the blockage of a major vessel brings on death within seconds.

Embolus, a dirty word, was especially dreaded in Patton's family. He had a history of embolisms—two instances, in fact, when he was hospitalized with a broken leg eight years before in Boston. He lived through them then. But now, with the infarct in the lung, he had only a slight margin left for such a complication.

THE FATEFUL TURN was sudden and unexpected. Patton had been comfortable the whole afternoon on this December 19. He talked and joked with his visitors, then slept intermittently without Seconal. Only an hour before the attack, he had a little eggnog, then forced down two glasses of water. But somehow they proved too much. The intake of the fluids was followed abruptly by shortage of breath and the "blue jaundice."

Atropine was prescribed to reduce excessive salivation and bronchial secretions. Oxygen was administered and it helped. But Patton was very ill by the morning of December 20. The coughing had subsided, and he rested quietly most of the time, but the improvement was superficial and deceptive. Encouraged by the good news the day before, Mrs. Patton had gone to General Keyes's residence for the night, but she was back in the hospital as soon as she heard of her husband's sudden turn. At two o'clock in the afternoon on this Thursday she was reading to him when there was another coughing spell and more sputum was produced. There was no external evidence of phlebitis. But the evidence of an embolism now became conclusive: Patton had turned cold and clammy and was perspiring. His heart action weakened, the pulse became more rapid, and his blood pressure plunged. The sputum that the cough produced was now more distinctly tinged with blood. And X-rays spotted the embolus in the upper part of his right lung.

A call was put in to Frankfurt for Lieutenant Colonel Herbert J. Pollock, the eminent internist serving as the chief medical consultant in the European Theater. At the hospital, Captain Kent, as competent as any, was making the most of what was left to prolong a life slipping away. An emergency regime of digitalis was prescribed, the drug given orally at intervals of four hours. To replenish the loss of salt, sodium chloride was administered intravenously, as was human plasma. But nothing appeared to help. Most of the time Patton remained fully conscious, even alert. But he was sleeping more and more and the intervals of lucidity were becoming ever shorter.

COLONEL POLLOCK arrived on the morning of December 21, only to confirm that there was really nothing more anybody in this world could do for George Patton. By then, his condition was no longer just critical. It was hopeless. But even as his life was ebbing away, the tide of memories made his bond with Beatrice ever stronger. She was reading to him—now it was *Through the Fog of War,* a 1938 book in which Captain Liddell Hart studied the personalities and events of World War I for clues to the next war. She was just beginning the chapter called "Three French Soldiers" when it seemed that Patton had dozed off again. To test him, Beatrice went back to the top of the page, but no sooner did she repeat the opening sentence— "Joseph Jacques Césaire Joffre, destined to become the first Marshal of the Third Republic"—than the general opened his eyes and said: "Oh, Bea, don't give me that crap again."

He was sleeping on and off most of the day, so quietly, in fact, that Mrs. Patton refused to accept the doctors' verdict. She had been with him most of the morning. Around 5:00 P.M., crocheting in her chair at the bedside, she looked at him, just as it seemed that her husband was forcing his eyes open again. "Are you all right, Georgie?" she asked. As she looked at him, she suddenly thought that there was greater eloquence in those bird-dog eyes than she had ever seen in them before—the whole story of their lives and love, a summing up of all that they had gone through together. She patted his hand gently, now all skin and bone, when she heard him speak in a distant voice, with some difficulty.

"It's so dark," he said. And a moment later, "It's so late."

The words came haltingly, and their meaning was obscure. Patton closed his eyes again, and dozed off, so soundly and quietly that Mrs. Patton thought it might be safe to leave him alone for a brief span. But he had spoken his last words to her. She would never see him alive again.

INSTEAD OF LETTING him pass away by just dozing off and getting the deep, deep rest his tired body craved, they kept him occupied with myriad discomforting chores. The dosage of the digitalis was raised. Pure protein was poured into him, and more needles punctured his skin and entered his exhausted veins.

"Why don't they just let me die?" Patton had asked Lieutenant Hohle during the night, without any of the bogus bathos of the B-pictures. But he was getting his wish. "I am going to die," he told Lieutenant Maertz several times in the morning, and more pointedly to Lieutenant Rondell when she arrived on her shift in the afternoon. "I am going to die," he said, "today."

"[GENERAL PATTON] died at 1745, 21 December 1945," Captain William Duane, Jr., wrote in the last entry—indeed, the last two lines—of his progress notes, "with sudden stopping of the heart." And Colonel Hill summed up the "progress"of his final hours: "On the morning of the

21st, increasing pulmonary signs were augmented by signs of right heart failure. Examined by the Theater Medical Consultant, an effort was made to compensate for this by increasing the output and digitalization, and adjustment of protein intake. However, at 1745, 21 December 1945, without warning, the patient passed away."

It was left to Margery Rondell, Patton's favorite nurse, who had stood the dog watch when he died, to describe the subdued drama. At 3:00 P.M., when she had relieved Ann Maertz, she found the patient sinking, to be sure, but refuting in his fashion Fielding's aphorism that dying was more terrible than death. George S. Patton was dying well.

A "very productive" coughing spell at half past three woke him up momentarily, and though he barely opened his eyelids, the nurse seized the opportunity to turn him first on one side, then on the other. Atropine sulfate—ordinary belladonna—was given him at a quarter to four, the last time he was bothered with a drug.

"Very drowsy," Lieutenant Rondell recorded his state at 4:00 P.M., and then:

"1616 . . . Sleeping. Breathing irregular.

"1630 . . . Very dyspnoic.

"1700 . . . Sleeping. Breathing more regular. Pulse 56 to 68.

"1730 . . . Still sleeping. Pulse 68. Res[piration] 36."

Then at 1745—at 5:45 P.M. Central European Time—as Patton was sleeping, the nurse looked at him because a sixth sense suddenly told her that it was all over. She beckoned to Captain Duane, who was sharing the vigil in the room, and he ran down the corridor to summon Beatrice. She came immediately, followed by Colonel Spurling. But Patton had died before they reached the bedside. The old soldier, whom no enemy bullet could fell, was killed by a wayward blood clot that struck him stealthily in his good lung.

The nurse picked up his chart and noted, "1745 . . . Expired."

She left it at that, the page unfinished.

The abbreviated cause of his death in the routine death certificate was given as "pulmonary edema and congestive heart failure." The cause was spelled out more precisely in the version of his death in the Adjutant General's report, which a clerk named Woodliff compiled for the files. It was given as "myelitis cromatic* transverse fourth cervical segment, pulmonary infarction, myocardial failure, acute." Patton was dead, and it did not matter to him one way or another how he had died. What would have chagrined him if he knew was what Woodliff chose to do with the printed form of the report. A stickler for bureaucratic accuracy, he added the prefix "Non" at the top of the sheet, whose regular caption was, "Battle Casualty Report."

That was how it went into the files, #347063 1-CC-2, for posterity.

"GENERAL PATTON DIES QUIETLY IN SLEEP" read the headline over the front-page story in the morning. He did pass away becalmed like Seneca, with the philosophy of the sage in the end—*Non amittuntur, sed praemittuntur*. Not lost, but gone before! In the privacy of his innermost world, he had set his soul in perfect order. "Patton died as he had lived," wrote Colonel Spurling. "Bravely."

And yet, for George Smith Patton, Jr., General, Serial Number 02605, it was an incongruous death.

---

*The word was a typographical error. "Cromatic" should have read "traumatic."

23.

$$\star \star \star \star$$

So May He Rest

"THROUGHOUT his illness," Colonel R. Glen Spurling wrote in his moving necrology of his most famous case, "there was never one word of complaint regarding a nurse or doctor or orderly. Each and every one was treated with the kindest consideration. He took orders without question—in fact, he was a model patient."

But the model patient quickly reverted to type in death and became a problem corpse. George S. Patton had no part in the series of behind-the-scenes squabbles that followed his demise. But somehow, the fracas, fray, and fuss that trailed him throughout his life pursued him also into his grave. First, there was a question about the autopsy. Then, problems arose about the mortuary arrangements that usually go with the American way of preparing the body for burial. And third, a controversy developed over the question of where to lay him to his final rest.

Spurling himself skirted the issue of the post mortem with a brief reference that was not quite candid and, as it turned out, not helpful in the long run. According to him, there was no qualified pathologist available to do the autopsy, and Mrs. Patton felt that under the circumstances she preferred not to have one performed. "I am sure, though," Spurling later wrote, "that had there been adequate facilities for careful study of the remains, she would have granted permission."

Though obliged by tact and by consideration for the widow's sensitivity, Colonel Hill was more outspoken but still not as blunt as the issue warranted. "An autopsy was

274

requested by Colonel Spurling," he wrote in his summary of the case, "but refused by the patient's wife, Mrs. Patton."

Mrs. Patton's refusal proved regrettable on several grounds. For one thing, history is interested in its heroes, even after death. For another, Patton's death was the result of an accident, and it was not yet known whether criminal negligence was involved.

In order to give Patton his rightful place in history or assign him his proper rank in the military arts, it would have been helpful if an autopsy could have established once and for all the extent to which his actions and moods—particularly those of these last days—had been caused by the physiological injuries he had sustained over the years. His brain, so vibrant, but so roughly handled in wars and in sports, held secrets of special interest to experts both in medicine and in history. Among the injuries he had sustained were two from his football days at West Point, on September 3, 1905, and on September 28, 1908. And there were two potentially significant ones sustained when he fell from his mount during those early years.

In the first fall, which occurred on April 5, 1913, while riding in a steeplechase in Fort Myer, Virginia, the injury was located in the frontoparietal region of his head. In the second one he was struck by the horse's shoe when the animal fell, and then was also kicked in the head while attempting to extricate himself. This accident caused a four-centimeter laceration in the left lateral region of his skull. Over the succeeding years his medical charts abounded with periodic incidence of headaches, the lasting symptoms of a severe concussion.

Those falls may have produced a subdural hematoma, a bloodclot within the cranium, that could exert undue pressure on the brain, especially under stress. One typical consequence of the damage from these accidents was that even a few drinks could make Patton tearful and maudlin in the privacy of his home, or turn him boisterous and aggressive in public. Patton was, of course, subject to erratic behavior, broad swings between temper and contrition. Without the benefit of an autopsy, we can never know the extent to

• • •

these aspects of Patton psychology may have had at least a partial physiological base.

DESIRABLE AS the nailing down of such medical hypotheses may have been, there were more urgent reasons for a post mortem. Rumors of a conspiracy started immediately after the accident. And debate and disputation were already afoot questioning the true motivations behind the controversial general's death. Was the mishap genuine and unavoidable? Or was it a setup? An ambush? Was somebody trying to kill Patton? Who? Why?

On the scene, at the time of the crash, the MPs' stock investigation was perfunctory and preliminary. It was cut short then and there, apparently with Patton's generous remark absolving both drivers. There was no formal inquest held after the general's death and no inquiry was conducted while he was alive—he himself was never questioned—and there seemed to be a deliberate effort to keep the accident unmentioned in his presence.

General Keyes did launch an informal probe, in the course of which the two drivers were heard but not interrogated. Woodring's version of the mishap was accepted at face value and he was absolved; the original charge that he drove carelessly proved baseless. Thompson, the driver of the truck, was quite a bit equivocal. He actually sounded, as Lieutenant Babalas put it, too good to be true. He had been on the way to deliver the truck to a depot, he said, and was a little too late in spotting the general's limousine, or else he would have not made the sharp left turn. As he did, he gave gas, in the hope that he could still avoid a collision, but unfortunately he could not make it. He insisted that he had not seen the four stars on Patton's limousine.

Thompson's testimony could have been challenged in every one of his separate statements. But it was not. And the case was left at that. Although it was still nominally open and pending on December 21, it was never pursued after that. The investigation of this historic accident was far less thorough than even that of a minor traffic incident that claimed no life and involved no figure even remotely as important as General Patton.

The appalling inadequacy of the investigation as far as it went was dramatized unintentionally by a summary of what did not happen and what was not there. Prepared for Major General William A. Bergin, who was then the Adjutant General of the U.S. Army, the record was assembled after a telegram had been received on November 18, 1953, from the *Post-Tribune* of Gary, Indiana, asking the Army to identify the driver of Patton's car. Two men—"a certain A. D. C. Atchison and one Horace Woodring"—both claimed to have been the driver at the time of the accident, the paper wrote.

"Report of investigation is not on file," the Army's record then stated blandly, "and details of the accident are not shown in 201 File. No indication as to driver. . . .

"Casualty Branch has no papers on file regarding accident.

"There is no information re the accident in General Gay's 201 File. . . .

"Mr. Litsey, Safety Branch, G-1, Extension 56811, said they have an *unofficial* report of the accident in their files. There is a signed statement by Horace L. Woodring *taken in 1952* that he was the driver of the car in which General Patton was riding."*

The case was filed and, indeed, forgotten, while the rumors proliferated and the controversy mushroomed, and before competent investigators could have established what it really was. Thus the case was closed in spite of the fact that even the preliminary report of Lieutenant Babalas stated in so many words that the accident resulted from "the care-

---

*Emphases added. Asked about the statement allegedly signed by him, Mr. Woodring told this writer in 1979 that he does not remember ever having made a statement or having signed one in 1952. A perusal of the alleged statement leaves some doubt about Woodring's authorship, if only because it contains references to the nature of Patton's injuries and the causes of his death that would presuppose some medical expertise which Woodring conspicuously lacked in 1945, in 1952, or at any time, for that matter.

lessness of both drivers"—Patton's own and the driver of the truck.*

Even if one considers the possibility of foul play or any premeditation on the part of the driver of the truck, one thing is certain on the face of it. There was no conspiracy afoot in the Kaeferthal, and General Patton was not the victim of a "Jackal" hired to kill him. The timetable of the outing, the itinerary of the journey, and the haphazard nature of his progress combine to rule out even the remote possibility of an engineered plot.

Horace Woodring survived the incident without a traumatic aftermath. His regrets are profound, of course, but he has no feeling of guilt about his part in the accident. The driver of the truck remains a shadowy figure in the drama; nothing is known about him to this day beyond the barest facts of his Army record. Unlike Woodring, he prefers to remain incommunicado. His violation of the rules and his moonlighting with a couple of friends, hung over as the case may have been, was never looked into. None of it is part of the official record.

---

*The scene of the accident no longer resembles the spot in the Kaeferthal as it existed in the fall of 1945. Witnesses, including the military policemen on the spot, vary in their recollections and versions. One of them, First Lieutenant Joseph F. Shanahan, now an attorney in Lambertville, New Jersey, who claims to have been "among the first at the scene" and who had subsequently "investigated the accident which involved America's most controversial general," went so far as to deny that Patton had been killed as a result of the accident. "Patton died of pneumonia," he said in January 1979, "three weeks after the crash." Others at the scene, including Senator Babalas, cannot recall that Mr. Shanahan was present, but Shanahan may have arrived in the Kaeferthal after the ambulance carrying Patton had left and Babalas had left. In spite of all the contradictory reports and the strange omission of an official investigation, I am satisfied that there was no foul play whatsoever in Patton's death and that his accident occurred exactly as it is described in this book.

    Note: The account of the accident presented in this book is, in fact, the result of the only proper but, of course, unofficial investigation ever conducted to ascertain the facts of the mishap and clear up whatever mysteries were left in its wake. It was undertaken on an elaborate scale by Mr. Farago in Germany and in the United States against considerable odds.

                                                                JMF

So Patton's death, either directly or indirectly, did not put an end to the Patton mystery. The enigma lived on after his puzzling death.

EUROPEANS do not indulge in the elaborate tribal rites that go with the interment of "the Loved Ones," as the dead are gently called in Evelyn Waugh's novel. They do not give corpses the benefit of cosmetic processing to improve their appearance and promote their attractiveness posthumously. No embalming preparations are injected into the dead veins to preserve the body from quick decay and perfume away the odor of death.

But Patton was a great American and the 130th Station Hospital was American soil. The ritual seemed mandatory in his case. A hurried search was made for morticians who would make up and dress the general for his lying-in-state. The ravages of his hospitalization had to be erased. The pallor of his skin had to be rouged over. The famous face had to be recreated, so to speak, to be the face of the vigorous Patton the world had known and not that of an invalid fresh from his deathbed.

There was no German undertaker in town, and no American-style funeral parlor anywhere in Germany, to meet the needs. Colonel Hill undertook a personal search for someone serving at the hospital whose regular vocation or even avocation in civilian life would have qualified him as a surrogate mortician, but the closest he could find was a plumber who, in fact, volunteered his services.

Two registered morticians were eventually found on duty with the U.S. Forces in the European Theater, and unlike a pathologist, were brought to Heidelberg. They did what they could, with such gratifying results that General Patton could be buried, not only with the fullest of military honors, but also in the best tradition of the American mortuary arts and sciences.

WHILE PREPARATIONS were being made for the funeral, Mrs. Patton expressed the wish to take the body to the United States and bury her husband in the old village cemetery where the Ayer family had their burial ground.

The Adjutant General's office was contacted in Washington, the papers were drawn up, the bureaucracy was grinding out the arrangements. The plans were nearly completed when General Keyes took Colonel Spurling aside and told him:

"There is something bothering me, Colonel. There hasn't been an American soldier, whether enlisted man or officer, taken home for burial since the beginning of the war. I am fearful of the adverse reaction on the part of the gold-star mothers of America whose boys have been buried overseas, if we make an exception in General Patton's case."

Keyes was emphatic in raising the issue, but seemed reluctant to do something about it. "I feel," he said, "that I cannot put this matter straight to Mrs. Patton, because of my long friendship with both her and the general. I fear she may misunderstand and resent my objection."

"What do you want me to do, General Keyes?" Dr. Spurling asked.

"I would appreciate it, Colonel Spurling," Keyes said, "if you would take up the matter with Mrs. Patton and explain the situation to her."

It was now Colonel Spurling's turn to take Mrs. Patton aside. As he later wrote, he put the proposition bluntly to her. "Of course!" Mrs. Patton agreed immediately. "He must be buried here. Why didn't I think of it! I know George would want to lie beside the men of his Army who have fallen."

All that was left then was to choose the site from among three large military cemeteries in which soldiers of the Third Army were buried, and Mrs. Patton selected the one in Luxembourg. It was there, she told Spurling, that the general had met some of the stiffest opposition and his Army had sustained the greatest casualties during the Battle of the Bulge.

Just then, too, Colonel Hill was accosted by Meeks, a sad-faced black sergeant with hash marks going up, in the Colonel's words, to his armpit. His eyes were sunken from crying, and he could barely talk, when he handed Hill a neatly folded American flag. "This was the general's storm flag, sir," he said (and Colonel Hill still does not know what a storm flag is). "I am sure the general would want to be laid to rest in it."

On Saturday, December 22, 1945, General Patton lay in state in the Villa Reiner, one of the stately homes of Heidelberg, on a hill high over the Neckar, near the residence of his friend, General Keyes, commander of the Seventh Army, who had taken personal charge of the arrangements. Old Blood and Guts was dead. Dispatches of sympathy and condolences were pouring in to General Joseph T. McNarney, who had succeeded General Eisenhower at the top in the Theater. "As an old comrade and admirer of George," Field Marshal Viscount Alexander cabled, "please accept my deepest sympathy on his death." Lieutenant General S. Kopanski, head of the Polish Military Mission, wrote from London: "One of the greatest army leaders in history; his memory will live forever." The hatchet buried at last, Field Marshal Montgomery signaled from his headquarters in Germany: "He was a great soldier and a warm-hearted friend."

Gone were the old resentments and animosities, high and low. Now the GIs claimed him as one of their own. They came in seemingly endless procession to pay their last respects to the great soldier and the grand old man who, unlike themselves, would not be going home soon, or ever. They were everywhere in Heidelberg: a company of the Third Armored Division at the church, a company of the First Armored Division at the railroad station, men of the 84th Infantry Division and of the 15th Cavalry, a unit once commanded by a much younger Patton, lining the streets.

The massed bands of the divisions furnished the music during the funeral at 3:00 P.M. on Sunday, conducted by Colonel Edwin R. Carter, the Episcopal chaplain of USFET, at Christ Church in the Old Town. Patton was sent on his long journey with Psalm 63, which King David had sung in the wilderness of Judah: *O God, thou art my God; early will I seek thee; my soul thirsteth for thee, my flesh longeth for thee in a dry and thirsty land, where no water is; To see thy power and thy glory, so as I have seen thee in the sanctuary.*

It was Patton's favorite psalm, devout but also defiant.

*My soul followeth hard after thee. Thy right hand uphol-
deth me. But those that seek my soul, to destroy it, shall
go into the lower parts of the earth. They shall fall by the
sword. They shall be a portion for foxes. But the king shall
rejoice in God; every one that sweareth by him shall glory,
but the mouth of them that speak lies shall be stopped.*

A company of the First Armored Division was at the
railroad station, and one of its batteries fired the farewell
salute when the two special trains left the station at 4:30
P.M. One carried Patton's body, accompanied by Mrs. Patton, Frederick Ayer, Jr., her brother, and a number of close
friends whom Beatrice had invited for this last trip with her
husband. In the other train rode General McNarney and all
the other general officers who had assembled in Heidelberg
to say farewell to George Patton.

He was buried in the drizzle of a fog-shrouded December
morning on the day before Christmas in the American Military Cemetery at Hamm in Luxembourg, where he joined
5,076 heroes of the Third Army under their crosses and
Stars of David.

PATTON'S PASSING was barely noticed in Germany,
even though he had been gaining a modicum of popularity
in a country his great army had helped to defeat. But his
fame or notoriety was mostly confined to Bavaria, for there
were no media outlets as yet that the Germans could have
used to make him nationally adopted as a friend of the
Germans.

The few regional newspapers licensed by the Allies in
their districts of occupation reported his accident and then
his death in minuscule headlines over brief dispatches taking
up, for example, one-third of a single column in the
Süddeutsche Zeitung of Munich, which had just started publishing on a franchise from the American military government.

Ten days before—because it had taken almost a week
for the news to make the papers—the accident was given
twelve lines at the bottom of an inside page. His death
received half a column under the headline: "General Patton

Dead." Yet it was left to the Luxembourg correspondent of the *Süddeutsche Zeitung* to write probably the best, certainly the most succinct report on the burial—brief and to the point, yet still managing somehow to be colorful and even a little warm.

The dateline of the story was December 26. It appeared in the paper on December 28. The news was traveling slowly in occupied Germany. But there it was at last, a shy farewell to the famous American general, the obit Patton would have liked, for it was a sort of tribute from the enemy. It read:

> General Patton's mortal remains were buried on December 24 at 10 o'clock in the morning in the military cemetery in Hamm, east of Luxembourg. He rests next to the grave of an American soldier who was killed in action last winter in the Battle of the Bulge. Preceding the burial, a funeral service was held in the Luxembourg Cathedral.
>
> In spite of the pouring rain, thousands lined the streets from the central railroad station along the tracks to the cemetery, in order to render this last homage to the dead general. Hundreds of people walked from the capital to attend the burial ceremonies. Representatives of nine countries and the highest-ranking officers of the American troops stationed in Europe followed the coffin. Also present were delegations from Luxembourg, France, Belgium, England, Italy, the Netherlands, Czechoslovakia and Yugoslavia.
>
> France and Belgium provided the honor guard. While the gun carriage with the coffin was on its way from the railroad station to the cemetery, a French battery fired a seventeen-round volley of salute. During the burial, a military band played the Third Army March. After a brief religious service, the coffin was lowered into the grave.
>
> The entire Grand Duchy of Luxembourg mourns the death of General Patton, the liberator of the country. Thirty thousand American soldiers are buried in Luxembourg. Many of them served with the Third U.S. Army under the command of General Patton.

At the cemetery in Hamm, standing at solemn attention beside contingents from the British, French, and Belgian armies, a composite battalion of infantry and cavalry soldiers represented the Third Army, under the personal command of Lieutenant General Lucian K. Truscott. Patton was seen to his final rest by a distinguished group of honorary pallbearers, remarkable for a last-minute change in its composition. The original list of thirteen included high-ranking officers in the Theater and three members of his staff, General Muller, General Williams, and Colonel Harkins. At the request of Mrs. Patton, however, one man was dropped and one man substituted. Dropped was the name of Lieutenant General Walter Bedell Smith, of whom Patton had told General Eisenhower during a friendly dinner on the evening of October 12, not yet three months before, to which Smith had been invited: "In light of what happened, I cannot hereafter eat at the same table with Beetle Smith." He did not care to see him at his bedside, and obviously he would not have wanted him at his funeral either. The friend Mrs. Patton asked to be substituted for General Smith was Master Sergeant William George Meeks.

Now, in the final moment of the ceremony in Luxembourg, the middle-aged black man who had served the general so faithfully for so long presented the flag that had draped the casket to Beatrice Ayer Patton—the "storm flag" Meeks had given Colonel Hill a couple of days before. There were tears in the sergeant's eyes, his face was screwed up tight.

He bowed slowly and handed the flag to Mrs. Patton. Then he saluted her. For an instant their eyes met and held. Sergeant Meeks turned away. A twelve-man honor squad raised its rifles and a three-round volley of salutes echoed into the Luxembourg hills. Then it was all over. Patton's last audience, the one he moved to tears, dispersed in the rain.

They buried him in what turned out to be his temporary grave—in Plot EE, Row 9, Grave 222—which was to serve him until 6:00 P.M. on March 19, 1947, when he was placed at the head of nine columns of his soldiers, with a simple cross for his marker, the embossed plate on it reading under his four stars: GEO. S. PATTON, GENERAL, 02605. 3RD ARMY.

The dead, most of whom had been killed fighting in the Battle of the Bulge, came from all of what were then the forty-eight states, from the District of Columbia, and from Alaska and Hawaii. In twenty-two instances, two brothers lie side by side. Originally laid to rest beside Private First Class John Hrzywarn of Detroit, Patton now lies separately, close to the memorial terrace, facing two Stars of David. Under them lie a couple of Jewish boys, one of whose names was Bonaparte. The mosaic above proclaims:

"In proud and grateful memory of those men of the Armed Services of the United States of America who in this region and in the skies above it endured all and gave all that justice among nations might prevail and that mankind might enjoy freedom and inherit peace."

THEY HAD COME, the princes and the paupers, the generals and the privates, the mourners and the scorners— except the two men whose absence appeared to be especially conspicuous. General Eisenhower was gone from the European Theater for good and apparently could not spare the time to fly back from Washington to pay his last tribute to his old friend. And Colonel R. Glen Spurling, who only two weeks before questioned the wisdom of risking the lives of a plane-load of people to save the life of the stricken general, was present neither at the funeral in Heidelberg nor at the burial in Luxembourg.

He was gone because, as he said, Mrs. Patton had "insisted" that he return to the United States so that he could be with his family for Christmas. He did not quite make it. He arrived on December 27, and immediately went to Washington to arrange for his return to civilian life.

"This time," he wrote in his notes on the Patton "episode," as he called his last case in uniform, "I took no chances about getting out of the Army. I processed my papers at the Pentagon on the 28th and was relieved of active duty on January 7, 1946. After all," he added with tongue in cheek, in a strange epitaph, as it were, "I didn't want to take a chance on another general's breaking his neck."

There was now only one last step left before Patton could be regarded as dead, indeed, and it was up to the Army, punctilious as always, to supply that final footnote.

Patton existed by the latest of his orders, that of December 7, 1945, granting him a leave of absence. As far as the Adjutant General was concerned, he was on leave. The book could be closed on him only when his leave was properly canceled.

On December 25 that last word was duly spoken. The Acting Adjutant General of USFET also bade General Patton his final farewell, by issuing him still another order. It read: "Letter Order AG 300.4 (5 Dec 45) 12-472, this headquarters, subject: Orders (Stat Code NPJ), dated 7 December 1945, pertaining to leave of absence of General George S. Patton, Jr., 0-2605, USA, is revoked."

Patton's death was official, at last.

Epilogue

★ ★ ★ ★

The Limited Assembly

Those gentlemen who reach posterity are not much more numerous than the planets.

—BENJAMIN DISRAELI *on June 3, 1862*

THE LONG ROAD out of Luxembourg City that leads to this vast burial ground of American heroes is named for him: the Boulevard General Patton in Hamm. The cemetery is an exclusive club. By order of the Department of the Army, its membership is restricted and complete. No further burials may be made in these hallowed grounds except of those remains that may still be found in these battlefields.

Close to the huge wrought-iron gate stands the white stone chapel in the woods, flanked at a lower level by two large pylons on which are posted colorful maps made of granite. They recall the feats of the American armies in the Battle of the Bulge and the advance to the Rhine. Also inscribed on the pylons are the names of 370 men whose remains were never recovered or could not be identified. Their roster looks down on rows and rows of headstones made of glistening white marble that follow each other along graceful curving lines. Fountains, trees and flower beds contribute to the exquisite beauty and dignity of this limited assembly.

Patton's grave under the chapel's plateau is tended in all weather by the American Battle Monument Commission, represented ably at the cemetery by David J. Pucket and Herery Akkermans, and by the Grand Ducal family, who

serve as volunteer custodians in observance of the wish of
the late Prince Felix, the general's good friend. It is also
cared for by the children of Pierre Mousty from nearby
Esch-sur-Alzette, in memory of their own father, who was
a member of the anti-Nazi underground. The trains to and
from Contern slow down each time they pass the southern
edge of this huge final resting place of 5,077 American
soldiers and blow their whistles. The planes from the nearby
airport dip their wings in rueful, respectful salute.

MRS. PATTON died in 1954, in an accident, like her
husband, of a broken neck after a fall from her horse. Her
wish, well known to her descendants, was to be buried with
her husband, side by side in a common grave. But since it
was still impossible to bring General Patton's remains to
the United States, Mrs. Patton's body was allegedly taken
to Hamm and buried surreptitiously in her husband's grave.
A rumor, indeed—and attested to though it is by certain
people supposedly in the know, it is still nothing but idle
talk, for it could not be verified without disturbing the General's grave.

INDEX

Dramatic and Revealing Historical Books From Berkley!

☐ 0-425-09881-8 **THE LAST DAYS OF PATTON** $3.95
Ladislas Farago

☐ 0-425-08480-9 **MONTE CASSINO** $3.95
David Hapgood and David Richardson

☐ 0-425-08481-7 **IVAN THE TERRIBLE** $3.95
Henri Troyat

☐ 0-425-07981-3 **CATHERINE THE GREAT** $3.95
Henri Troyat

☐ 0-425-07699-7 **REFLECTIONS OF THE CIVIL WAR** $3.95
Bruce Catton and John Leekley, eds.

☐ 0-425-07578-8 **THE MURDER OF NAPOLEON** $3.50
Ben Weider and David Hapgood